A RINGSIDE
AFFAIR

A RINGSIDE AFFAIR

BOXING'S LAST GOLDEN AGE

JAMES LAWTON

BLOOMSBURY

LONDON · OXFORD · NEW YORK · NEW DELHI · SYDNEY

Bloomsbury Sport
An imprint of Bloomsbury Publishing Plc

50 Bedford Square   1385 Broadway
London   New York
WC1B 3DP   NY 10018
UK   USA

www.bloomsbury.com

BLOOMSBURY and the Diana logo are trademarks of Bloomsbury Publishing Plc

First published 2017

British Library Cataloguing-in-Publication Data
A catalogue record for this book is available from the British Library.

Library of Congress Cataloguing-in-Publication data has been applied for.

ISBN: HB: 978-1-4729-4563-1
ePub: 978-1-4729-4565-5

2 4 6 8 10 9 7 5 3 1

Typeset in Minion by Deanta Global Publishing Services, Chennai, India
Printed and bound in Great Britain by CPI Group (UK) Ltd, Croydon CR0 4YY

To find out more about our authors and books visit www.bloomsbury.com.
Here you will find extracts, author interviews, details of forthcoming
events and the option to sign up for our newsletters.

For my daughters Jacinta, Victoria and Hannah

Contents

CONTENTS

Prologue

I first met Muhammad Ali soon after he had reinvaded the imagination of the world with his astonishing victory over George Foreman in Kinshasa in 1974. I last saw him in his hometown of Louisville, Kentucky, 34 years later when, from the wheelchair in which he had been so long imprisoned, he welcomed the Ryder Cup teams of America and Europe. The great, multimillionaire golfers might as well have been awestruck schoolboys.

They reminded me of how I felt when I went to interview him at the Café Royal in London and of what he had come to mean to me and, no doubt, his millions of admirers across the world. He was so much more than a fabled sportsman. He was a touchstone for the possibilities of life, for the rewards of courage; and now when I come to recount all the years I would spend at ringside I see more clearly than ever that without him it would be an account lacking not only its first impetus but also an unchanging focus.

This isn't the story of Muhammad Ali, though – I came too late to it for that – but of the deeds he bequeathed, the bar he set, the demands he made on the performances of the greatest of the fighters who followed him.

At the Café Royal, I didn't know I would see the last of his fights – his most stirring, final triumph and then his last agony in the ring – and that was maybe why, when I sat down with him, I rushed somewhat to an ending. I asked him what he would like written on his gravestone.

He told me at some length. He wanted it said that he had never ducked a challenge, in or out of the ring, that he stood for certain principles of truth and fellowship and kindness, and that he had loved all people of good faith, whatever the colour of their skin. He didn't have an argument with the Vietcong, not when his own people were treated so badly back home in Kentucky, and that was why he had refused to serve in Vietnam. It went on like that to the point where he saw that my note-taking had become less diligent. At the end of his eulogy to himself, he leant across the table and demanded, 'Read that back.'

I left him somewhat chastened but, like so many before and after me, convinced that I had felt a uniquely compelling presence.

It was a feeling that would linger down all the years and never more forcibly than when, on a spring morning in a café in the village in the Veneto to where I had retreated when the sports-writing days were over, I saw flashed on the television screen the news that Muhammad Ali had died. There was a stirring in the café, even in the corner where the old men played their cards. I wanted to add to it, I wanted to shout that I knew that man, had seen him fight, had felt his force, and that we would all be lucky if such a one ever passed our way again. Instead, I went into the sunlight weighing again the privileges that came to me in the years that had their starting point in a panelled salon of the Café Royal.

What follows, I hope, is a small measure of the gratitude I will always feel for having time around a great fighter and a great man. And seeing so much of the best of his legacy to the world's oldest and most embattled sport. Of seeing fights that, from the moment they unfolded, I knew would rank among the greatest of all time. For being able to say, maybe, that I saw the last great age of boxing.

Chapter One

New York, September 1977

When Muhammad Ali came into the ring everyone agreed there was more than the usual thunder in the air. It was apprehension, so tangible you could almost touch it. I felt it first on the Eighth Avenue sidewalk when I stepped out of the yellow cab. I could see it on the faces and hear it on the lips of the throng pressing into Madison Square Garden. It warned me that maybe I had come to see not my first Ali fight but his last rite of survival.

Either way, I had one certainty as I took my seat at ringside. I had never known before, and might never again, such a heightened sense of being present at a moment so filled with impending drama.

Ali had once defined the fascination of a big fight in the simplest terms. He said that for a little while the world was obsessed with the question, 'Who's gonna win? Who's gonna win?' and then it would move on. In one way, it was like the pursuit of a beautiful girl: a driving imperative one moment, a passing whim the next.

Here though, as Ali faced the menacing power of Earnie Shavers of Ohio, the implications ran deeper and, potentially, with permanence. At 35, Ali had in front of him nothing less than a visceral examination of his will to go on, to take blows that might prove as destructive – sooner or later – as any he had received down the years, and announce yet again not only his ability to withstand them but to add still more lustre to his name.

Two years earlier he had fought Joe Frazier to a standstill in Manila in a third fight so elemental, so invasive of both men's body and psyche, that some extremely seasoned observers could hardly bear to watch. The Thrilla in Manila was stopped only when, at the end of the 14th round, the superb veteran trainer Eddie Futch concluded that another round might irreparably damage, if not kill, his man Frazier. Frazier was near blind, with one eye closed and the other the merest bloodied slit, when Futch reached a decision that would always be resented by the fighter and much of his family.

Twenty years later, Futch, then in his eighties and recently the winner of a unanimous decision over an abusive racist in a Las Vegas car park, would tell me how a young woman came to him in a shopping mall, embraced him and thanked him for what he did in Manila. 'I have wanted to say this for a long time,' she said. 'Thank you for the courage you showed, thank you for saving my father's life. My father may still resent you for what you did, and some of my family may hate you. But down the years I've come to realise you were right.'

Futch was touched by this sentiment of one of Frazier's daughters but no man who ever influenced a significant fist fight was in less need of reinforcement. When he died in 2001, at the age of 90, he was widely celebrated as one of the most astute educators and tacticians boxing had ever known.

He moved with his family from Mississippi to Detroit as a five-year-old as part of the vast migration of the former slave population swapping the toils of sharecropping and cotton picking for the industrial mills of the north. His family lived in the Black Bottom section of Detroit and his early life in a fight gym included sparring with Joe Louis.

Futch was an able lightweight fighter but a heart problem thwarted his hopes of a professional career. He went to Los Angeles, en route, he thought, to work on the Alaska pipeline, but he lingered there after being drawn into the local fight milieu. In his time he tutored a small army of world champions. Astonishingly, he trained four of the five men to beat Ali – Ken Norton, Frazier, Larry Holmes and Trevor Berbick, though Berbick's triumph was less a victory than an act of plunder amid the ruins of the great man's career.

When Futch was asked to take over the training of Riddick Bowe, the world heavyweight champion of great talent but questionable commitment, he issued demands on the fighter that had to be met unequivocally if he was to proceed. They included the need for serious road work, starting the following morning. He took the assignment, but only after rising before dawn and stealthily parking his car in woods beside a mountain road outside Reno, Nevada.

When he saw Bowe pounding up the hill, Futch, as trim and as vital in his eighties as he had been in his Detroit youth, decided Bowe might be worth the trouble. One consequence was that Bowe delivered the first defeat of Evander Holyfield in a superb battle for the undisputed heavyweight crown.

In a Las Vegas coffee shop Futch told me, 'I always believed there was a way to beat Ali, and I gave Shavers a good shot that night at the Garden, but that had nothing to do with any thought that Ali wasn't a great fighter, maybe the greatest of them all. My doubts about him were not to do with his fighting ability, his skill or his imagination or, least of all, his courage. No, the vulnerability I saw was in part of his nature, his urge to show off, to express himself in a new way. He loved to intrigue the world. That, and Joe Frazier's strength and determination and great hooking brought that first win at Madison Square Garden in what they called the fight of the century.

'But then Ali's genius was to find a way to win, and he did that in Manila, as he had in Africa against Foreman. I never had any doubts about my decision to stop the fight in Manila – Joe needed saving from himself. I had a duty to him and his family, even if he didn't see it, quite literally. Ali was hitting him freely in the 14th round, landing head shots which Joe just couldn't pick up.'

Against Shavers, Ali would have no free shots at a defenceless, unseeing victim. He would, as he was in the decisive stages of the Manila fight and the triumphant Rumble in the Jungle against Foreman a year earlier, be stretched to the limits of his nerve and his ingenuity and all that was left of once-phenomenal physical resources.

In the sparkling fall days leading up to the fight there was, however, no indication from Ali that he was facing a moment when he might be laid bare. His exuberance spilled into the thoroughfares of Manhattan, as it had done in so many of the places along the road from his Olympic gold medal in Rome 17 years earlier.

The day before the fight he gathered his entourage in the lobby of the Statler Hilton hotel, formerly the venerable Pennsylvania where a solitary guest, jazz composer Jerry Gray, penned Glenn Miller's classic swing hit, 'Pennsylvania 6–5000', a telephone number that would thus be preserved through the ages.

Ali told his people that he wanted to walk along Seventh Avenue. He wanted to draw strength from his people, those whom he had claimed for so long, and perhaps remind himself of what he meant to the watching world. If that was indeed so, he could hardly have been more gratified. The traffic stopped. It was a parade that lacked only ticker tape. A shoe-shine boy provided a free service. Flowers were thrown down from apartment windows, and garment workers cheered to the rafters above their abandoned work benches. It was part embrace, part salutation. A cab driver and his passengers joined the crowd, and the New York constabulary looked on benignly. A notably pretty girl found her way into the great man's arms, albeit chastely, because whatever his private inclinations publicly he had long been a minister of Islam. 'I'm still the king,' he shouted to the great crowd. The response was wild in its agreement.

He had been no less charged with elation in his final sparring sessions at the Felt Forum, an intimate arena in the Garden now named the Paramount Theater and given over to stage shows and graduation ceremonies. After a few rounds with Jimmy Ellis, a former holder of the World Boxing Association heavyweight belt after the title splintered during Ali's suspension from the ring following his refusal to enlist for Vietnam, he was in the mood for mockery. He waved his fist in the direction of Ellis and declared, 'Last night he dreamed he beat me but the first thing he did this morning was apologise.'

The denizens of ringside laughed – and Ellis gave a small grimace. He too had his pride. He won his title against the dangerous Jerry Quarry. He defended it successfully against the remnants of the once formidable Floyd Patterson (before he was bulldozed into long years of pain and self-effacement by Liston, and beaten quite formally by Ali) and surrendered it only to the scything hooks of Frazier. But now Ellis, who had also grown up in the streets of Louisville, was part of the Ali show, a hireling, another extra, another stooge. However, beneath all this hubris one question would not go away. Would Shavers, who had been christened 'the Ohio Acorn' by Ali for his shaven head, be quite so willing to play his part?

Back in the dressing room at the Felt Forum, Ali was in no mood to ponder and, still less, debate the worry. He preferred to make his jokes, and maybe his trainer Angelo Dundee guessed, by an expression on my face, that I was about to intrude into the champion's revelry. I was, though on this occasion my question would not have been to do with the wording of his epitaph but the degree of his concern over the power of Shavers' punch.

Dundee squeezed my arm and whispered, 'Not now, buddy, it's not the time. The champ needs his space.'

The question would be raised soon enough, and not in a stutter but a fusillade. It came in the second round and it bore the intimation of impending doom. Ali had won the first round with a familiar formula of jabs and right hands, delivered with no apparent loss of speed or facility or certainty. There was a swagger in his return to his corner, where Dundee spoke quietly and meaningfully amid the blandishments of the manager, Herbert Muhammad, and the ultimate cheerleader, Bundini Brown.

Dundee had long been a member of the hierarchy of great trainers. He was a more waspish, bespectacled version of Futch, and someone who had every reason to be relaxed in the company of such legendary ancients as Ray Arcel, whose work in helping create 20 world champions began and ended with two superb lightweights in a span of more than 50 years, Benny Leonard and Roberto Durán. Another of the circle was Freddie Brown, who did some of his most brilliant corner work on behalf of Rocky Marciano.

Dundee had already pulled off a coup before Ali and Shavers entered the ring. Having learned that NBC television would air the judges' scorecards round by round, he stationed a man in front of a television set in Ali's dressing room. Thus prepared, Dundee's fight strategy would be armed with some certainties as he received his signals between each round.

In that second round, however, there were disturbing signs that Dundee might have won only an academic advantage. On three separate occasions Shavers produced daunting evidence that he might well supply his own adjudication. They arrived in the form of long, crunching right hands. After the first of them, Ali mimed mocking, fake distress to the crowd, but it was clear at ringside, as it must have been in the furthest corners of the arena, that he protested too much. Certainly, when Shavers landed two more blows of similar force, Ali's reaction was shorn of all theatrics.

His stool in the corner was, suddenly, no longer a stage but a refuge, and the only voice that mattered now – in fact it had become the only one in his corner against the rising clamour of the arena – was Dundee's. His counsel was for watchful caution, a more careful assessment of the challenge before him. Ali had come into the ring to the music of *Star Wars* but now the need to go to ground, at least for a while, had become critical.

The tactic worked well enough in that the news from the dressing room persuaded Dundee that Ali could afford to eke out his stamina and his ability to conjure scoring blows from any part of the ring. Yet if Ali accumulated enough points to build a lead there was no escaping the threat of the Shavers' power. Later, Ali would revive his old joke that he was hit so hard the blows must have been felt by his kinfolk back in Africa. There was an extremely harsh reality behind the jest. Shavers did hit hard, some believed at least as hard as any heavyweight in history, and he did it frequently enough to maintain the possibility of a life-changing victory.

In the fourth round, another Shavers right landed with shuddering effect, and again in the seventh Ali's head was snapped back with a force that would surely have brought down a less resolute man. The pattern was unchanging. Ali scored in swift flurries, Shavers advanced with the wrecking ball potential of his right hand.

By the later rounds, Dundee could reassure Ali that he was obliged only to stay on his feet to retain his undisputed world title – and preserve the idea that he remained the master of his career destiny – but neither man had reason to be complacent. Shavers may have lagged on points but he retained the potential to make an utterly decisive intervention. The threat exploded again, most seriously since the onslaught of the second round, in the 13th.

Shavers measured Ali and delivered and again the champion's head was cruelly battered. He fell back on the ropes before enveloping Shavers in a clinch, but no longer was he providing a derisive commentary. It was as much as he could do to make it to the end of the round. He was sucking in his stinging breath and staunching as best he could the revived tide of Shavers' aggression.

The 14th was a hiatus, and featured another largely successful attempt by Ali to subdue the late Shavers' surge. It gave no guide, certainly, to the furies of the last round, which was the most bone-deep riveting passage of sport I had ever seen.

Shavers didn't know the scorecards but his imperative could not have been more explicit in everything he brought to the 15th round. Maybe he had pushed Ali to the point of breakdown, perhaps the cumulative effect of his thudding blows could now be exploited. He rushed into the round, wielding his right hand like a club, and he scored again. Ali retreated, drew in his breath even as he shook his head in defiance, and absorbed the charge in another clinch.

Then it came, the great and maybe last moving statement by Muhammad Ali in the boxing ring. For, although he would have one more victory – a scuffling, underwhelming act of revenge against the still raw Leon Spinks in New Orleans a year later – here in Madison Square Garden we had the last of the best.

We had Ali taking up the fight, striding forward, summoning all he had left in a reservoir of spirit and strength that for some time, had invited the suspicion that it had become less than inexhaustible. Shavers was caught in a tide that lapped into every corner of the arena. He was required not only to retreat but to stare into the face of an improbable reality. Not only was the man he had hit so hard, so frequently, still standing, he was rampaging again, throwing punches of still astounding speed and originality.

When the cards were read out – 9-6, 9-6, 9-5 in Ali's favour – there were some murmurings of disbelief because this scoring did not speak of the essence of what we had seen, the fineness of the line between two men who had ransacked their spirit and their knowledge of themselves to gain a decisive edge. Ali had won, on points but also in the matter of stunning resistance to a most serious threat.

For at least one moment you could believe again in one of Ali's philosophical statements that was shorn of fancy and the most outrageous hyperbole. It wasn't about 'floating like a butterfly stinging like a bee'. It didn't concern wrestling with an alligator, tussling with a whale, handcuffing lightning or throwing thunder into jail. No, it was about something you had to believe we had seen rise up this night in Madison Square Garden.

After distilling all that he had learned and felt in the ring, Ali had declared, 'Champions aren't made in the gym. Champions are made from something they have deep inside them, a drive, a dream, a vision. They have the last-minute stamina, they are a little faster. They have the skill and the will. But the will has to be stronger than the skill.'

He might, when he said those words, have been foretelling his final great public performance, his last successful statement about who he was and what he had come to represent down all the years. As in Africa against Foreman and in the Philippines against Frazier, and so much earlier in Miami Beach against Sonny Liston, he had been indomitable.

In the arena, the jubilation lasted until every seat emptied. That was understandable enough. For most, it would take a little time to learn of the terrible cost of Ali's defiance. For others, though – and especially those who had joined the charge behind Ali down a riotous corridor – that was clear enough when he reached his dressing room. There, he screamed for the lights to be turned off. He said they were burning in his eyes like needles.

I got one foot into the pandemonium of that dressing room, I heard the scream of Ali, but no more that could be easily identified. A formidably large security guard checked me with a forearm across my throat and I was volleyed back into the corridor. I remained close enough, though, to hear a persistent chorus of cries, a noise that suggested anything but the normal euphoria of a great victory. That it was so was confirmed to me in an act of professional kindness I would never forget. It came from a senior colleague, Frank McGhee of the *Daily Mirror*.

McGhee, a veteran of many big fights and the great events of world sport, had taken his chance as the guard was heaving me back into the corridor. He slipped into the dressing room with a well-practised air of unobtrusive authority, and when he emerged he said to me, 'You better take some notes, it was quite a scene in there.'

Most dramatically, Ali's medical adviser, Ferdie Pacheco, had called time on his ability to continue serving the great man in anything like good conscience. His speech was that of a man contemplating the point where he could no longer look comfortably at himself in the mirror. It was said of Ali, by Hugh McIlvanney of the *Observer*, that he was a man who when he looked into the mirror each morning reinvented himself. Pacheco's contention now was that no flight of fancy could any longer recreate a fighter who could still go in the ring without grave risk to the quality of the rest of his life.

'Muhammad, you cannot go on,' he said. 'Tonight you took terrible punishment to all parts of your body: your head, your liver, your kidneys, right down to your bowels. As your doctor, I can't be a party to it.' For corroboration, he cited a report of the New York State Athletic Commission's medical staff, which claimed that Ali's kidneys were 'falling to bits'.

Some elements of the Ali camp, notably manager Herbert Muhammad and the eternally optimistic Bundini Brown, were unmoved by the bleak forecasts. Ali would have four more fights and lose three of them. The position of the devoted Dundee was different and more complicated. He heard what Pacheco was saying, he didn't need the perils underlining, but he also felt he had a duty to see through the job that had come to define his superb career.

If Ali continued to insist on going into the ring, he needed to be there. While he was around, drawing from his vast experience, he might be able to help avoid the worst possibilities, at least in the ring if not the long haul of the rest of the champion's life. In this, at least, his continued service was of great value to Ali, especially when he saw, unlike some other members of the camp, that Ali's situation in the ring had become simply too hazardous.

Dundee, who had first tutored the novice professional in the Fifth Street gym in Miami, said, 'I cannot tell Muhammad what to do, no more than anyone else on this earth can. But I can look after him around the ring and before fights as best I can.'

It was a resolve that gave substance to at least one pronouncement of Howard Cosell, the former lawyer who became a giant of TV sports broadcasting. Cosell had a pompous manner on and off the screen. Once, at a Manhattan cocktail party, he was involved in an argument about the relative merits of certain sportscasters, including his own, and sought the arbitration of the great columnist Red Smith. 'Hey, Red Smith,' he called, 'will you tell these bozos how many great sports broadcasters there are in this world?'

Smith, never a man to shout his opinions, deadpanned, 'One less than you think, Howard.' Still, he wouldn't have argued with Cosell's assessment of Dundee when he said, 'If I ever had a son who wanted to be a fighter, and I couldn't talk him out of it, I would send him to Angelo Dundee.' In a suddenly uncertain world, Ali indeed could be sure of Dundee's loyalty and concern for him in any situation. In the tumult of Madison Square Garden, he had said, 'Whatever happens, whatever decisions are made, I'm here for Muhammad Ali, good or bad. Look, he's my kid.'

He was, however, for all the courage and the unfathomable skill he had trailed as new clouds of glory along Eighth Avenue, no longer the favourite son of the world's most famous fight emporium. This was made clear when the Madison Square Garden matchmaker Teddy Brenner aligned himself with Pacheco. It was the crushing verdict of a much respected boxing expert.

Brenner was a former shirt salesman who had graduated from the small, smoky old fight halls of the New York area to the pinnacle of his profession at the Garden. He had brought along the Olympic and world heavyweight champion Floyd Patterson and unfurled him at the Garden. He had pulled off the coup of his career when he set up the 1971 Fight of the Century between Ali and Frazier, one so compelling Frank Sinatra appeared with a press photographer's credential in his hatband. Brenner made the deal only after promising both fighters the then stunning purse of $5 million each.

That seemed to be a long way into the past, though, in the wake of Ali–Shavers. Brenner shook his head and said, 'I never thought I'd live to see the day when Muhammad Ali's greatest asset was his ability to take a punch.' It was a solemn statement and it came with an assertion that Ali had made his last appearance at Madison Square Garden.

These were weighty considerations for someone covering his first significant fight, and with a London deadline stretching to noon the following day I moved from the frenzies of the press room to a bar in Greenwich Village, not altogether inappropriately named the Bells of Hell. There, I weighed the storyline options over a couple of drinks and a few riffs of jazz. I was still weighing them as noon approached and a knock sounded on the door of my room at the Statler Hilton.

It was Frank McGhee, clad now in a silk dressing gown and still with the concern he had shown for a young colleague in that chaotic, tumultuous back corridor of Madison Square Garden. He had filed his copy in the small hours of the morning while I was tentatively sipping my drink and feeling a knot tightening in my stomach.

'Remember, my boy,' he said. 'If you can't send a good story on deadline, send a bad one.' Elementary advice, perhaps, but the delivery was timely, as was the encouraging pat on the back. I clattered out my piece and was not too abashed when I dictated it to London. The desk seemed happy enough and said I should enjoy a few days in New York before flying home.

There are not many less onerous commands but if those days still glitter like the diamonds in the window of Tiffany's on Fifth Avenue, they did not obscure the terrible price Muhammad Ali might have to pay for his last supreme act of brilliant gallantry.

They were days underpinned by extraordinary circumstance. Between that night of the fight, 29 September, and the Sunday afternoon of 2 October, not one but three of the greatest sportsmen of all time were required to define, in one way or another, the meaning of their careers.

First there was the glorious defiance of Ali. Then there was the last professional appearance of Pelé, the world's greatest soccer player, at the sold-out Giants Stadium in the New Jersey Meadowlands. Finally, in Watkins Glen in upstate New York, Niki Lauda, less than a year after receiving the last rites following his narrow escape from incineration at the Nürburgring, won back his Formula One title with a drive of nerveless precision.

Ali, bruised but still publicly exulting in his heroic victory, rallied to join the crowd at Giants Stadium, and when his arrival ran like a charge of electricity into every corner it was a reminder, if any were needed, that he still had no rival in his genius for touching the people. No one, certainly, had gone more willingly into the darkening night; no one had so clearly, so bravely, proclaimed his defiance of the odds accumulating against him. That was the hardest – and most worrying – conclusion I took from my first watch over a legend as I rode the late bus to Kennedy airport.

I didn't know if I would ever see Ali fight again – if men of good judgement like Teddy Brenner prevailed over those who saw in him the last branches of a fabulous money tree, I wouldn't – but at least I could say I had been present when he made something rather more than a desperate last stand. It was never that, even when Shavers bore down so hard and so optimistically. It was a man, however battered, rejoicing in the fact that he could still find some of the best of himself. And, of course, no man was ever more conscious of what he had brought into the ring and to the wider world.

In the months that followed many notable American writers, including Norman Mailer and the king of gonzo journalism, Hunter S. Thompson, wrote essays that were essentially professional obituaries. When Thompson penned his for *Rolling Stone* magazine, he enlisted the help of Ali's own sweeping view of his place in history. He seized on the declaration, 'When I'm gone boxing will be nothing again. The fans with their cigars and hats turned down will be there, but no more housewives and little men in the street and foreign presidents. It's going to be back to the fighter who comes to town, smells a flower, visits a hospital, blows a horn and says he's in shape. Old hat. I was the only fighter to be asked questions as though I was a senator.'

There were truths in there that would survive the erosions of any gravestone inscription. But it wasn't the whole story, the final statement of boxing, and it would be my thrilling if sometimes haunting assignment, as I fell asleep before the end of the opening credits of the in-flight movie, to be around to see that **that** was indeed not the case.

Chapter Two

Montreal, June 1980

Muhammad Ali was hardly alone in believing his departure from the ring would signal the beginning of the end of the sport he had entranced and illuminated for so long. Almost everyone was saying it. Certainly, it was my instinct when I collected my credentials for the world welterweight title fight between Sugar Ray Leonard and Roberto Durán at the Olympic Stadium. The surging pulse of Madison Square Garden might have been a hundred years earlier.

An intriguing and extremely rich fight, no doubt – Leonard would become the latest record-breaking earner in the ring – and one to be waged by two outstanding performers at their weight, but the launch of a new era, a thrilling redefinition of all that boxing had to offer?

It would take some massive stirring of the blood, something wild and unforeseen. And then, there it was, staring in front of me: the demonic fight face of Roberto Durán.

He arrived in Montreal so far from Ali's discouraging image of tame and workaday successors he might have come not from the raw and volatile streets of Panama City but from a separate planet devoted exclusively to waging war. His dark eyes blazed and even the smallest phrases of his body language spoke of a coiled aggression. It spilled over from its principal target, the welterweight champion and Olympic gold medallist Leonard, into what might have been mistaken for an assault on the sensitivities of the world at large. He was inflamed and committed way beyond the routine braggadocio of a big-fight participant working both the box office and his own reserves of self-belief. For the conservative burghers of a city where it is said you cannot throw a stone in any direction without breaking a church window, he was a shock as much as a revelation. Wherever he went he announced the most singular and ferocious vision. He was primed to fight, he announced, in a way that perhaps he had never been before. This was a huge statement of intent because whatever else he was, Roberto Durán was a natural-born fighter.

Now, he might have been accompanied by an army of demons. So, it was observed before he stepped into the ring, you had to pity the waiter who was laggardly with his steak and potatoes in the opulent restaurant of his five-star hotel. Or the fellow diner misguided enough to complain about the music that boomed from the ghetto blaster he slammed down on the table.

Back at home in his youth he had famously knocked down, for a bet, a horse hitched outside a raucous bodega. Some first read that for an apocryphal take on the nature of a man who had dominated the lightweight division with a violent hauteur that had beaten so many opponents before the sound of the first bell. Here, against an authentic welterweight and – with respect to the great, upright Scottish lightweight Kenny Buchanan – unquestionably the most talented fighter he had ever faced, the strategy of raging psychological fury had been brought to full working order. He spat out contempt for Leonard. He questioned his courage, his ability, even his manhood. 'Leonard? A *maricon*, not a real man. I will expose him,' he sneered.

Rarely had someone come into an important fight making such a show of his determination to give everything he had. An old native warrior once said, 'Bury my heart at Wounded Knee.' Now, if he couldn't win, it was as though Durán was nominating Montreal as a resting place for his deepest fighting instinct.

Dave Anderson, the Pulitzer Prize-winning sportswriter of the *New York Times*, was especially impressed by Durán's expression of commitment. It took him back, he said, nine years to the huge impact of Joe Frazier when he arrived in Madison Square Garden for his 'Fight of the Century' with Ali.

Anderson was so taken with the comparison he approached Frazier at ringside and asked him if in the last few days Durán had reminded him of anyone. Anderson was hoping that Frazier would confirm that he had seen a mirror image of himself as Durán thrust his way through the ropes. Instead, Frazier reflected for a moment and said, 'Yeah, Charles Manson, the murderer.' What couldn't be denied was that Durán was wearing a glare of homicidal intent.

However, behind the venom, the barrage of insult he aimed at Leonard, it was also possible to see the coldest of tactics. Leonard's superior skills, his beautiful ring-craft, provided a fascinating and, many believed, winning counter to the rampaging style of this ultimate street fighter.

Styles make fights, they say, and here was one being shaped in a way that might have been conceived in some fistic Valhalla. The key to everything was whether Durán could draw Leonard away from his strengths, his superb timing and ability to shape a fight from the middle of the ring. As Durán piled one slur upon another, conveyed a hostility that threatened to brim over at any point in the pre-fight formalities of press conferences and the weigh-in, his best hope was increasingly self-evident. He had to drag Leonard down from Mount Olympus and into the street.

For those weighing Durán's chances of success most optimistically, there was an eight-year-old precedent. It lay in that defeat of Buchanan at Madison Square Garden. Durán, just 21, was given little chance of upsetting the classical Scottish fighter, a 2-1 favourite.

Buchanan, six years Durán's senior, had honed his art to a fine degree. He had, said most of the experts, too much craft, too many options to be ambushed by the rough furies and presumptions of the young challenger.

The Scot's American trainer, Gil Clancy, said his man had one great imperative. He had to bring to his third world-title defence all the authority that had already earned unusual levels of respect for a fighter from across the Atlantic. It was true he had a boxer's style unseen in the alleys of the Bronx, or Panama City, but it was one leavened by a tough-minded understanding of how a ringside judge filled in his card.

In 1972 there was a clear parallel with the fight about to break out in Montreal. It had been Buchanan's fight to control, to shape, as it would be Leonard's. The question was whether Durán could batter aside Buchanan's more stately approach and impose his own understanding of who was the better, stronger man. It would have been a bold battle-plan for any challenger, however seasoned, but in New York, as in Montreal eight years later, it would be underpinned by a pre-fight confidence that at times touched the astounding.

Against Buchanan there was an instant reward. Durán landed a right hand that brought a flash knockdown and, if Buchanan was quickly back on his feet, it was already apparent that Clancy's best hopes were under the gravest threat. Durán, at his first opportunity, had indeed dragged the man who had grown up amid the broad thoroughfares of Edinburgh into his own kind of terrain. Durán suffocated Buchanan with his unceasing pressure, and when the fight reached its controversial breaking point in the seconds following the end of the 13th round he led hugely on every scorecard.

Referee Johnny LoBianco had it 8–3–1, judge Bill Recht 9–2–1 and Jack Gordon agreed precisely with the referee. The Associated Press scored it for Durán 9–3. The young Panamanian fighting devil had crossed the line between technique and competitive will and had he lost the decision he might have cursed for a lifetime the misadventure of barely a second.

Down all the years, and not least in the darkest of the days when he had been obliged to fight against the most insidious of opponents, alcoholism, Buchanan could never shake the belief that he had been cheated out of his title. But if it was true that Durán had landed a low blow in a brief exchange after the bell sounded for the end of the round – and after watching several reruns the referee sheepishly agreed that he almost certainly had – it still seemed unthinkable that he might have been denied the title.

Buchanan insisted, 'The low blow dented my protector and metal burst into my right testicle. I was peeing blood for days. I didn't receive any protection from the referee all night.' Naturally, Durán's reaction was to scowl – and take the embrace of a crowd who had been stunned, like Buchanan, by the extent of his aggression, the reach of his ambition.

Would it be the same in Montreal's Olympic complex, where four years earlier Leonard had been handed a gold medal, a fragment of the riches that now lay at his disposal?

Some were more sceptical than others, though a vote of 30 accredited fight reporters had Durán the favourite by a margin of 17-13, with 16 of the majority predicting a knockout. However, among those impressed by Leonard's apparent tight control over his emotions, and insistent determination not to be lured into the bad place that had seen Buchanan's downfall, was Leonard Gardner.

Gardner's 1969 novel *Fat City* is still regarded as one of the finest portrayals of boxing's darker side. As Ernest Hemingway did in his short story 'Fifty Grand', Gardner superbly delineated the lonely, morally challenging imperatives of the professional fighter. He did much of his research in a gym in the gritty Californian town of Stockton, where the fine Mexican-born light-heavyweight world champion Yaqui López became one of the most illustrious of the bruised inhabitants.

In his more nostalgic moments, López reran the movie based on Gardner's work, a haunting adaption starring Stacy Keach and Jeff Bridges. He also said of Durán, 'At that time in Montreal he was, as maybe he would never be quite so completely again, all fighter, all the way down to his toes. What he brought to that fight with Leonard was incredible. He had great technique, aggression, but more than anything he had desire and he wore it like a coat.'

Yet the author of *Fat City* had a suspicion that Leonard, while much less experienced than Durán, had a deep composure born of his Olympic gold medal and his impressive passage to the world title. He wrote, 'Both Durán and Leonard worked out in a [ice] hockey arena converted into a gym. Leonard boxed brilliantly, hitting on the move, slipping punches and countering with combinations that seemed to flow from him effortlessly. Once he knocked down a sparring partner so picturesquely that the young man from Leonard's home-town boxing club got up with what seemed a smile of aesthetic appreciation.'

It was true that Leonard mostly wore a mask of confidence, the bearing of a fighter who had answered satisfactorily the most searching questions he had asked himself. These had been posed most significantly seven months earlier at Caesars Palace in Las Vegas, where he separated the precocious, 21-year-old Wilfred Benítez from his World Boxing Council world title.

For Leonard – two years older than the prodigy who was born in the Bronx, grew up in Puerto Rico, and had thrilled the home crowd in San Juan when he took the crown by defeating the formidable Mexican Carlos Palomino on a split decision – it was by far his most testing examination. But soon it was clear that it would be a rite of passage. He won on a TKO in the 15th round, when he was ahead on the cards of all the judges and had been quite relentless in his carrying of the fight with a performance of perfectly judged assertiveness.

He put Benítez down in the third round and never allowed that psychological advantage to fade. Three months before arriving in Montreal he had delighted a home crowd in Maryland by dispatching Britain's game but utterly outclassed contender Dave 'Boy' Green. He did it with a left hook of such blistering venom that Green's manager, Andy Smith, seemed almost as stunned as his charge, who was several minutes prone on the canvas. Smith said, eventually, 'I think we are seeing the emergence of one of the world's great fighters.'

Certainly, Leonard's body language, as Gardner suggested, was generally not at variance with that widely held assumption. But then there were moments when his guard dropped. After one of his workouts, he demanded to know of a knot of reporters who had gathered in his dressing room which of us had joined the majority calling a victory for Durán. Sheepishly, some of us raised our hands. I was one of those asked to explain his reasoning. I cited Durán's greater experience, his pre-fight demeanour but, of course, allowed that it would be very close. His expression was almost as withering as the left hook that had left Dave 'Boy' Green dreaming of the gentle meadows of his native Cambridgeshire. 'Well, you're an expert,' he scowled. 'So maybe I should be worried.'

In response to the claim of Durán's co-trainer, Freddie Brown, that Leonard's trainer, Angelo Dundee, had wished to avoid the fight, Dundee said it was quite to the contrary. He believed the champion would deliver a knockout victory of even greater impact than his masterful deconstruction of the much lauded Benítez. He said, 'Durán's a heel-to-toe guy. He takes two steps to get to you. So the idea is don't give him the two steps. Don't move too far away. The more distance you give Durán the more effective he is. What you don't do against aggression is run from it because then he picks up momentum. My guy won't run from him.

'Durán waves at you with his hand. He gives you movement of his body, slipping from side to side. He won't come straight in. He'll try to fake you. He misses you with an overhand right. He turns southpaw, comes back with a left hook to the body. My guy's going to be moving side to side. And he's going to the body. No one ever hit Durán in his weak spot.'

If Leonard did have any worries about the extent of the challenge, and the choice of Durán as an opponent, they were not shared by his bank – or his manager Mike Trainer and his ally, promoter Bob Arum. Financially Leonard could already be proclaimed the winner, the biggest in boxing history, and this was despite Durán's Panamanian manager insisting on Don King's role as a co-promoter. Carlos Eleta, a Panamanian diplomat, had been impressed by King's capacity to prise money out of governments and cities and television companies, and if his man should beat Leonard, well, who knew what the limits might be?

Leonard would earn more than any previous fighter. He was guaranteed no less than $7.5 million, and when all the ancillaries were added to the $3.5 million contribution of the Olympics Installations Board, and the assorted rights from television outlets came in, Leonard could reasonably contemplate earnings close to $10 million. For all the guile of King, Durán would receive far less, a maximum of $1.5 million. But he was hardly downcast. Back in the *barrio* such riches would have been a fantasy, and now they were underpinned by the possibility of a glory that would make his name immortal in the minds of his people.

On the night of boxing's new El Dorado it was cold and wet. The rain was beating down on the stadium so hard that plastic bin bags were handed out to the bedraggled press corps making its way to ringside in the centre of the infield. The undercard had hardly been lavished with the riches bestowed upon the principals, and for the most part it proceeded while drawing only passing attention, shockingly so for those of us who only later discovered that the lightweight Cleveland Denny had sustained blows from the local hero, Gaétan Hart, that would claim his life.

Durán burst through the ropes to the sound of war drums. If ever there was a fight to set to such a rhythm, it was this one. Durán's assault was immediate and unrelenting. He had set the agenda in and out of the ring. Before the first round was over, it was clear that he had indeed drawn Leonard out of his own most secure territory, he had probed and needled, sneered and jeered, and now we could see that all the wisdom of Angelo Dundee and the talent of his fighter were gravely imperilled. Leonard had to win Durán's fight, and as each round slipped by, and Durán's fury matched the warrior glow in his eyes, the challenge became more intense. Increasingly it seemed that Durán had already won the battle of the minds and only something quite extraordinary from Leonard – a steeling of his will and maybe a piece of raw power – might adjust the balance.

The first round was a torrential statement of Durán's most serious intent, a hugely bullish invasion of Leonard's time and space and composure. He went inside with jabs and hooks and a thudding overhand right. In the second round, there was the first crisis for Leonard. Durán connected with a short, vicious hook and right-hand lead and Leonard could not disguise his shock and distress. He covered up and won a little time and later he claimed, 'I showed I could take a punch. I didn't want to, it wasn't part of my plan, but he left me with no alternative.'

As the battle wore on there was joy in Durán's corner. The old warriors Ray Arcel and Freddie Brown were seeing a scenario they might have painted in their best dreams, right down to the fact that the referee, Carlos Padilla, had apparently heard and heeded Brown's gruff injunction during a first-round clinch, 'Let them fight.'

Padilla allowed Durán to fight in his own inimitable way. It was almost as if the official was, like most everyone in the stadium, caught up not in a fist fight but in the whirlwind of one man's intense ambition. Arcel checked faithfully with Durán on his state of mind at the end of each round but it was the merest formality, rather like a sea captain constantly turning to the barometer in the fury of a storm. 'How do you feel?' he cried above the din and each time the reply was the same. 'I'm good, I'm good.'

Arcel would later insist Durán had been fighting to orders, saying, 'He did what he was told. He fought the kind of fight he was told to fight. Leonard couldn't work his jab. We never let him execute. And Roberto set a hell of a pace. I said to him, "Keep setting the pace, keep crowding him."' Few men in boxing ever had, and legitimately so, more weight attached to their words than Arcel but here there was maybe a sense that for once he might just have been exaggerating his influence. His claim, after all, did seem to suggest an unlikely degree of control over something that had come to resemble a force of nature.

That, anyway, was a theory somewhat supported by Durán at the end of a collision so fierce that Leonard's wife Juanita, always an emotional figure at ringside, was weeping by the third round and had passed out by the eighth. In French-speaking Montreal the fight had been billed as *Le Face-à-Face Historique* – An Historic Face-to-Face. Don King, however, preferred the catchier 'Brawl in Montreal', and he was right. To his added delight, it was Durán's brawl, a fact the fighter was eager to stress the following morning.

He declared, 'I'm very content. Many people did not believe I could make it but I did. Many people believed I was too old to win but I was not. Many people said I could not beat Sugar Ray Leonard. Before the fight, I asked, "Why can't I beat him?" I wondered, "Maybe he's a phantom and you can't beat him." Maybe they thought I was going to stand in the ring and let him beat me, like I had my hands tied. That's the only way he can beat me. I would have to be tied to a tree, with my hands tied behind my back . . . He would have to break me down a thousand times. He was strong but he did not hurt me. My rage was very big. When I get into the ring to fight I always give my best.'

Leonard found some measure of effectiveness in the middle rounds, inevitably landing shots that came from an inherent brilliance in timing and force, but it was not enough to disrupt the certainties of Durán's assault and with some grace he owned up to this reality. He said, 'I did the best I could. I think I pretty much fought from the heart.' This, of course, went to the core of his problem. The clinical sharpness that, round by round, had undermined Benítez was missing in Montreal. Dundee, his head bowed, admitted it was so. He said, 'You never fight to a guy's strength. You try to offset it and Ray didn't. He tried to out-strong the guy. Durán was being Durán and Ray was going with him. It was strictly Durán's stuff, elbows and knees, his head to Ray's face. Leonard has lumps all over the place. The guy who had more practice at that won the fight. It was all Durán. He pushes. He comes at you from different angles. He feints and wings. When a guy comes at you, you move. You counter and move. Ray didn't.'

The fact that it could have been different did come in isolated, brilliant flashes. The judges agreed that Leonard carried the sixth round, as they did that rounds seven and nine were even. In the sixth the old masterful Leonard, the one in charge of everything around him, made his appearance. He put together a series of jabs and left-right combinations that were among the most perfectly sculpted punches he had ever thrown.

Dundee's eyes sparkled briefly with passing hope. Had his guy emerged from an extremely bad place? Unfortunately for him, Durán still had the keys to the gate and when the discomfort of the sixth round had passed he was wielding them once again, beating once more a tattoo on Leonard's head and body.

The most extraordinary round was the 13th. If you ever needed to identify the three minutes in which boxing proved that it had the capacity to reproduce some of the best of the Ali years, the riveting, all-consuming glory of their drama and their commitment, these surely had all that you would want. There was no pause, not one moment of restraint. A clap of thunder and a flash of lightning were all that this shuddering climax lacked. Yes, climax, because when the bell sounded there was something utterly emphatic in Durán's strutting return to his corner. It was filled with a strange but tangible certainty, as though a fever had passed and the last crisis was over.

He fought the last two rounds almost as though they were a victory parade, despite his opponent producing some of his best and sharp-est work, and when the final bell sounded, and Leonard half-heartedly raised his arms in the old formality, Durán might have been shaken from a deep reverie. Outraged, he pursued Leonard across the ring and aimed a kick at the seat of his pants. He was a man punishing a gross impertinence.

The judges ruled that Durán was right. He had scored a narrow but still profound triumph. Raymond Baldeyrou of France had it 6–4–5, Britain's Harry Gibbs 6–5–4 and the scorecard of Italy's Angelo Poletti, after an initial misreading of a draw and the announcement of a majority decision, read 3–2–10. William Nack of *Sports Illustrated* sniffed that Poletti had built a monument to indecision. More endur-ing, though, was the edifice of power and will that Durán had put together, brick by ferociously laid brick, and sent climbing into the dark, moist sky.

In the morning, a hint of softness had come to Roberto Durán's fearsome glare. He played with his son and showed off the two diamond rings his wife had presented to him as birthday presents. And he posed with the belt of the world champion, saying, 'I am proud for myself, my family and my country. I did everything I came here to do.'

It was a mellow summer's afternoon when I arrived home on the Pacific Coast, to where I had moved to work for the *Vancouver Sun*. Sunshine dappled the forests running to the shore and glistened against the still snowy peaks of the mountains. There was also a remarkable sensation. It was, after the discovery that there might still be vibrant boxing life after Muhammad Ali, an invitation to draw breath.

Chapter Three

Las Vegas, October 1980

In the early summer I was in Philadelphia covering the Stanley Cup finals between the Flyers and the New York Islanders, a brilliant series of fights enhanced by the certainty that whenever a game of ice hockey broke out it would be of the highest quality. There was, however, a stronger lure up in the hills of the Amish country, a two-hour drive along the interstate. It was Muhammad Ali's training camp at Deer Lake.

For a while there had been talk of his return to the ring. It had not warmed the hearts of those who loved him most. They had been relieved 18 months earlier when he won back the world title from which he had been separated by Leon Spinks, the raw Olympic champion who had previously fought just eight times as a professional. That potentially shocking denouement of a legendary career – Ali left the Las Vegas ring with a distorted face and an excruciating loss of pride – had been redeemed, at least to some extent, in New Orleans by the more serious training regime demanded by Angelo Dundee. But, still, it was not so much a triumph as a deliverance, an escape from the cruellest possible postscript to the fighting life and name Ali had defended so valiantly in New York against Shavers. The rematch win over Spinks had also brought him the distinction of becoming the first to win the world heavyweight title three times.

Now he planned to fight again, but not against someone he might reasonably anticipate outwitting and overwhelming with the sheer weight of his presence. No, the proposed opponent was Larry Holmes, a man of daunting strength and technical accomplishment unbeaten in 35 fights and with such formidable victims as Shavers (twice), Ken Norton and Mike Weaver. Ali pointed out that Holmes was his former sparring partner; yes, he was a good pro, but when the first bell sounded he would know his place.

Seven million dollars were on the table – a substantial retirement plan, no doubt – but on the drive past the pony-and-traps and the painted barns of the Amish land the bright sunshine hardly bathed the project in such an encouraging light. A retirement plan, you had to ask yourself, or a death wish?

At the camp, an impressive installation of sturdy wooden buildings, a Canadian colleague, magazine writer Hal Quinn, and I were given a surprisingly warm welcome by Ali's faithful retainer, Gene Kilroy. 'Writers, great!' he exclaimed. 'We haven't seen a writer in weeks and the champion has been getting restive. He said to me over breakfast this morning, "Hey, Gene where are the writers and the TV guys? Has the world forgotten me already? I want everyone ready to welcome me back as the king."'

Kilroy offered the quote without any input of his own. He knew boxing well enough, having enlisted in Ali's army, and become, along with Dundee, one of only two white American bedrock members of his entourage, 20 years earlier at the Rome Olympics. But if he knew boxing, better still he knew Ali. And most of all he understood that you couldn't challenge his idea of reality. Or his measuring of the odds against him.

In Rome in 1960 Kilroy, a young lawyer and army officer, was entranced by the magic of the then Cassius Clay. He had never seen such a magnetic performer in any branch of sport – or life. When Ali was banished from the ring after his refusal to serve in Vietnam, Kilroy became his business manager. That, at least, was his official title. Really, he was the day-by-day monitor of all his moods, hopes, fears and, far from least, his foibles.

Most famously, Kilroy was consulted when Ali's flight entered the descent path to Kinshasa for the awesome challenge of subduing the power and the menace of George Foreman, who had so recently come close to dismembering Joe Frazier. Ali knew that a great gathering awaited him at the airport and the question for Kilroy, the trained lawyer, the man of the world, was how best he might connect with his African 'kinfolk'.

When he sat down beside Ali he was asked, 'Who do these people most hate?' Kilroy said that he was not an expert on Africa but it was certainly true that the old Belgian regime had been among the hardest, most repressive in the history of colonisation. He added, 'On that basis, Champ, I'd take a guess at the Belgians.'

When Ali came down the steps of the plane he was, as expected, greeted by a vast throng. He stopped and waved for quiet. And then announced, 'George Foreman is a Belgian.'

For Kilroy, there would never be a drama quite like that of the Rumble in the Jungle. Of course the Frazier trilogy was epic, the downing of Liston sensational, and almost always there had been a sense of travelling into new terrain of the mind and the spirit. But then no one had loomed larger than Foreman, and Kilroy recalled the grim picture he took back to Ali after serving as his representative in Foreman's pre-fight dressing room. There, he saw Foreman pounding his great fists together and heard his distinguished camp helper, Archie Moore, speak of the stench of death. Ali asked for Kilroy's impression of the scene and added a pointed question, 'What did the nigger say?' Kilroy felt obliged to say it as it had been said, reporting, 'He said he was going to make your children orphans.'

There was no such foreboding at Deer Lake – but it was hard not to believe there should have been.

As Kilroy predicted, we had a warm welcome from Ali. We were greeted not as interlopers but as reassuring confirmation that the world still wanted to hear what he had to say. What looked like a leisurely workout was almost at its end but we were invited to sit with him while he was massaged. Had we not been impressed by the new moves he was putting together in the gym? He was disappointed when we confessed to missing most of his work. 'Well, you just have to come again tomorrow and see it with your own eyes. Come for breakfast.' Kilroy was right. He was in the mood to welcome beggars from the street for whatever reinforcement they might bring.

'My business is to delight the world and to shock it and keep it in suspense, asking, "What's he going to do now, what's he got planned?" And I'm ready to do it again,' said Ali. 'I've done it so many times before and I'll do it again. They said that I would be crushed by Liston and that Joe Frazier would end my story, and then George Foreman was going to kill me. Now the boogie man is Larry Holmes. Some people don't think I can find a way to beat him. When will they ever learn not to doubt me?'

I asked him if he ever fretted over the warnings he had received, and especially the one that came from his medical adviser, Ferdie Pacheco, after the Shavers fight. Did he not feel sometimes that he had done war enough and that every warrior had to choose the time when he must put down his arms? It was a question I would put to so many of the great fighters and, almost invariably, it produced a response tinged with a little anger, a suspicion of impertinence.

On this occasion, though, it was as though Ali had blithely put aside all thoughts of his worst possibilities. He said that he was still primed to fight, to feel the great sensation of going into the ring and proving all over again that he was indeed the Greatest, the one who would always set his own agenda.

'Look at me,' he said, 'do you think I'm ready to walk away? Do I look like someone ready to quit on the thing he does best?'

Certainly, for good or bad, that was not the sense carried back into the rush-hour traffic of Philadelphia. Ali, after some promotional false steps, would have his fight, his latest rite of reinvention. And who was ready to say that the story of Muhammad Ali, the great champion, would be over before the end of the year?

No doubt it was a logical conclusion when the work patterns of Ali and Holmes over the last few years were seriously reviewed. That of Holmes spoke impressively of the maturing of a fine and increasingly brutal talent. He had long shed the anonymity of the sparring partner who lined up in pursuit of the casual labour offering payment that, given the pain, the unremitting punishment the labour brought, was never likely to attract even the most desperate longshoreman or fruit picker. Big, immensely strong and equipped with a powerful, perfectly thrown jab and a punishing right hand, Holmes also had the steel of a deeply motivated professional.

He had sampled the rewards for himself and his family and he carried around with him diagrams of the fine house – and heart-shaped swimming pool – he was having built in his hometown of Easton.

A hard-working community on the confluence of the Delaware and Lehigh rivers in Pennsylvania, 55 miles north of Philadelphia and 70 miles west of New York City, Easton was not a place for adventurers or opportunists, and Holmes, after the hardest application, had come to be its wealthiest and most famous citizen. Such status was not likely to be easily surrendered, even to the man who had so dominated the dreams of every heavyweight fighter for so long.

The original plan had been for Ali to fight John Tate, the new World Boxing Association world champion, but it fell apart when he lost that title to Weaver in March. The new champion was next in line but Ali, when naming Holmes as his opponent in October, put on a pained expression and said, in the fashion of an exasperated businessman, the demands of Weaver's promoter, Bob Arum, were 'totally unacceptable'. That sounded almost prissy on the lips of the man who had so spectacularly led the greening of boxing, but then the prospect of his fight with Holmes produced a quite different perspective. Everyone knew – and perhaps even Ali in the small hours of the night – that he was again standing on the edge of the abyss.

Soon though, the fight acquired inevitability. Ali, in his inimitable way, had planted it in the mind of the boxing public. He had talked it up in bursts of bravura – 'the pupil thinks he can teach the master but that makes it clear he's a chump not a champ' – but much more significantly he had not picked out a soft option for maybe his last major payday in the ring. He had elected someone guaranteed to provide an ultimate test of his right to continue calling himself 'the People's Champion'.

He did have one hurdle to overcome, however. It was a legacy of the controversy provoked by that terrible scene in his dressing room after the Shavers fight, one that his former medical adviser, Ferdie Pacheco, returned to at regular intervals. The Nevada Athletic Commission said Ali must be cleared medically. He went to the prestigious Mayo Clinic in Minnesota.

The report, which was not made public until after the fight (and was then lost somewhat in a wider controversy), contained some disquieting observations but none of them were, in the view of the commission, serious enough to cause the fight to be cancelled. The neurological findings noted that Ali's speech was not always easily co-ordinated with muscles that controlled the function, his agility while hopping on one foot was less than perfect, as was his ability to touch his nose with his finger. In another, even less fastidious age of boxing, and without knowledge of the early development of Parkinson's disease, Ali might have been said to be exhibiting the first signs of being punch drunk.

However, in the days before the fight the queasiness that assessment might have provoked was consumed, at least for some optimists, by another possibility. It was that Ali had made of medical science what he had of some other of life's cautions. He looked miraculously well. He was, at least an illusion said, alive again at the peak of his powers.

At the weigh-in there were gasps when Ali stepped off the scales weighing a mere 15 stone 7 pounds, his lightest since taking down Foreman six years earlier. Ali lived on beautifully; at least, it was pretty to think so. Some, though, were not inclined to bury their reservations. They included Hugh McIlvanney, who had written so memorably over the years on the theme of the great man's power to reinvent himself, and not least when reporting from Kinshasa. Then, he introduced his report to the *Observer* thus, 'We should have known that Muhammad Ali would not have settled for any old resurrection. His had to have an additional flourish. So, having rolled back the rock, he hit George Foreman on the head with it.'

Yet every man is ultimately rooted in the tyranny of time and wear and I shouldn't have been surprised when, on a drive into the desert to escape for a little while the orchestrated frenzies of the Vegas Strip, McIlvanney frowned and emitted a small groan when I volunteered that I had not, in my fight preview for the Vancouver paper, precluded the possibility of another feat to astound the world. 'Ali has been astonishing,' he said, 'but everyone has their limits and I fear that he may well discover this here.'

It was a salutary warning, along with the one he offered after briefly sharing my table at a roadside casino and watching my novice attempts to win at blackjack. 'You may think it's a simple game,' he said, 'but there are some very important rules. You should take the time to learn all of them, son.'

But then, of course, there are some points in your life when there is no weightier counsel than the promptings of what you like to think of grandly as your heart and your soul. Neither could have been more influential when the reincarnated Ali came into the ring.

I was back in Madison Square Garden, transfixed by a possibility that, looking back, had been dissipating too long under the weight of some unforgiving years. Now, though, reality would arrive without a sliver of doubt, a moment of dispute or, for Ali, respite. It would envelop him, drain from him every ounce of the old hubris. Strong men cried at the ringside. They wept for the end of something that they believed had ennobled their experience of life and an understanding of the potential great men would always see in the challenges it brought.

It wasn't that Ali didn't fight – that idea at least would not haunt for ever all those who had come into the cool desert night for maybe one last taste of the glory. No, the problem was much more fundamental than any of failure of nerve or will, some defection, at the very last moments, of all that had made his career so unique. He couldn't fight; he had become disabled.

Pat Putnam of *Sports Illustrated*, who had been around the Fifth Street gym in Miami in the early sixties when Ali first flourished under the guidance of Dundee, reported the phenomenon with the most admirable detachment for a man who had invested so much of his professional life in telling every phase of the story.

He wrote, 'Round one had ended and Muhammad Ali, slumped on his stool in his corner, knew then what the world would soon discover. The recently gained body beautiful was no more than a clever counterfeit. Ali was a Ferrari without an engine, a Rolex with the works missing. There was nothing inside. As Ali sat half-listening to his trainer Angelo Dundee, sadly he understood that the career that had burst so brilliantly into being 20 years earlier at the Olympics in Rome would end this night in humiliation and defeat in a Las Vegas parking lot.'

Later there would be a welter of analysis, most of it around the fact that Ali had been treated for the errant diagnosis of a thyroid problem with a drug that had the side effect of a powerful, weight-losing diuretic. But first there was the ordeal: Ali's and all those who loved him. It was the undiluted horror of helplessness that came to a man whose forte had almost always been his ability to grow under the gaze of a bewitched and expectant world.

Now he wilted a little more with each new round. Dundee beseeched him to make a show, however futile, warning Ali by the mid-rounds that he had to do something, even if it was illusory, to prevent referee Richard Greene stopping the fight. It was one of many prospects that haunted Dundee to the point of tears as Ali threw jabs that had no pace and launched right hands that were a parody of the old spontaneous, shattering brilliance.

Before the fight, Holmes said that if he could dispatch Ali with one punch, he would. But then when that proved impossible he simply did his work with a relentless efficiency, even if some had the sentimental idea – which he disavowed – that something deep in his psyche held him back from one single moment of ultimate, crushing ruthlessness.

By the fourth round Dundee had looked into the eyes of Ali, one of which was now half-closed, long enough to know that all they could see were reasons for a growing despair. Dundee recalled, 'I was trying to find some familiar chord, activate something that might still be deep inside him, but the more I tried the more elusive it seemed to be. I was trying to pump him up but you cannot pump up what isn't there. You can't get water out of a dry well. You can't make your own reality, you can only work with what you have.'

Ali, it was clear now, surely even in the seats closest to the desert, had nothing. He ransacked what was left of his resources, you could see in the desperate expression of a face that, beneath the dyed hair, had so recently seemed to have shed at least several years, and found only a scrap of surviving resistance to the idea of surrendering the fight.

Holmes thought it might well be over in the fourth when he landed a thunderous right to Ali's kidneys and believed he saw every sign of his subsiding. He said later, 'When the hook hit him he moaned and started to fall. Then all of a sudden he jerked himself up. His damned pride just wouldn't let him fall. There's not another man on earth who would have been on his feet after that punch.'

At the end of the tenth Dundee could no longer bear the sight of Muhammad Ali's travail. The ever-faithful, besotted fan Bundini Brown begged for one more round, but one more round of what, Dundee wanted to know in a flash of fierce indignation. Another round of Ali's pain and humiliation, another chance to see him gaze so forlornly at a horizon lost to him for ever.

The tenth had been purgatory for Ali. Holmes hit him at will as he stumbled into range: hooks, jabs, combinations too quick for his jaded reactions rained upon his head and his body. It was the end, there could be no more of this cruel and artificially extended ordeal. If fighting doesn't have intrigue, the possibility of something uncharted and mysterious, it descends into plain brutality and that was now the fate of the man who some of us had been foolish enough to believe might have one more stupendous act to play.

'That's it, it's over,' Dundee yelled at the referee, Greene, as Ali dragged himself back to his corner. Bundini's entreaties to Dundee rose above the yells – and included a plaintive attempt to embrace the trainer. Dundee was snarling now. 'Take your goddam hands off me,' he shouted at Brown. 'He can't take any more. He's defenceless. Get the hell away from me. I'm boss here. It's over.'

Ali's manager, Herbert Muhammad, was wise to heed Dundee's general warning against any encroachment on his field command. The referee would later say that he would have made his own decision to end the fight if Dundee hadn't thrown in the towel. Ali? He continued to gaze into the blur of the middle distance. If he retained that scrap of defiance, he no longer voiced it.

When he was helped the short distance to his opulent hotel suite, he whispered hoarsely that all he wanted to do was lie down. He was 38 years and nine months old, beaten, or so it seemed, beyond even the limits of his own self-belief. Soon enough he would feel the stirrings of a degenerative disease. It was a scenario so bleak that perhaps only he could have found in it the smallest gleam of light.

Inevitably he did so, after exchanging some banter with a Holmes who came to his suite in no mood of triumphalism. Indeed, he was keen to once again bend his knee to the meaning of a great career and said that his beating of a man he still revered had brought him no relish. 'So why did you do it?' Ali asked with a weary smile. Holmes asked for an assurance that his hero would never fight again but, as he left the room with his brother Jake, Ali began a low and now familiar chant: 'I want Larry Holmes, I want Larry Holmes, I want Larry Holmes.' Holmes laughed thinly and said to his brother, 'Oh Lord, let's get out of here.'

He had hardly shut the door when Ali was up on his feet, preparing for an appearance, behind dark glasses, on the 4 a.m. Western time first showing of *Good Morning America*. By then, though, the target had shifted. 'I want Mike Weaver, the WBA champion,' he told his interviewer.

A fantasy, no doubt, but how could it possibly live in the shell of someone so profoundly battered just a few hours earlier?

It was because there was one last evasion of reality. Ali, even as he winced in pain, had decided that his defeat was not due to the erosion of time, nor a surfeit of brutal punishment, but the medical misadventure of the thyroid diagnosis and the use, beyond the ordered dosage, of a drug called Thyrolar. Thomas Hauser wrote a searing account of the episode in his definitive work *Muhammad Ali: His Life and Times*. He reported that Dr Charles Williams, a member of Ali's reformed medical team, had prescribed Thyrolar after believing he had detected a thyroid imbalance. Hauser wrote of the drug Ali had embraced as both a vitamin and an aid to weight loss, '[It] is a potentially lethal drug and no one on Thyrolar should engage in a professional fight.'

Among the side effects were fatigue, sluggishness, headaches, increased blood pressure, tremors, nausea, increased heart rate, frequent urination and weight loss. Apart from that last cosmetic benefit, all in all it was not exactly a boon to the cause of an ageing warrior. Later, Dr Williams conceded, 'I may have placed him in jeopardy inadvertently,' and at the same time the University of California Los Angeles Medical Center concluded that Ali's thyroid had been functioning normally before the administering of the drug.

Inevitably, Hauser found an obliging witness in the man who had first proclaimed publicly the growing hazards Ali faced in the ring. Said Pacheco, 'Ali was a walking time bomb in the ring that night. He could have had anything from a stroke to a heart attack to all kinds of bleeding in the head.'

In the best of all worlds Ali might have celebrated his escape from such a fate before the eyes of the world; he might have looked into the mirror not for another act of reinvention but for an acceptance that, along with all men at a certain point in their existence, he had had the best of his time and now he had another challenge. It was to see the world, and the rest of his journey through it, as it was and not as he would have liked it to have been.

He couldn't do it. He told *Good Morning America* that he would return. His story wasn't over. But of course it was, and if anyone still nursed the slightest of doubt it was dispelled with infinite sadness in Nassau in the Bahamas 14 months later. He lost a unanimous decision to Trevor Berbick over ten rounds. Ali took some considerable punishment from a stronger, much younger man who would five years later win a share of the heavyweight title before immediately surrendering it to Mike Tyson.

At last Ali, nearing his 40th birthday, made his concession. He said, 'Father Time has finally caught up with me. I'm gonna retire. And I don't think I'm going to wake up and change my mind. I came out all right for an old man. We all lose sometimes. We all grow old.'

In that most modest of ambitions he succeeded, for all the difficulties he encountered, at least in a way denied Berbick, the fifth and last of his conquerors. Twenty-five years after the Nassau fight, Berbick was murdered while he attended church in his native Port Antonio in Jamaica, battered with a steel pipe wielded by a relative with whom he was involved in a land dispute.

When Ali died he was attended, of course, by presidents and the common people who poured into the streets of hometown Louisville, Kentucky. That was a valediction that was never in doubt at any stage in the 35 years that came after the night in Las Vegas when the strong men cried at ringside.

And perhaps in the sad exodus from the gaudy site of his most devastating trial, his most desperate experience in a boxing ring, there was still one last consolation in his forlorn cry to America and the world that he would return.

It was the deeper truth that he would never leave the hearts of all who had seen him, however fleetingly, march to a fate that his life, his nature and the trade he distinguished so uniquely had in the end made inevitable.

Chapter Four

Any doubt that Durán–Leonard II had achieved the status of a 'Super Fight', the first post-Ali collision to enjoy that unquestioned ranking, was largely dispelled when I stepped fresh from the airport into the lift of the big hotel next to the Superdome.

My only companion was dressed in a shimmering gold lamé hot-pant suit, and hanging from around her neck was a Leica camera. She was also, like Frank Sinatra in that Fight of the Century between Ali and Frazier at Madison Square Garden in 1971, wearing an official working photographer's credential. It was Christie Brinkley, the Uptown Girl who would soon become Billy Joel's second wife.

There were many more flurries of celebrity spreading into the French Quarter where even the jazz and the blues seemed to be enjoying a revived resonance. Ray Charles, the namesake of Leonard, who seemed to have shed so many of the uncertainties that had undone him in Montreal, would intone 'America the Beautiful' with an especially haunting cadence before the first bell. The place was alive with the electricity peculiar to great events. Boxing, which seemed so imperilled in Las Vegas barely a month earlier as Ali submitted to the reach of time and the clubbing power of Larry Holmes, had gone down deep and found old reasons to proclaim the continued appeal of its brash and so frequently troubling existence.

If there was any strengthening currency in the theory that boxing had indeed gone beyond its time, that no longer could an advanced society support the concept of one man hitting another on the head, with the possibility of fatal consequences, as legitimate public entertainment, it was hardly negotiable in New Orleans.

In the dense and animated arboreal lobby of the fight hotel someone shouted, 'Does anyone know where Durán is?' and Ed Schuyler Junior, the Associated Press boxing man whose cutting wit would for so long irrigate some of the harder days on the road, put down his bourbon and said, 'No, but Ray Arcel just came by with a whip and a stool in his hands so I guess he's gone to the gym.'

Unfortunately, we would learn soon enough, Arcel and his tough old co-worker, Freddie Brown, would have needed rather more than such basic training aids to recreate the fighter who had appeared so ferociously in the ring of the Olympic Stadium six months earlier.

Then, Durán wore his hunger for glory, and Leonard's title, on his face and every fibre of a taut and perfectly prepared body. Here in New Orleans he was a man whose appetite for much beyond the dining table and nights of unending celebration was said to have been largely sated.

The fight would always be remembered for the words of Durán that shook boxing to its foundations and traumatised his adoring nation, Panama. They were words of both pain and irony. 'No mas, no mas – No more, no more,' he said with a wave of his hand in the eighth round. It was a phrase that his superb veteran trainers, and his devoted manager, Carlos Eleta, had longed to hear in the months of excess that followed the great triumph over Leonard. When the first drama was spent, but the mystery was still being explored with much intensity, Eleta would make a long and detailed statement on Panama's main television channel. It was boxing's version of an address to the nation. It spoke of Durán's collapse as a disciplined fighting man and it contained the shattering opinion that he should never return to the ring.

Eleta's revelations would be vital to any understanding of Durán's state of mind, and expectations, in New Orleans. However, even without them, and with a Durán more easily recognisable as the man who had reported to Montreal, there was another huge factor in play. It was that we also had a different Sugar Ray Leonard.

In Montreal, there were times when he'd appeared to be submerged by the furies of his opponent. Here he was bursting with a slick, buoyant composure. After one late workout, when he had moved with a thrilling poise, he briefly resurrected his inquisition of writers who were calling a Durán triumph. They were reduced in numbers now, partly because of Leonard's regained aura, partly because of those disturbing, but initially fiercely denied, stories of Durán's slide towards anarchy.

This time when we raised our guilty hands, Leonard's expression was more quizzical than outraged. He shook his head, grinned and commented, 'That's very interesting.' His favourite's odds had shortened to 6-5, three points narrower than before the first fight, but if you had spent a few days in New Orleans without any knowledge of events in Montreal you would still have been tempted by a gift beckoning at the betting window.

The regained faith in his old powers was quickly justified. Tommy 'Hitman' Hearns, who would take on the winner, leant forward at ringside with the rapt gaze of an assigned assassin dressed, appropriately, in a black suit. As early as the second round he muttered, 'Leonard looks good. He looks like the one who has come to fight this time.' But not only to fight, also to parade his skills and mock the audacity and presumption of the man who had brought him down.

The doyen of American sportswriters, Red Smith, was pushing deep into his seventies now but his antennae were both acute and tuned by more than 50 years of experience, and he was quick to see that Leonard was involved in a work of elaborate, showy revenge, something more than a mere display of beautiful timing and masterful ring-craft. 'He wants to strip down Durán, physically and mentally,' said the man who had been scathing about some of the ring antics of the young Cassius Clay.

Later, against the pressure of his East Coast *New York Times* deadline, Smith wrote, 'When the match ended, officially a knockout in the eighth, Leonard was ahead on the cards of all three judges. Acting as his own judge, Leonard obviously felt that he had it all the way. In the third round when Durán lunged at him and fell far short, Leonard laughed and stuck out his tongue. In the seventh he thrust his face out toward Durán and taunted him with a grimacing, shoulder-shrugging boogaloo. He was not a spectacularly gracious winner.'

Something of Leonard's mood was expressed in a conversation he had with his manager, Mike Trainer, as he left the dressing room to go down to the ring. He was dressed in black shorts and plain black boots and he asked Trainer how he looked. The manager replied, 'You look like a mix of the Grim Reaper and an assassin.' Leonard smiled and said, 'Good.'

By the eighth round his combination of superb boxing, filled with all the strength and adroitness and timing that had become stretched and frayed in Montreal, and his unrestrained assault on Durán's psyche – and specifically his huge macho pride – had become overwhelming. A fight that had generated $38 million, and guaranteed Durán $8 million and Leonard $7 million, had dwindled in value so much, as a contest if not a lurid spectacle, that it might have become some cameo of a fractious schoolyard.

It was one in which Leonard's mastery had become total if not, as Red Smith suggested, admirable.

In Montreal Durán had made an immediate statement of intent. He had gone into Leonard with an ultimately unanswerable authority.

In New Orleans, despite the reinforcement provided by the first triumph – and a record of 72–1 with 55 knockouts – he was markedly more tentative. Indeed, half of the first round had elapsed before he sought to dominate and when he did so, driving Leonard into the ropes, it was only to see his victim escape almost nonchalantly before landing with a crisply dismissive right hand. And then Leonard said, in so many words, 'OK, let's do a little trading,' and there was no question who had most to barter. Leonard jabbed cleanly, was plainly sharper and more intent on taking control. He ended the round with a left-right combination that left a rueful smile on Durán's much less than serene face.

Already there was something of the matador in Leonard's strut, the way he engaged Durán with the boldest of moves, then extricated himself so elegantly, and arrogantly, he might have been dressed in a suit of lights and trailing a cape in the sand. In the second round, he went more quickly about his work, landing heavy right hands, jarring back Durán's head, and then retreating sure-footedly behind perfectly thrown jabs.

If this had indeed been a *corrida*, the man from Panama was beginning to look like the bemused bull in search of his *querencia*, that part of the ring where he feels most confident, most at home. But then it was impossible to believe that Durán would not produce something in the way of meaningful aggression and, sure enough, he generated enough of it to win the third round unanimously and shade the fifth. But they were brief flashes of defiance. For all the showy pyrotechnics, Leonard's performance was plainly built on the soundest foundations.

By the eighth Durán could do no more than confirm that he was lost. In the face of Leonard's disdain, the whirling of his fist in the action of a bolo punch that never came, in the showing of his tongue and the now permanent, gleeful sneer on his face, Durán had reached down into all his experience and found nothing on which he might draw.

So he turned his back on his tormentor and said to referee Octavio Meyran, '*No mas, no mas.*' Bewildered, Meyran asked simply, '*Por què? – Why?*' Durán muttered the shocking words again, this time adding the English translation, 'No more box.'

In the hours that followed there were many theories. Durán had been injured, he had seriously overeaten after the midday weigh-in on the day of the fight and was afflicted by cramps in the fifth round. But a medical examination the following day, while Durán's purse was being withheld, failed to show up any injury or physical disorder.

It seemed to me that two conclusions had to be reached. One was underpinned by a mountain of evidence that almost from the moment he left Montreal's Olympic Stadium in triumph, Durán had shed the bearing and the instincts of a proud champion. That made the first verdict a formality. Durán had lost his title in the months and the weeks and the days, even the hours, before he entered the Superdome ring.

The second determination had to be arrived at just as urgently as the imminence of the deadline gnawed more deeply than usual. Had Durán made a statement of cowardice? Had he simply refused to take the punishment that his negligence on the road and in the gym had made inevitable? I found that belief absurd at the time, and still do, and it was reassuring to have the agreement of the doyen Smith over a late Scotch.

'I agree with you,' said Smith. 'I believe Durán would rather have been taken out into the street and shot than suffer any more of that humiliation which Leonard was so intent on piling on him. A man like Durán can take anything, absorb anything, apart from having his manhood, his fighting ability, mocked and scorned in the eyes of the world. He would have taken his punishment but he couldn't accept the role of being Leonard's dupe, a prop for comedy.'

In the morning, in the press huddle that awaited further illumination, I had less reason to be uplifted by Hugh McIlvanney's reaction to my confession that, as in Vegas before the Ali–Holmes fight, I had invested somewhat too heavily in my idea of a man still capable, for all the imperfections of his preparation, of summoning an extraordinary fighting will. I said, sheepishly, that I had described Durán as 'an implacable warrior'. I can still hear McIlvanney's hoots of laughter. 'It would seem,' he chortled, 'that the bottom has fallen out of the implacability business.'

That morning there was illumination enough of Durán's professional dereliction. Much of it was fuelled by the raw anger of Ray Arcel and Freddie Brown and the saddened resignation of Eleta. William Nack of *Sports Illustrated* portrayed fight men shattered by the betrayal of their most fundamental values.

Arcel had demanded an explanation from his fighter, only to be told, 'I quit. No gonna fight any more.' Brown, who had once healed a gaping gash in the nose of the remorseless, unbeaten heavyweight champion Rocky Marciano, was equally bemused. He said, 'I've been with the guy nine years and I can't explain it. The guy's supposed to be an animal, right? And he quit. You'd think an animal would fight right up to the end.'

Arcel's wife Stevie stood in the disconsolate, bewildered group and reported, 'I went to his room to commiserate with him, to console him, and I could hardly get in. There was a party in the room, Roberto was singing with his wife.'

Arcel delivered a final, crushing statement of disgust, telling Nack, 'I've had it. This is terrible. I've handled thousands of fighters and this is the first time one has quit on me. I think this guy needs a psychiatrist more than he needs anything else. What happens in the human mind? Who knows?

'I've been associated with guys like Ezzard Charles and Barney Ross, guys who gave their all. Durán always possessed the same courage, the same determination. He was a fighter. If anyone had ever come to Freddie and me and said, "This guy will quit on you," I'd have spit in the guy's eye. Durán quitting? Never. He would never quit.'

Some of the details of Durán's self-indulgence might have been imagined by those who dreamed up the myth of the vomiting rooms of Ancient Rome. The outline of Durán's preparation, as it emerged piece by piece, binge by binge, was bleak enough. One report had Durán near 200 pounds, or 53 beyond the welterweight limit, shortly before he was dispatched to his training camp in the Catskill Mountains of New York State three months before the fight.

Brown stated that Durán had been 173 pounds when he reported in in September, and at the start of November, less than a month before the fight, he had still to lose another 13 pounds to make the weight.

On the day of the fight he made it at the lunchtime weigh-in with a pound to spare. However, it was not exactly a triumph of careful husbanding of a champion's strength. Carlos Eleta admitted that three days earlier Durán had, like Ali so disastrously before the Holmes fight, sought the help of diuretics. He had dried himself out and then, when he stepped from the scales, swigged a thermos of consommé and half a flask of hot tea. He then sat down to two large T-bone steaks, fried potatoes, four large glasses of orange juice, two glasses of water and a cup of tea. He then demolished a very large orange.

Four hours later, he had half a T-bone and several cups of tea. By comparison, Leonard, who had reported to training camp early and in fine condition, had consumed a substantial breakfast before the weigh-in: two eggs, grits, two pieces of toast, peaches and a glass of fruit juice. His pre-fight dinner was a model of restraint – a little fried chicken, peas, a glass of water and a fruit drink.

His greatest appetite was to fight, and when it was done, when so many were accusing Durán of betraying the meaning of all that he had achieved, he could not spare himself his own bout of self-indulgence. It was a most generous helping of self-vindication. He announced, 'They said Ray can't get up. Ray's not angry enough. Ray doesn't have that killer instinct. Ray's not that kind of person. Ray's too nice. But I didn't lose track of what must be done to carry out the mission – and it was a mission. It was like going to the Olympics.

'I proved myself in New Orleans. I proved to him what I could do. I made him quit, to make Roberto Durán quit was better than knocking him out.'

This, no doubt, said far more about the degree of pain and humiliation Leonard suffered in Montreal than his essential fighting nature. In the years to come Leonard would repeatedly assert his pride under the fiercest pressure. He had fights to come that would stretch his resources to their most impressive limits, gut-wrenching battles in which the antics he performed in the Superdome would have been as inappropriate as tasteless jocularity at a funeral. Maybe he needed to purge his system of all the frippery that crowded into his subjection of Durán. Perhaps, more even than in his quelling of Wilfred Benítez, when he announced the quality of his fighting pedigree, it was his rite of passage, his graduation from mere virtuoso to the status of pure, honed-down warrior.

From Durán we had precisely the reverse. Or so it seemed when Eleta walked with his heavy heart into the Panamanian television studio. He told the nation of his failed attempt to return Durán to the closed, committed world of a working world champion. He spoke of the devastating impact of a small army of hangers-on, their number reaching a peak at around 100 – and of his need to put the bulk of Durán's eventually released purse of $7 million into a trust fund in an effort to protect his fighter, with whom he never had a formal contract, from the worst of his own behaviour.

Later in an interview with the *New York Times*, syndicated across North America, Eleta underlined the weight of the burden he had carried to and from New Orleans. He said, 'I explained to the people

A RINGSIDE AFFAIR

of Panama what happened. I told them he had a problem in the life he led before the fight. Now the situation is good. The people understand what happened and why he got the "reaction" during the fight.

'After the first fight in Montreal everybody was inviting him to parties. He is like a god in his country. His house was like a hotel. It was impossible for his trainers to put him to work. When I sent him to Grossinger's [a resort in the Catskills] for the training camp he weighed 183 pounds. He had to train hard but even in the camp the people around him were kidding him and feeding him. There were 60 persons from Panama around him, and asking for money and worshipping him. They went to New Orleans invited by him. I had a lot of trouble with them. I told him I didn't want any of these people around him any more. They were bad for him in Panama and in New Orleans. When the trainers were telling him to do things these people were shouting, "Don't listen to them, you're fine." So if Durán said he wanted to eat more, they said, "Well, eat more, it will not hurt you."

'I wanted to fight with all of them. They don't give a damn about anyone. All they want is money from Durán. They were destroying him.'

Eleta was speaking from a great well of sadness. It was fashioned by what he considered a tragic loss of a reputation built on a character forged out of the difficulties and the challenges that he considered inseparable from the lives of young people in the American ghetto and the *barrios* of his homeland.

He went on, 'I'm so discouraged because I work all my life that Roberto Durán will retire as one of the best fighters of all time. You know how honourable Ray Arcel and Freddie Brown are. Now everybody is talking bad about them. I am very sad. Why did he quit in the ring? Something happened to him mentally, he says to himself, "Leonard is not going to make fun of me." Something strange happened to him. He was not in bad shape. He was not hurt. Yet he cannot be a coward – not someone who has such a record for so long. He was

52

trying to do what the body wouldn't let him do. His body wasn't there, so in the end he said, "To hell with it."'

Without Eleta's help, at least officially, Durán would return to the career he said was over in the aftermath of New Orleans. He would regather his pride, and sufficient standing, to return to the ring in the very highest company of Leonard, Marvin Hagler and Tommy Hearns. The results would be mixed but the worst of his New Orleans stigma would dissolve in his willingness to go in once more against such opponents and take whatever might come to him. He would never again walk away from an opponent.

In this at least he would vindicate the instinct I had shared with the great Red Smith in the face of all those cries that he was guilty not of a refusal to play another man's game, one that he thought did not belong in a place where men went to fight, but of physical cowardice.

We agreed that Durán had not made a nonsense of his life in such an easily identifiable way, and before Smith returned to his home in Connecticut, where he wrote his daily column for the *New York Times* in a well-upholstered garden shed, we had a parting drink. It was in the lounge where the departed fight crowd would soon be replaced by the latest army of conventioneers wearing their corporate smiles and company name tags, and another point of agreement was that we should not forget the privilege of the job we did and the things we saw.

I never saw the 75-year-old Red Smith again. It was one of his last journeys on the road that he travelled – he was never too proud to admit – with at least half an eye on his potential to get things wrong, to jump too easily to a conclusion that might just not stand the test of time.

He died just a year and one month later, shortly after reducing his workload to three columns a week, all of them pared down to shining examples of concision and insight and, not least, an understanding that so many things, in life and sport, were not always as they first seemed.

That capacity helped win him a Pulitzer Prize for commentary, but the wider accolade he claimed was the respect of all those who saw that he was a man prepared to admit that indeed he had not always been right.

Most significantly, he conceded that his first dismissal of Muhammad Ali as a shrill braggart and a 'column dodger' who would always be beaten by a man like Joe Frazier had been turned to ashes by the years. It was no hardship, he said, to admit to being wrong. Ali had proved himself a great athlete, a great fighter and a great man.

Smith also said that writing was 'Easy . . . all you had to do was open a vein and bleed'. And, most certainly, step back from the kind of reflex assertion that in New Orleans said that Roberto Durán, of all fighters, had turned yellow.

Time, and far more of it than Red Smith had left, would continue to remind me of that.

Chapter Five

Las Vegas, September 1981

Sometimes if you are very lucky you see something you know will always be with you. It takes hold of you so completely you might be held in a vice. You know that when it is over it will be like the breaking of a spell, the cessation of a storm – and the triumph of a most dominant spirit.

That was how it was at ringside when Sugar Ray Leonard did what he knew he had to do in the 14th round of his fight with Tommy Hearns for the undisputed welterweight title of the world. He had to go into the loneliest, most challenging place a fighter ever occupies. He had to strip away every inhibition.

He had to act. He had to blast his way through a crisis that might just have borne him a lifetime of regrets.

Many say it was the best fight they ever saw. I am one of them. It had a cadence, a violent beauty that would always run before my eyes and sound in my heart.

'You're blowing it, son,' said Leonard's trainer, Angelo Dundee. It was a warning taken less as a rebuke than a call to action. He moved on to another level. He threw a series of withering punches, perfectly timed jabs, searing hooks, powerful right hands. He had always been celebrated for his superb technique. He came into the professional ring both an Olympic champion and a beautiful stylist.

But this was a different Leonard. This was a fighter as hard and elemental as anyone had seen.

The onslaught was his final option and he took it so unanswerably that if it had been the last thing he ever did in a boxing ring there would have been no doubt about the legacy he would leave.

Earlier in the fight his wife Juanita's piercing cries rose from near to ringside. 'No more, no more, Baby,' she wailed, but she had swooned and lapsed into semi-consciousness when Leonard found all his power and his conviction. Now, her yells would have sounded weirdly discordant.

And as Hearns – who led, controversially, on every card when referee Davey Pearl stopped the fight with one minute and 15 seconds left in that astonishing round – was helped away from the ring, his feet trailing behind him, there was another stunning reality.

It was that the new age of boxing, the one that had to make itself amid the ruins of Ali's fall, had done more than set out an impressive stall. It had given itself an extraordinary point of reference, an indelible, timeless stamp that would have been no less impressive had it come around the prime of a fabled figure who drew applause when he took his place at ringside. It was Sugar Ray Robinson, who was fêted in Paris when he came to Europe as he had been in America. He had a head start in the City of Light through his subjection of the Raging Bull, Jake LaMotta, who was the recent conqueror of the French hero Marcel Cerdan, but here, in a place that had been no more than gritty scrubland when he was at the peak of his powers, his meaning lingered on.

Leonard was accused of impertinence when he took the appellation Sugar. It was, some said, an affront to the achievements of a man still regarded by many as the greatest pound-for-pound fighter of all time. But not any more, at least not by those who left ringside for the Caesars Palace casino convinced that they had seen one of the most compelling fights in the history of the ring. A cascade of fireworks blazed in the desert sky. For once Vegas could not be charged with garish overstatement.

However, more than a decade later I was given an older perspective when I happened upon the Raging Bull in one of his favourite New York haunts, P. J. Clarke's on Third Avenue.

He had been in the company of a striking younger woman but she had left, rather peremptorily with an exasperated flounce, and so, putting aside any degree of risk, I asked him if I could buy him a drink. Yes, I could, he grunted. I was working on a piece about Oscar De La Hoya, the world welterweight champion who was the toast of East Los Angeles and boxing's current sensation, and I was interested in LaMotta's opinion on how he would have rated in those days when he was battling, mostly unavailingly, against the great Robinson. 'Oh, I guess he might have made the top ten,' said LaMotta. A little surprised, I asked, 'Pound for pound?'

'Naw,' he said, 'as a welterweight.' It was a rough and arbitrary verdict and betrayed a generational prejudice that Leonard had no doubt challenged when he overcame Hearns. Still, there was much poignancy in the assessment. De La Hoya was already a multimillionaire, celebrated in the mansions of Bel Air and Malibu as well as the clapboard houses of his youth, while Robinson spent his last years struggling for cash, as did his great contemporary Joe Louis, who ended his life as a casino greeter sitting in a wheelchair.

Such a spectre of impoverishment had long been banished by Leonard and Hearns when they fought so brilliantly before the gaze of Robinson – and just a few months after Louis's death. Leonard–Hearns I grossed $38 million. Leonard's share was $11 million and Hearns took $8 million back to Detroit.

It was a financial coup that had been in the making for a year. But if the fight was glorious, less uplifting was so much of the scheming that went into its making. Indeed, the machinations had been so cynical the competitive perfection of Las Vegas was made to seem like a reward that boxing hardly deserved.

Certainly, it was not a high road on which Leonard and his management travelled, by way of Syracuse, New York, and Houston, Texas, to lay their hands on the riches that awaited them at Caesars Palace.

Hearns had made a powerful case for his place in the Vegas 'Showdown'. Three months before 'No mas, no mas', which he witnessed with the expression of a gunfighter who had arrived in town with some serious business in hand, he had laid waste to the vaunted Pipino Cuevas before an exultant home crowd in the Joe Louis Arena in Detroit.

The Mexican virtuoso was making his 12th defence of the World Boxing Association's welterweight crown but he was consumed by the reach and the power of Hearns and never made it through the second round. He left Motown a broken man who would never again fight for a title, and for Hearns, the most dynamic graduate of Emanuel Steward's famed inner-city Kronk Gym in Detroit, the future was made. Just so long, that was, as his people could make the deal with Leonard's manager and financial guru Mike Trainer.

It was not the formality it should have been. By the time 20,000 had been persuaded to pay to watch Leonard fight Larry Bonds – a waspish southpaw whose principal income for some time had been from collecting rubbish for the city of Denver – on the campus of Syracuse University, the imperative was not to watch the fight but to monitor the backroom negotiations. There were two main candidates to fight Leonard in Las Vegas six months and two fights later: Hearns, and the formidable, undisputed middleweight champion Marvin Hagler.

Bonds, incomprehensibly rated number six by the World Boxing Council, was picked from a long list, which at one point included Wilfred Benítez (but his memory of Leonard was still too vivid). It meant that Bonds arrived in Syracuse with the expression of someone down on his luck who had just been handed a winning scratchcard. He was being paid $100,000 as Leonard's first challenger in his second reign as WBC world welterweight champion. It was a $98,150 improvement on his best previous pay night.

Understandably enough, he was both incredulous and delighted over this first summons to action in a year – and after fighting just ten rounds in 18 months. Trainer was unrepentant, saying, 'All we are doing is following the rules. We wanted to fight Clint Jackson, which would have been a better fight, but he isn't ranked. And the WBC says a champion has to fight every four months against a rated fighter.'

It was then that Bonds, a 29-year-old musing over retirement from the ring, received the call. It was a huge lift for both his finances and his self-regard. When the phone rang he was trailing his wife on the family pool table.

For the Leonard camp, Bonds served an additional purpose. As a southpaw, he would provide a little useful practice for Leonard's next assignment just over two months later in Houston, when he was due to meet the reigning World Boxing Association world junior middleweight champion from Uganda, Ayub Kalule, in the Houston Astrodome. Leonard had faced just two southpaws, and Bonds, despite his meagre haul of knockouts in a 29–3 record forged among the lower orders, proceeded to inflict a degree of frustration upon Leonard before being overwhelmed in the tenth round.

Leonard headed back to Maryland nettled by being held up for many rounds, but at least he could agree with his advisers. It had been one more accident-free step on the way to the El Dorado in the desert.

In Houston I applied late for a credential and was rewarded with a place in the Astrodome's overflow baseball box. It left me only marginally nearer earth than if the local National Aeronautics and Space Administration had assigned a place on one of their inter-planetary observation satellites. But then it was also true that what happened in the Astrodome did not demand the closest examination.

This time, Leonard's people had not interrupted the rounds of a garbage man in pursuit of an opponent. However, the Hearns camp were in that kind of terrain when they picked out Pablo Baez for their fighter's place on the Houston undercard. At least Leonard's latest opponent was a reigning world champion.

Hearns won in the fourth round when he hit Baez in the mouth hard enough to make him collapse with tragicomic haste. The victim's consolation was that he was in receipt of by far his biggest pay cheque at $75,000, which was $69,000 more than he received for his last fight. Hearns was paid $525,000. By comparison, the $2.5 million Leonard received for dispatching world champion Kalule in the ninth round, while suffering an injury to his left hand, came to look almost deflationary. There was huge relief when Leonard knocked down Kalule and applied enough pressure to provoke a shake of the African champion's head when he was asked if he was ready to carry on. The Leonard–Hearns Super Fight, at last, was moving from the counting house to its desert arena.

Yes, Leonard–Hearns would prove to be worth all the trouble, and the machinations, but if Leonard would define himself as a fighter, once and for all, on the steamy night of 16 September – and Hearns would have a lifetime to regret the slippage of his control – there would be unanimous agreement only on its status as one of the great fights.

Always there would be the one pivotal question: when Leonard took hold of the fight, battered it beyond any possibility but the dictates of his own will, what was he doing precisely? Was he performing an act of indomitable defiance against heavy odds? Or was he smashing down what some will always say had the potential to be among the most outrageous ringside scoring in the history of boxing?

Four decades on, the question would still burn on with the life of a newly kindled fire.

One position remains particularly fierce, immutable. It says that Leonard's crisis was created not so much by the surprise of the decision of Thomas 'Hitman' Hearns to box Leonard rather than rely on the big right hand that had scythed down 30 of his 32 victims but by the unfathomable operation of the ten-point scoring system by the ringside judges Lou Tabat, Chuck Minker and Duane Ford.

When Leonard's ferocious eruption in the 14th round overwhelmed Hearns, left him draped against the ropes from where he was led to his corner by referee Davey Pearl, Leonard trailed on all three cards. Tabat had it 125–122 for Hearns, Minkner 125–121, and Ford 124–122.

Such scoring, some claimed when the storm of Leonard's equalisation had passed, was a grotesque distortion of the reality of the fight. Pat Putnam of *Sports Illustrated* was especially vehement, prefacing his argument that Leonard had always been the stronger, most vital and damaging force with this damning indictment of the judging: 'The scoring was on the ten-point system, which is a fair method if competently applied. The winner of a round receives ten points while the loser must settle for nine points or less. It is the "less" which seems to have been miscalculated by the judges Lou Tabat – who has been known to count punches on his fingers – Duane Ford and Chuck Minker.

'The flaw in the scoring is plainly evident when you compare the scoring for rounds one and two with that for six and seven. Hearns won rounds one and two with a 10–9 edge, mainly because he was the one moving forward. Leonard's powerful domination of rounds six and seven was unjustly rewarded by one-point margins also.'

Pearl gave some weighty support to this argument when he reflected on his decision to stop the fight with Hearns, theoretically at least, just four minutes and 15 seconds of fighting time away from what would have been his greatest victory. The referee said, 'I figured Hearns was winning all those light-hitting rounds. But Leonard was doing all the heavy damage. I thought it was close. Jeez, what if I had let the fight go on and Ray just barely won the last round and they gave Hearns the decision. Caesars wouldn't have had to tear down the stadium for the Grand Prix auto race next month. The people would have done it for them.'

The other case, one to which I will always hold, gives Hearns much more credit. If it was a great fight, if it still has the power to sweep you back into a maelstrom that might have burst forth only yesterday, it was shaped by not just one but two fighters. They made action that would always unite them. They went into the pantheon of the great fights – the company of Ali and Frazier, Dempsey and Tunney, Robinson and LaMotta – and doing that carried one great requirement. It was the creation of a superb competitive balance, one that needed nothing more in the way of endorsement than the moment Dundee breathed into Leonard's ear the grievous warning, 'You're blowing it, son.'

That desperate statement was not some prophetic anticipation of bizarre judging – this time he hadn't been able to arrange its arrival in his corner at the end of each round – but his understanding that Hearns had indeed brought both tactical surprise and a performance guaranteed to cast doubt over the outcome.

In the end Leonard brilliantly exerted the best of himself, and this was what made the greatness of the fight. Even he, though, couldn't have it both ways. He couldn't have made himself a titan of the boxing ages, couldn't have achieved a reputation to hold for ever, while merely overcoming the passing difficulty of some disordered scoring. The fight could never be explained in such terms.

The one I saw asked of Leonard a supreme effort, and when it came it was so fine, so concentrated, that all that had come before was made to seem like one superb crescendo. And, then, a climax for the ages.

Certainly, it didn't happen according to the confident battle-plan fashioned by Janks Morton, Leonard's mentor and trainer, and

Dundee, a corner strategist of unquestioned calibre. They saw Leonard's superior ring-craft as the vital advantage on a night that was still so oppressively hot it would surely challenge the 6 foot 1 inch Hearns the more profoundly. He had spent long hours in the sauna to make the 147lb limit.

Leonard's fight-plan could hardly have been more explicit. He had to fight smartly, make Hearns carry the fight and then watch an opponent three inches taller dwindle as his stamina inevitably drained away, almost certainly no later than the middle rounds.

Morton was emphatic, saying, 'Hearns can't go but one way, turning to his right. Everyone lets him because they are trying to get away from the jab. And there's no way he's going to jab Ray.' But there was, and by the third round Leonard had felt enough of it to step sharply away from the strategy laid down by Morton and Dundee. He made a fleeting but effective switch to southpaw, then promptly reverted to some classic in-fighting culminating in a powerful right hand. It prevented Hearns winning a third straight round but it did not delight Dundee, who shouted into Leonard's ear, 'What are you doing fighting him? Don't fight him. Move, make him move.' Hearns was, however, moving well enough by his own volition. He was boxing Leonard and sufficiently well to win the fourth and fifth rounds, an advantage that Dundee and Morton by now had good reason to recognise required some swift and dramatic dislodging.

Leonard could not have done much more towards satisfying the demand in those sixth and seventh rounds in which he not only seized control with a sharp increase in aggression but persuaded his corner, if not the judges, that he had both stopped dead a developing crisis and moved to the point of victory in six minutes of furious and biting attack. In fact both corners agreed that Leonard had produced devastating work. Steward conceded that Hearns had never truly recovered from a low-slung hook that smashed into his ribs near the end of the sixth, and Morton reflected later, 'The sixth should have been the last round. Ray had him but he got a little excited. If he had just shortened up his punches he would have knocked him out.'

But then he didn't, and having survived another beating in the seventh, Hearns again began to win rounds. That he did so legitimately rather than by judging miscalculation right through to the bell for the 13th would be another strand of post-fight dispute. Yet no one could question that Hearns carried the fight into its final phase with regained authority in the 11th round.

Leonard had picked up an injury to his left eye in sparring and now it was beginning to close, something that plainly distracted him as much as it encouraged Hearns. Certainly, the man from Detroit had his best round. His jab had regained snap and one short right to Leonard's head suggested that he might be turning a reprieve into triumph.

It was a possibility enhanced by another winning performance from Hearns in the 12th, when the resurrected jab again did most to shape the action. Or so it seemed. The last reality was that what Hearns had been doing, more than anything, was defining precisely what Sugar Ray Leonard had to do when he came out for the 13th.

What it was had the force of an earth movement. Leonard delivered a right to Hearns' head that sent him wobbling from right to left, briefly assessed the effect, and then launched a torrent of unanswered punches. There was initial confusion, at least in the mind of the referee, as to whether Hearns was left sprawling on the ropes as the result of the Leonard fusillade or a push. Had it been a push it would have been of the order of an avalanche, and there was no doubt about the consequence, either way. It was a count of nine.

In the 14th all intrigue flew into the desert night. Leonard came out of his corner with an executioner's intent. His attack was as fierce as it was clinical, and when Hearns later asked how long he had to survive the round before the referee led him to his corner, and was told one minute and 15 seconds, his nod of resignation seemed to be his agreement that it might just as well have been eternity.

There was no great cry for a rematch. Few fights, after all, had asked – and answered – quite so many questions, and though they would fight again eight years later, everyone knew, and not least themselves, that they had already covered ground they could never hope to regain. It was terrain they had anointed, for all time, with their sweat and their blood and their fighting glory.

Chapter Six

Las Vegas, November 1983

It was just three years since Roberto Durán retreated from New Orleans with the self-inflicted wound that for a while had threatened never to heal. But that was perhaps not quite right. Three years for those of us who came here merely to witness a surviving fragment of boxing history, maybe, but for Durán himself it might have been another lifetime.

In the moments of his greatest success he had always carried the hauteur of a warrior. Now he had something of the penitent. The eyes that blazed fiercely in Montreal, then became so clouded in New Orleans, had still another quality, though one not quite so easy to categorise. They showed some hurt but also much resolve. Certainly, they held your gaze in a way they hadn't after he walked away from Sugar Ray Leonard.

They seemed to say, most of all, that if we didn't know it, he had come back a long way from the ignominy of the Superdome. He had remade the pride that he once carried like a sword. He had gone back to the place of his first great triumph, Madison Square Garden, and become a world champion again, beating Davey Moore to take the super-welterweight title. And now in a few days he would step into the ring with Marvellous Marvin Hagler. No, you had to agree, it was not the modus operandi of any old irredeemable coward.

Hagler was not only a 4-1 favourite, he was bigger and stronger and arguably the most formidable pound-for-pound fighter in the world. He had beaten his seven challengers for the middleweight title inside the distance. He was relentless, merciless and, most everybody agreed, a stride too far for Durán on his Redemption Road.

This was despite it being true that since New Orleans Durán had indeed restored himself beyond his best hopes when he returned to Panama as a pariah rather than a national hero. Yes, he had been emphatic that he had left the Superdome ring not out of fear of a beating but as a refusal to play the stooge of Sugar Ray Leonard. But that didn't stop the hate mail or the white feathers, and it was something he wanted to address even under the advancing shadow of Marvin Hagler.

'One day,' he said, 'I want to step into the ring with Leonard again. Yes, I know he is a great fighter. He has proved that many times, he proved it in this place against Tommy Hearns. But I have never feared him and never would, and I want the chance to prove this before I leave the ring. You will see my determination when I fight Hagler.'

Maybe he saw on my face a willingness to believe when I wished him luck and we shook hands, and he said, with the flicker of a smile, that he had brought everything he still had to this fight.

His first step came nine months after New Orleans in the Public Auditorium, Cleveland, against Nino Gonzalez, a tough, hirsute 22-year-old from Bayonne, New Jersey, who had 24 wins and just one defeat and a hunger for success that he wore almost as ferociously as had the young Durán.

Larry Holmes, the reigning heavyweight champion, was in an audience of 8,000 that seemed prepared to go back to before the Superdome and remember a Durán who had come to represent ring ambition at its most committed. That fighter had a thinner waist – and in his corner, unlike the new and notorious Carlos 'Panama' Lewis, the two great trainers Ray Arcel and Freddie Brown – but still the crowd seemed ready to celebrate again the best of his past. They clapped and cheered him into the ring and were maybe mindful that Lewis – who would later be sentenced to prison for his involvement in one of boxing's most infamous incidents – had revealed that Durán had taken off 30 pounds in three weeks, when they applauded his victory by unanimous decision, which came despite signs of dwindling stamina in the later rounds.

Durán had reassembled some familiar strengths of his past. His right hand might not carry so much destructive force in still another heavier weight division but it was hard and discouraging, and his left hook to the body still carried a draining effect. Clearly Lewis had, on this occasion, put his time to good and creative use. But then no one ever doubted his understanding of some of the ring's most basic demands. The problem – his, not Durán's – was a persistent failure to observe even the roughest of fighting morality.

In the years to come Lewis would hit depths that would make Durán's New Orleans behaviour seem no worse than a mere strategic misadventure. His most egregious offence came two years after the Cleveland fight – and, ironically enough, on the undercard of the Madison Square Garden bill that would most significantly restore Durán's reputation with the victory over Davey Moore.

Lewis's fighter Luis Resto ended the undefeated record of 'Irish' Billy Collins over ten bloody rounds. The blood came almost entirely from the young prospect's battered face. At the end of the fight Resto, who won a unanimous decision, walked over to the loser's corner and offered his gloved hand to the anguished father and trainer, Billy Collins Senior. Collins Senior was horrified when he felt the thinness of Resto's glove. The padding had been removed and holes had been made in both gloves. The damning evidence was impounded and both trainer and fighter would serve prison time. Lewis was charged with possession of weapons for criminal purposes. The weapons were Resto's hands, which had cut the face of Billy Collins so brutally they had torn an iris in one eye and left him with permanently blurred vision.

When Collins was later killed when his car plunged off a bridge near his home in Tennessee, it was widely believed that he had taken his own life in the depression that came with the end of a promising career.

Lewis was banned from ever holding an official position in a sport in which he had displayed much talent, not least for his handling of the outstanding lightweight champion Aaron Pryor, though even this success was mired in controversy when a television sound system caught him yelling to a corner assistant to give Pryor the bottle of 'water' that had been specially mixed.

In Cleveland, however, Lewis compromised neither himself nor the man he prepared so diligently for his return to the ring. Holmes was also agreeably surprised by Durán's visit to the American rustbelt. He said, 'He was off [his best] but he showed a lot of determination. I was very pleased with the look of him after a long layoff. A month before he looked like a heavyweight. If he keeps fighting, he will be back.'

He was fighting again in less than two months, against Luigi Minchillo, middleweight champion of Europe and billed as 'the Italian Warrior'. The fight was on the undercard of Leonard–Hearns I and on that account alone was never likely to reverberate for too long.

Durán was still a work of reconstruction but he picked up another unanimous decision, which was considered enough reason to give him a world title shot against Wilfred Benítez. This was hungrily accepted as something more than a chance to win his third title in a different division. Certainly, it said more about Durán's enduring mystique than the clearest evidence that he was already a remade fighter of the highest quality. He was returning to Caesars Palace in Las Vegas, he would receive half a million dollars, and in the opposite corner would be one of the most admired fighters of his generation. Benítez would surely, properly investigate the authenticity of Durán's return to the highest level of fighting.

Durán's regained legitimacy was helped by a parting gift from his previously exhausted protector, Eleta. Though still deeply disillusioned by events in New Orleans, he retained feeling enough to worry about the fighter's future, his ability to live with himself comfortably when the days of action were over. And there were valuable services he felt he could perform.

One was to re-recruit Ray Arcel, who was more aghast than anyone in the wake of *No mas*. Another was to continue to argue for the vital clearing away of Durán's large and ruinous entourage. Finally, he could arrange, by the presidential decree of Panama dictator General Omar Torrijos Herrera, that Durán be taken, virtually in military custody, to a penal colony 15 miles off the Panama coast.

Durán had the softer ambience of southern California in mind, but in the company of some of his country's most desperate criminals he was obliged to face up to the demands of a physical trial that would surely help shape the rest of his career, and maybe his life. He worked as he had rarely done before, and when he came to the ring against Benítez he said, 'Well, I have done all I can.'

Durán didn't beat Benítez. He lost on every card, but given all the ground he had been required to cover, the margins were more than respectable. Indeed, they were tinged with glory. Judge Hal Miller gave it to Benítez by one round, Dave Morretti by three and Lou Tabat, the butt of so much criticism after scoring Leonard–Hearns I, by four.

Durán did his best work in the sixth round. There were times when, it seemed, he was battling for nothing less than his continued existence as a top-flight fighter. He hit Benítez with a series of clean, perfectly delivered rights to the head, then glumly concluded that they had less than the desired effect. Arcel reflected, 'It's the size. He hits a lightweight like that and he goes. But while he can hurt these bigger guys, they are strong enough and have enough endurance to come right back.'

Benítez did that but not to the point where he could put out the fire that still burned in Durán. 'I can promise you this,' Arcel added. 'If Durán ever thought he would do again what he did against Leonard in New Orleans, he'd kill himself first.'

Pat Putnam of *Sports Illustrated*, who had been among the more unforgiving in New Orleans, added his own rider, saying, 'Durán proved that in the 15th round. Exhausted, hardly able to hold up his arms, he whaled against Benítez in a corner of the ring and for most of the final three minutes they slammed each other with abandon. It is the way people should remember Roberto Durán. Although he knew he couldn't win, the indomitable and courageous Panamanian warrior who gave us years of fierce joy was giving his all until the final bell.'

One of boxing's most incisive, and forthright, writers believed he was witnessing Robert Durán's final statement, but he was premature. Durán would fight on for many more years, and what he did in Las Vegas against Benítez was the underpinning of all that he would continue to do – the good and the bad, the gallant and the exhausted. None of it would ever again provoke the smallest hint of cowardice. The regained respect would hold against all the highs and lows of a career that would stretch, incredibly, into the late nineties and the age of 47.

What was now beyond him though, coming into the Hagler fight, was the fierce consistency of his prime, the days when he was a lightweight with the fabled hands of stone.

This was clear in Detroit six months after the Benítez fight. He was beaten comfortably, despite the unfathomable scorecard of one judge that created a split decision, by the talented but less than ferocious Jamaican, Kirkland Laing. Don King, mortified by what he feared was a massive loss of earning potential, delivered a dressing-room diatribe, which was later sharply modified at a post-fight press conference. Behind the closed door, he had trashed Durán's performance and said he should quit on the spot. Before the media he put on a solemn face and declared, 'I will not only urge Roberto to retire, I will implore this great man whom I love and understand to go out with the dignity his career deserves.' On this occasion, Durán reacted not with hands but with ears of stone.

He would fight on – and with sensational results. Not initially, however. His next fight, two months later in Miami, would have gone unregistered on the Richter scale in any circumstances but was made to look especially humdrum on the undercard of Aaron Pryor's tumultuous knockout defeat of the revered world lightweight champion, Alexis Argüello.

Durán won a unanimous decision over British journeyman Jimmy Batten, but with it came a rare sense of operating in the margins of an arena in which he had so often been the most compelling presence.

What he needed now was not the respectability that he had re-established with his performance against Benítez – and much less any battle for parity with such moderate performers as Kirkland Laing and Jimmy Batten – but the adrenalin that came with a big fight. His next opponent, Pipino Cuevas, had passed the point where he could automatically bestow that status but he still had some to bring into the ring of the Sports Arena in Los Angeles in January 1983. After Durán's defeat by Laing and his laboured showing against Batten, and Cuevas's loss to Roger Stafford in his last fight 14 months earlier, the hard view was that both men were taking their last pickings.

The Ring magazine had nominated the Stafford defeat as the Upset of the Year but Cuevas's career was already in a descent, signalled in 1980 when he was overwhelmed by Tommy Hearns in the Joe Louis Arena in Detroit. Against Stafford, the Mexican fans at the Hacienda Hotel in Las Vegas were stunned when he was knocked down in the second round, a blow from which he never recovered as Stafford eased his way to a unanimous decision.

In Los Angeles, the Mexican and Panamanian supporters strived to recreate the glories of the past, but there was another reality written into the fight contracts. Durán and Cuevas were fighting for $50,000 each, a figure that would once have brought from them only sneers of disbelief. There was, though, one streak of light in the Californian sky. It was the potential of the 12-round world title eliminator to carry the winner to Madison Square Garden and a shot against the champion Davey Moore.

Durán didn't so much beat Cuevas as dismantle him. By the fourth round he was in absolute control, knocking Cuevas down for a second time with a combination of two rights and a left that stopped the fight.

Moore was unsure of what to make of Durán's untroubled passage. He asked, 'Was that Durán looking so good or Cuevas so bad?' If he was whistling in the dark, his worst fears would be confirmed in New York five months later. Durán celebrated both his 32nd birthday and his rebirth as a major fighter with an eighth-round victory barely more difficult than the dismissal of Cuevas. Had Durán, or his new promoter Bob Arum, written their own scenario, they would have been hard pressed to add any more positive embellishments.

The 24-year-old defending champion had grown up in the Bronx and had a meteoric start to his professional career, winning his world title in Tokyo after just eight fights. He was local and, it was said, filled with great potential, but it was Durán who was coming home.

Moore found an opponent ransacking his memory for every strength – and every dark trick. He had, with devastating effect, unfurled one of the latter before the end of the first round: a thumb in Moore's right eye which progressively reduced his vision. Had it been 20/20 in every phase, however, Moore would have been at his limits in tracing the pattern of Durán's fast spilling aggression. Durán dictated almost every exchange. In the seventh round, Moore took a count of eight before stumbling back to his corner. The eighth was so punishing for Moore that his mother and girlfriend had passed out, and with 52 seconds left in the round the referee called the end.

The new champion believed he had vindicated his pre-fight assertion that the sleeker line of his body was grounded in the hardest of work and not long hours in the sauna. He said, 'People think I've been in the sauna because of the way I look. What they don't realise is that I've been working out for four months. Forget about those defeats before I beat Cuevas. I'm not the same person.'

He also moved his fight for redemption onto a higher plane, saying, 'I can't find words to express how I failed in the past. There are no excuses. Once I thought I was a man, now I am a man and I know it. In truth, I have so much enthusiasm, like it was the first time I came to New York to fight for the title and the people were with me all the time. I'm the old lion. I don't fight for the money. I want to show myself that I'm a champion. I do this in search of glory.'

He found plenty of that as he drank champagne in one of his favourite New York haunts, Victor's Café on 52nd Street, where among those who came to salute his achievement was Muhammad Ali. A more meticulous man than Durán might have pushed aside the emptying bottles and made a list of his reasons for satisfaction. Prominent would have been the fact that he had just elected himself to a permanent place among boxing's elite. He had become the seventh fighter to win world titles in three different divisions, joining the company of Alexis Argüello, Wilfred Benítez, Bob Fitzsimmons, Henry Armstrong, Tony Canzoneri and Barney Ross. There was the sight of Ali paying his respects, homage from the mountaintop indeed, and maybe most delicious of all, at the end of the fight Sugar Ray Leonard had stepped into the ring to shake his hand.

More exhilarating still, though, were the possibilities of a future, which had come so close to lying in ruins. That prospect had been officially banished by the headline about to adorn the fight coverage of *Sports Illustrated*'s William Nack, a man much respected not only for his perceptive, eloquent reporting of classic horse racing and the ring but also an ability to recite backwards, and in Spanish and at any time of night or morning, the final pages of *The Great Gatsby*. The headline read, 'He That Was Lost Has Been Found'.

Any doubts about this disappeared when promoter Bob Arum triumphantly announced the result of his winning gamble on the man so many had assigned to the past. It was Marvin Hagler versus Roberto Durán at Caesars Palace, Las Vegas, on 10 November 1983, for the undisputed middleweight championship of the world. The resurrection had a time and place to confirm that it was indeed a reality.

There was also the reassurance of a return to old riches. Durán's recent willingness to fight for $50,000 had resembled a last desperate reach. Now it was the equivalent of hitting the Caesars Palace jackpot.

Hagler – as befitting a man of such unimpeachable antecedents, of an aura so formidable that some winced on behalf of Durán when the fight was announced – would enjoy the bulk of the purse at $5 million, but Durán was guaranteed $1.5 million and would receive a percentage of revenue. Whatever happened in the ring, his table at Victor's would be secure for some time.

What happened in the ring was a slow-burning drama that would become so engrossing that you forgot both the chill of the desert night and all the apprehensions that had grown on behalf of Durán before the sound of the first bell.

He produced something he had not shown before. Against Buchanan all those years before he had been tumultuous, unstoppable in his hunger for victory. In Montreal he had displayed the will and the courage of a lion. And just six months earlier at Madison Square Garden he had engulfed the young and psychologically ill-prepared Moore.

Against Hagler, Durán couldn't begin to anticipate such mastery. The quality of his opponent had seen to that. But what he could do, in a way that made your blood run fast and your mind open up to astounding possibilities, was distil all that he had learned, from the *barrios* of Panama to the peaks of boxing. He stripped all of that down and chose from it only that which he believed would work against a man of Hagler's strength and experience and apparently bone-deep belief in his power to negotiate any challenge. At ringside, you could only say that the result was amazing. Not only were Hagler's plans for a formal destruction frustrated and confounded, increasingly he wore the expression of someone caught in disabling uncertainty.

Later, Hagler confessed, 'I wasn't getting my jab off the way I generally do. It seemed that everybody was disappointed I didn't knock him out. I felt that way myself. But he wasn't that vulnerable to a knockout. I didn't catch him with a solid shot.'

In fact, he did and most memorably in the sixth round, when he briefly took mostly unanswered control as Durán was forced to adapt to the fact that a round earlier he felt a sharp pain in his right hand, a difficulty that would develop through the fight. Afterwards, he was less than flattering about Hagler's approach. He said, 'He came to tear my head off but when he saw that I could hit hard, with strength, he got scared and became a coward. That's why he didn't take too many chances and mix it up with me. Everyone told me he was a destroyer but when he hit me he didn't do anything to me. His punches absolutely did me no damage. He got scared every time he threw a jab because I could get my right under it. That's why he held off so much.'

There would be echoes of the debate over scoring that followed Leonard–Hearns I. The consensus was that Hagler, for all the doubts created in his mind and his heart by Durán's mobility and craft, had landed more and heavier punches through the course of the fight. However, no one argued that Durán hadn't presented Hagler with a set of questions that he had not anticipated. Or that the result was a fight that was in the balance until Hagler produced some of his heaviest artillery in the 14th and 15th rounds.

Hagler won those rounds as unequivocally as his situation demanded. Going into the 14th round, he was behind on two cards by one point and even on the other. He retained his title by one point on two cards and two on the third. The Danish judge, Ove Ovesen, who had Durán leading before the penultimate round, explained his awarding of the first two rounds persuasively enough, saying, 'Durán was fighting the smarter, more composed fight. He made Marvin miss and countered on his own. I made those first two rounds for Durán, but not by much.'

So, it went: stalking and feinting, then fierce bursts of action in which both men knew they could not afford to give ground for the fear of surrendering everything they had come to believe they represented.

Goody Petronelli, Hagler's trainer, was not slow to recognise the impending crisis. The tough-minded, emotional New Englander had, with his brother Pat, shepherded the young southpaw middleweight away from the discouragement of two early defeats in the fierce battle-ground of the Philadelphia fight milieu in which he had been obliged, given his quickly established reputation as a most difficult opponent, to prosecute his trade.

The brothers had been appalled by what they considered an outrageous decision to award the defending – and blood-spattered – middleweight champion, Vito Antuofermo, a draw in Las Vegas three years before this fight. They hated the idea that Hagler might suffer another such injustice and later Goody reflected, 'Durán waited and waited and waited for Marvin to lead. We had to change our tactics and go on the offensive, which isn't really Marvin's style. At the end of the fifth round, I told him, "This isn't going too well. Put the pressure on him."'

At that point Durán's fight-plan was working near to perfection. He recalled, 'I fought him at half distance. I was waiting for him to unload so I could score on him. Whichever hand he unloaded [at one point Hagler switched from his southpaw stance to bring him closer to Durán] I was ready to counter. He didn't confuse me with anything. I was beating him without mixing it up too much.'

Durán came so close in the 12th and 13th rounds, stealing back the lead and inspiring his manager and tactician Luis Spada to send him into the 14th round with a battle cry. Above the din, Spada yelled, 'You win the last two rounds, you win the fight. Throw punches, make points. You have to win the last two rounds.' This was being echoed by the Petronelli brothers. 'I want a strong 14th and 15th. You can't make the fight close. You've got to win these last two rounds,' shouted Goody.

Durán knew how close he was to glory scarcely imaginable recently. At times – and especially in that desperate sixth round when Hagler seemed to have properly adjusted his sights – he appeared to have dredged it up from the depths of his fighting soul. The pain in his right hand had become discountable, an endurable inconvenience. He had stood and faced both the demons that had pursued him since New Orleans and the power of boxing's most formidable figure.

Hagler knew well enough that he was in a different and less inspiring place. He had to retrieve the authority on which his reputation was most impressively built. He had to restate who he was, draw a line beyond which he could no longer retreat a single step. He didn't.

He pummelled Durán, closed the ring down to a small rectangle filled with pressure. If you want this so badly, Hagler seemed to be saying, you must take this and you must overcome it. But Durán couldn't. He had given everything he had, as he had promised to on the eve of the fight, and now it was all spent. Yet if it hadn't brought the prize his courage and resolution and bursts of shining optimism had promised, there was a reward on which no boxing money man, no wheeler or scuffler, no Don King or Bob Arum, could ever set a price.

When the scores came in Durán nodded resignedly and muttered, '*Si*, the better man won.'

There it was, a moment of truth that Roberto Durán filled with grace. It was the statement of a born fighter who, it was warming to think before the sun rose again over the desert, was thankful for the great mercy of being able to bring himself home.

Chapter Seven

Las Vegas, April 1985

By now I had developed a pre-fight routine which I liked to think was a sign of developing maturity, at least professionally. I would have a light lunch before retiring for a siesta, which would sustain me when the post-fight rituals stretched into the small hours, and I'd then return to my room, lonely as a mouse in a cloister, to do the writing that was often still unfinished when the sun rose.

It didn't always work. Sometimes the idea of afternoon sleep was bombarded too heavily by the portents of the night. It was certainly so in the hours before Marvin Hagler and Tommy Hearns came to the ring at Caesars Palace with an intent so serious, so utterly explicit and intense, it seemed doubtful that they would be able to restrain themselves long enough to hear the first bell.

In the long hours of the afternoon, with the first stirrings of a high wind tugging at the huge Stars and Stripes attached to a tower overlooking the ring, I wandered the Strip. I played a few hands of blackjack, distractedly and unsuccessfully. I ran the possibilities of Hagler–Hearns over and over in my mind and, looking back, it seems clear that I was in the grip of a premonition. It said that something tumultuous, maybe unprecedented, was about to happen. And, so it was.

I would never have to refresh or nourish the images of a fury I had not witnessed before. I see it exploding again and again. I see the unchanging profile of Tommy Hearns with his back to the ropes swinging and pounding at the shaven, bobbing head of Marvin Hagler, and I wonder once more how it was that the harder Hagler was hit, the more resolve he seemed to find.

If Hearns had the look of an Assyrian warrior with his long coiffed hair, which lacked only the framing of a battle visor, and his beautiful musculature, Hagler resembled more a tank.

The fight lasted just one second more than eight minutes, yet when it was over, and Hagler stood alone and awesomely triumphant, it was as though we had been carried to a distant, previously unimagined place.

Budd Schulberg, who won an Oscar for his screenplay *On the Waterfront* and had followed the fights avidly since boyhood in New York, where he worshipped the superb Jewish lightweight world champion Benny Leonard, sat down in the ringside seat beside me. He rubbed his head and he said, 'I never thought I would see anything so intense outside of war.'

When Schulberg mentioned war, he knew well of what he spoke. In his US Navy service he was assigned to the Office of Strategic Services, where he worked with the Hollywood director John Ford's documentary unit. It saw him among the first Allied troops liberating the concentration camps. He was present at the arrest of Hitler's favourite filmmaker, Leni Riefenstahl, while gathering evidence for the Nuremberg trials. He had been drawn into the terrible pressures and ambiguities of the McCarthy Un-American Activities Committee when it descended on the Hollywood liberals. He had sparred with Ernest Hemingway, an assault of ego more than fisticuffs, and survived a lost weekend with F. Scott Fitzgerald. He was not a man to be easily impressed and here he was at ringside, his white hair ruffled by the wind and with a tremble in his voice.

Some gnarled old men argued that what we had seen here was the most violently compressed fighting since, 62 years earlier, Jack Dempsey and Luis Ángel Firpo, the Wild Bull of the Pampas, tore at each other at the Polo Grounds in New York. Dempsey, the reigning heavyweight champion of the world, kayoed Firpo in the second round. In the first, he had knocked the Argentinian down seven times – and had himself been driven through the ropes.

In Las Vegas there were many stunned witnesses carrying unimpeachable credentials. Willie Pep, arguably the greatest featherweight of all time, was in town as a guest at the latest marriage ceremony of Jake LaMotta, and he was in sparkling form at the reception at Maxim's Casino across the Strip and around the corner from Caesars. He said he was looking forward hugely to the fight – he thought Hearns had great talent but had probably found his nemesis in Hagler – and was happy to trot out his classic line on the vicissitudes of marriage, at least out of the earshot of the Raging Bull. 'All my wives were great housekeepers,' he recalled. 'After each divorce, they kept the house.'

After Hagler–Hearns, he was not nearly so flippant. 'There are times,' he reflected, 'when boxing makes you stop and realise that it will always have the ability to surprise you. You try to read a fight, imagine how it will go based on all your knowledge and experience, and then something else happens to blow your mind. That's what happened tonight.'

Five years later I saw Hearns in the company of his friend Sir Tom Jones, who was performing at the MGM in Las Vegas. When the Welshman left his dressing room and went onto the stage, Hearns and I followed him to the curtains. We smiled at his greeting to a rapturous audience, which had come down from places like Nebraska and Minnesota. 'Ladies,' he said, 'I've been singing to you for 30 years and you know right now it doesn't seem a second less than that.' It was my cue to ask the Hitman if time ever stalled when he thought of the Hagler fight.

He shook his head and said, 'It might have been last night. There is hardly a day when I do not return to that fight, live it again and run back through my performance. I suppose it is true that some things never leave you, you spend a lot of the rest of your life in their company.'

Hearns still speaks in the most vivid way of the emotions and instincts he carried against Hagler, and if some of it is tinged with regret, he also recognises a residual glory: 'It is something, I guess, to have been in a fight that no one forgets.'

It was a fight that from its inception had a life and momentum of extraordinary force. Both men had purged themselves of disappointment – Hearns the ebbing of his advantage over Leonard three and a half years earlier, and Hagler his failure to deepen his mystique against Roberto Durán. The wounds were not visible, however, when they stepped into the ring at Caesars and a trumpeter played the national anthem and that desert wind now tore at the great flag, making it flap and groan. Hearns had the warrior bearing, while Hagler was coiled for action so intensely that as he beat his gloves against his head Hugh McIlvanney remarked that if the national anthem had taken a little longer he might have knocked himself out.

There was no doubt that both men had restored their fighting aura. Hearns had probably enhanced his a little more, to the point where his status as the potential favourite had enraged Hagler. Since losing to Leonard, Hearns had won eight straight fights, culminating in a searing dismissal of Fred Hutchings in the Civic Center in Saginaw, Michigan. Hutchings, ranked number three challenger to Hearns' WBC super-welterweight title, was knocked down twice in the first round and led back to his corner in the third. But when Hearns came to stand against Hagler it was two other victories that gave him most reason to believe that he had remade himself.

One was Wilfred Benítez and the other was Durán. Durán was not so much beaten as caught in a hurricane. However, it was the victory over

Benítez, which came 18 months after the defeat by Leonard and brought the super-welterweight crown, that lingered most encouragingly.

Before going into the ring in New Orleans, the Hitman spelled out some new priorities. He said, 'I've worked hard on some things since I lost to Leonard. I've worked on all aspects of my approach, my jab, my boxing. I've been learning how to move my head to get away from shots. Learning how to tie up a man inside. Leonard gave me the inspiration to do all this, to make me look at myself from top to bottom. Whatever Benítez does, I am ready.'

Benítez was singularly unimpressed by this progress report. When he came into the ring he flashed Hearns a look of dismissal and said, very deliberately, 'I could beat you and Leonard on the same night.'

Leonard had already made a nonsense of the assertion and Hearns would soon leave it in further ruins with his most rounded and resilient performance. Pat Putnam's ringside verdict displayed his usual sharp and pithy acumen. 'The Hitman,' he wrote, 'also proved that he could run.'

That course became a necessity when Hearns hurt his right hand on Benítez's head in the eighth round, but it was at no cost to his scoring in a majority decision that had him winning by five and four rounds on two cards and drawing on another. Most satisfying for Hearns, and his mentor Emanuel Steward, was his ability to dictate the course of the fight against arguably the best pure technician in the ring and then make the necessary adjustments when the pain came to his right hand. His jab had never worked so fluently; Durán had made one serious miscalculation on his Redemption Road. Hearns absorbed everything Durán had to offer and tossed it away like a man shelling a peanut.

For Durán there would be other fights – including, improbably enough, one with Sugar Ray Leonard – but the raw details of his experience at the hands (principally the right one) of Hearns would never soften. Hearns put him down twice in the first round and his senses were so scrambled that when the bell sounded his team had to retrieve him from the neutral corner to which he had stumbled. There was not an eddy of relief. After crashing a right hand into Durán's chin in the second round, Hearns, with a fine sense of choreography, stepped backwards so that Durán could complete his free fall flat on his face. There had rarely been less need for the formality of a count.

Hearns' victory over Benítez had established the extended range of his talent, his ability to fight in different ways. However, there had been a price, and it was concern over the strength and durability of his greatest weapon, the right hand that had levied 32 knockouts. The hand was in a cast for three months after the Benítez fight, and when he returned to the ring against Luigi Minchillo and Murray Sutherland, something was missing. Both fights went the distance and the collision with Hagler was twice postponed. An old freedom returned, however, with the overwhelming of Durán, one that was made all the more significant by the difficulties Hagler had encountered seven months earlier against the same opponent.

Whatever the implications of his fight with Durán, Hagler had restored much of his old authority. He was indignant when referee Tony Perez ruled he had been knocked down in his next fight, which was his eighth defence of the middleweight crown, against the hard-hitting number-one challenger Juan Domingo Roldán of Argentina. He was also angered by the Argentinian's assertion that he had put a thumb in his eye. 'It was a clean shot right off the bridge of the eye,' said Hagler. All of this became extremely academic, however, when Roldán was sent careering through the ropes in the third and by the tenth was able only to give a small, just perceptible shake of his head when the referee asked him if he could carry on.

Hagler's ninth defence was even more imperious. Mustafa Hamsho was stopped in three rounds at Madison Square Garden. He was sickened by the force of Hagler's opening barrage, and by the third round he was unable to defend himself. Privately, Hagler fretted over the uncertainties he had displaced against Durán. It had been a disorientating experience, but the victories over Roldán and Hamsho had consigned it to his past.

When he was reminded of the venom of Hearns' punching, how he had first acquired his Hitman's aura, he sneered, 'Remember he ain't never hit Marvin Hagler. I've taken the best shots of the biggest hitters in the middleweight division and I've never been off my feet. And this guy isn't even a middleweight. Hitman, my ass.'

This was the Hagler who pounded his gloves against his head to the strains of the national anthem. This was the Hagler who, deep down, had always believed that he had been given something less than his due amid the hierarchy of his brutal business.

Sugar Ray Leonard had led him down several garden paths with the promise of showdown fights that would have, finally, given him the appropriate stage on which to announce his pound-for-pound superiority over all rivals. But Leonard was a will-o'-the-wisp.

Hagler, at 30, had never invaded the imagination of boxing. He was the foot soldier, the enforcer of strength and that confidence that comes when you know you have done your work. Now, though, there was perhaps something else, another dimension to explore. If at times he had been underrated and under-honoured – if he was cheated out of the middleweight title against Antuofermo and then, when he ascended to the title a year later in London, had his glory marred by riotous supporters of the beaten Tony Sibson – this could be a moment he could claim for himself down all the years.

Goody Petronelli, his trainer, would report that Hagler had never been so perfectly attuned to a challenge – or better prepared. He went through his warm-up in the dressing room with an uncanny, metronomic efficiency and there was no question of his lingering there while his challenger went on alone to first feel the weight of an expectant crowd. He wanted all of this desert night for himself, every surge of excitement, every particle of sand whipped up by the still rising wind. Dressed in a blue robe, he was at Hearns' heels when he came into the ring.

Hearns looked exuberant enough in his red robe with a yellow trim – and superbly conditioned. He had come in at just a quarter of a pound under the 160 limit.

Hagler scowled at Hearns, locked him in a glare, which reached new levels of intensity when referee Richard Steele called the fighters into the middle of the ring. Hagler had been wearing a cap emblazoned with the word 'War'. Now, with the sound of the bell, it broke out. Hagler's initial assault had been anticipated by Steward, who said, 'I think Marvin may come out so fired up that we will just have Tommy sticking and moving. Hagler will be so juiced up after seven or eight rounds it will rob his strength. Then we'll go for the late knockout.'

Hagler indeed laid down a stunning, almost primeval assault. Stick and move? It was never an option for Hearns. His requirement was to punch, which he tended to do inordinately well, and survive. Hearns did fire off a smattering of jabs but, far from wielding influence, they were barely punctuation marks. The essay of violence built layer upon layer. Later, the computer spat out astonishing facts. One hundred and sixty-five punches were thrown in that first round, 82 by Hagler (but not a single jab) and 83, 22 of which were jabs, by Hearns. It was a record prosecution of all-out ring violence. What the computer couldn't convey, though, was the impact of such a convulsion.

Years later Hearns recalled, 'I never believed he would come in like that, not in the first seconds of the fight, and without a pause. Of course, what it meant was that any fight-plan I'd discussed with Emanuel went straight through the window. The fight wasn't seconds old when I realised I had to slug it out, not to win the fight but just to survive. It was as simple and as brutal as that.'

In the unremitting cyclone of the first round, the fighters went toe to toe and landed punches so powerful that it was astounding neither went down. By the middle of the round Hearns drew the encouragement, however illusory it would prove to be, of seeing Hagler's face seeping blood. The champion's forehead was cut open above his right eye – it was never established whether it was by a punch or a flying elbow – and in this gruesome sight Hearns believed he had another reason to continue to unload the big right hand. Yet while the ring-doctor inspected Hagler's wound at the end of the round – and decided the fight should go on – Steward was beseeching Hearns to change his tactics.

'What are you doing?' Steward cried. 'You've got to stick and move, jab, don't fight him.' Later the trainer said that his man had fought 12 rounds in one. There was no doubt that this was true but Hearns had lived it, and suffered it, and, in his desperation, he concluded that he had been left with just one chance of survival.

In the second round the pressure abated to some small degree; however, it was not the result of evolving tactics – the Hagler corner was delighted with their sense that Hearns was already at the point of irrecoverable decline – but rather the consequence of an ultimately unsustainable fury. Yet neither the drama nor the commitment showed any sign of dwindling. Hearns signalled his determination – and power – with a perfectly thrown right cross midway through the round but instead of stopping Hagler, and making him think, it served only to fuel momentum. At the end of the first round he had told his corner, 'No, I won't worry about the cut. If you go to war you are going to get wounded. When I see blood I become a bull.'

At the end of the second the doctor came again to inspect the gash on his forehead, which had continued to spill torrents of blood. He asked Hagler if he could see clearly. According to Pat Putnam the champion's response was splendidly rhetoric. 'I ain't missing him, am I?'

he was alleged to say. In fact this, it turned out, was a ringside invention, but a superior one on a night that had made no call for workaday mythology.

But then maybe the champion wasn't quite as sanguine as he sounded. Perhaps he was haunted by the possibility that his fate might not be decided by his own pounding fists. Certainly, his urgency was renewed with devastating effect at the start of the third. Again, he advanced on Hearns, again he delivered crashing blows: first a short, jolting left, then a clubbing right against the side of Hearns' head. Stunned, Hearns retreated unsteadily across the ring. Hagler caught him, found him with a perfect combination of left and right and then landed a big overhead right. Summoning his last instincts for survival, Hearns reached out to clinch.

Hearns had been driven to his last act of gallantry. He got to his feet at the count of nine but the effort had left him, anyone could see, completely hollow. The experienced referee had only to take a cursory look into his eyes before waving that the fight was over.

For Hagler this was the defining triumph of his career, the time when he took control of every situation so profoundly that not even the flow of his own blood brought a pause.

Both the conqueror and the vanquished would know other dramas, but when they looked back they did not need telling they had left much of the best of themselves in the Vegas ring.

Many concluded that there had never been such a first round, and never would be again, and when Hagler and Sugar Ray Leonard finally faced each other in the ring, one burden they did not carry was the expectation that they would stir up quite the kind of violent storm that two years earlier had blown in from the desert.

That was something Hearns would always share with Marvin Hagler. But then if it would always be a source of pride it would never, he also made clear to me on that more gentle and amiable occasion of the Tom Jones concert, be free of haunting memories. He told me, 'When I fought Hagler I knew I had to go to my limit. I had to gamble. But when I lost the gamble I didn't have any regrets. I made an honest decision about my best chance of winning, and winning well. Maybe I should have stayed away from him more, used my reach, tried to outbox him. But I knew how strong he was, how he would keep coming at me, and I decided I would go for him. I would hang out there, on the edge.

'Man, that was a night. I worked so hard for the fight. When I got in the ring I might have had a smile on my face but my legs felt so tired I didn't believe I could go 12 rounds with a fighter as strong as Hagler. I felt I had to get him out of there. I don't blame my trainer Manny Steward. We had our rows over the years but they were never about how good he was at his job. He tried to rein me in against Hagler. But you cannot get your time back. If I could I wouldn't fight Hagler in the same way. I would trust my legs a little more, fight through that feeling of tiredness. I would box him, use my longer reach, attempt to drive him crazy with frustration.

'That was always going to be the strategy and I had fought it a thousand times in my head. But then the bell rings and you are in reality. The reality that night was heavy, the crowd was going mad, there was a huge flag hanging down the side of Caesars Palace, and so what do you do when your legs feel like lead and all that frenzy is building up around you? You hit the guy as many times as you can.

'People still tell me it was the greatest fight they ever saw, even though it went less than three rounds, and that they will remember it when they forget my other fights against men like Sugar Ray Leonard, Wilfred Benítez and Roberto Durán – all great fighters. I suppose what I took from it most was that I put everything I had into that ring. Yes, maybe I could have fought a smarter fight, but something told me that it just wouldn't work against Marvin Hagler that night.

'Maybe I should have listened more to Manny Steward, one of the great fight men, who had taught me so much down the years. But when I think about this, I always return to the same point. It is that a lot of us are remembered when we are gone, sure, but there are different ways of being remembered. The best way for a fighter to be remembered, I will always believe, is that he was never afraid to go to the edge. That is what I hope they will always say about me.'

Out on the stage, his friend Tom Jones was entrancing his mostly matronly audience with the lyric that it was not unusual to be loved by anyone. In the shadows, Tommy Hearns gave a small sigh as he reflected on another and not inconsiderable solace. It was that in a small, fierce fragment of his life he had made himself forever honoured in a rather rougher trade.

Chapter Eight

New York, January 1987

So now there was one great drama left in the story that had dominated the days since Muhammad Ali. It would play out soon enough back in Las Vegas when Sugar Ray Leonard and Marvin Hagler finally shared the same ring. Then, the last question would be answered – or at least it was reasonable to think so as I stood in the pre-dawn dark of Manhattan.

Why was I there? It was to take a first impression of what might just be the next phenomenon, one threatening to usher the great quartet of Leonard, Hagler, Tommy Hearns and Roberto Durán away from their stronghold at the heart of boxing. There was a new warrior at the gates, fierce and compelling and brutally intent on dominating the trade he had been practising professionally for not yet two years. One thing was certain. If it happened, it would be a most disorderly process. That much I knew when I stepped into the big black limousine with Mike Tyson.

What I could not know was along how many byways of a deeply troubled psyche this journey would take me. Or how it would carry me to places like Tokyo and Louisville and Memphis, to prison gates in Indianapolis, to a mosque and more casino nights and dawns in Vegas and Atlantic City than I could too comfortably recall. And, always, with the feeling that I might be travelling, ultimately, to an abyss.

Along the way one of his trainers, Richie Giachetti, would give me the bleak prediction that Tyson would probably die by gunshots, fired by the boyfriend of one girl too many who attracted him in some dimly lit meat factory of a bar or a nightclub. That wouldn't happen, but most else that could have gone wrong did.

Yet as the sky lightened over Queensboro Bridge on the way to the high school in Queens where Tyson was due to speak to pupils, there was still some reason to give to this story, which I was covering on my way back to England after a seven-year stint in North America, a touch of optimism. No one at that point could deny that it was more about survival than doom.

Up on the high-school stage he was gauche. His body language had none of the certainty that, at the age of 20, had made him the youngest heavyweight champion in history. His stance was hunched and his high-pitched, lisping voice quavered at times. But then his message was unequivocal enough. 'If I can tell you anything,' he said, 'it is that you should never lose hope that you can make something of your life. I never dreamed that I would be standing on a stage like this talking to kids like you who didn't grow up in the streets, who didn't live by stealing, who didn't lack respect for anyone whoever they were or whatever they had done or however good the intentions they had.

'If I looked up to anyone it was drug-dealers and pimps, the ones who wore jewels and rings and had cars. OK, the chances were that they would end up dead or locked up but they were the kings of the street, at least for a little while. But I got lucky, some people saw I had some potential as a fighter – and so I was saved from the worst that could have happened. I was luckier than most of the people I knew as a boy. Most of them are in prison now – or dead from drugs. I robbed in the streets. I put on a ski mask and went about my work. I stole from people and I terrified them and I got pleasure from that. But I'm here this morning. I survived.'

'Survived,' he said, and we said. But what kind of survival? It would take another 30 years and the publication of an autobiography – which, for the most part, might have been written and dispatched from a corner of hell – to get any kind of measure of it. Hardly a page would go by without some lacerating account of betrayal and pain and a growing addiction to both drugs and casual sex.

It was, though, clear enough in the beautifully upholstered limousine that thus far he had been on a most perilous journey. When I told him that later in the day I would head to his streets in Brownsville, the most scabrous corner of Brooklyn where life was still as cheap as the rent in the big, gaunt, rat-infested apartment buildings, he laughed and held his head in his hands. And then he said, 'Man, are you serious? You don't have a passport for a place like that. It's the baddest place on the planet ... it is a world someone like you will never understand.'

He was sent to a reformatory school as a 13-year-old with 38 convictions for street crimes, but he hardly saw it as a refuge and when he arrived he was considered all but unmanageable, an opinion shared by a member of the staff who would go on to recognise his boxing talent and profoundly change his prospects. 'If you live in hell,' Tyson would philosophise later, 'the worst things probably come to seem quite normal.'

Despite Tyson's scorn, I did go to Brownsville and came to understand a little better the reason for his peals of laughter when I told him of my plan to stroll around the old neighbourhood. It was indeed a bleak and menacing place. There was no incentive to dawdle on streets that had at their corners knots of the pimps and the pushers and the brooding wannabes whose company Mike Tyson had escaped. But for how long, how cleanly? Not, certainly, with any sense that these streets would quickly relax their hold over the instincts of those who had known them. For a day, maybe, or a week and, then, who knew, the moment when everything gained in a boxing ring would be put at risk by some sudden urge to go back. And what would that take? A flash of envy provoked by the sight of his Rolls Corniche gleaming on the meanest of sidewalks, a beacon for the foxiest of the 'hos' and the 'nasty bitches' who so recently would not have looked twice at the street kid with the high voice known derisively as 'Fairy Boy'.

I looked at the notices on the board in the police precinct house, and they might indeed have been bulletins from hell. One would linger with some force. It was attached to a picture of a middle-aged man with a predilection for assaulting and raping elderly women.

In her small office, a young policewoman whose job was to counsel young offenders wept when she told me of her days working out in the street among them. 'Some days you come in beaten, in despair because conditions are so bad and the prospects for these kids so poor. You feel useless, powerless. Mike Tyson has escaped a situation as bad as you can imagine. His mother, who died a few years ago, was deserted by her partner when Mike was just a baby. It is hard to believe some of the things you see. You can go in some of the apartments and see rats running across tables to eat scraps of abandoned food. You see mothers sleeping off the effects of drugs. You see toddlers playing amid filth.'

In Tyson's family background there was little to engender the hope that one day he might be picked up at an opulent East Side apartment and driven by limousine to a borough of the city where daily life did not routinely resemble a war zone – and then advise high-school students on how best to meet the challenges of life.

According to his birth certificate his natural father came from Jamaica, but he never knew him and if he had anyone to resemble a father figure, however vaguely, it was Jimmy Kirkpatrick, who in his youth excelled as a baseball player in his native North Carolina. Kirkpatrick lived briefly with Tyson's mother, Lorna Mae, but left soon after the birth of her youngest child, Mike, in 1966. To the boy, his 'father' was just part of the fauna of the street. He would recall that he was 'just a regular street guy caught up in that world.'

So the boy roamed the streets, unfettered, until he was sent to the reformatory. Apart from his own extraordinary arrival at the possibility of another kind of life, there would be one other wonderment in the story of a family waylaid by the dysfunctions shaped in such a harsh environment.

Tyson's mother died when he was 16, and eight years later he lost his sister Denise, so often his only ally in the worst of the domestic stress, to a heart attack. It all might have added up to a saga of insuperable futility and sadness for a lost, doomed family but for the destructive violence its youngest member released, at unimaginable profit, in the boxing ring – and one other, utterly separate success.

Some years later I would discover it for myself when I spoke with Tyson's elder brother, Rodney, in Los Angeles. The brothers, I found, had the same blood but inhabited completely different worlds. 'I love my brother and whatever happens, good or bad, he will always be that in my heart,' he told me. 'But it is true we have lived different lives, gone on different roads, and no, they don't really meet up.'

Rodney was a qualified pharmacist living contentedly in California. He had studied hard in high school, won his credentials and would become a surgical assistant in a leading hospital. Rodney Tyson was hardly a unique story of one man's victory over the most oppressive circumstances. What seemed remarkable, though, was the nature of his triumph. It was one of normalcy, of a safely tethered view of what life might reasonably offer – and certainly it would be something to reflect upon when, down the road, his brother was declared bankrupt after using up a fortune estimated to have approached a billion dollars.

In Brownsville in 1987, though, there was enough to consider when weighing the odds that Mike Tyson had beaten with his escape from the hopeless streets. It wouldn't have happened but for the prescience of a former Golden Gloves champion who gave boxing instruction in the reformatory.

In a place that in so many other respects seemed designed to further distort and break the spirit of a troubled young man, Bobby Stewart saw extraordinary potential in the boy with the troubled, angry countenance and a voice pitched to provoke scorn. He saw unbridled power. He saw a vast anger that might be channelled into the ring. And when he had taken him as far as he could, when he had installed some rudiments of ring-craft, he thought of all the men he knew in professional boxing, all those who would value most the chance to guide and nurture such extraordinary raw material. And then, with not a second thought, he called an ageing, cranky guru of a fight man who had already made his reputation by rescuing a young victim of the Brooklyn streets and making him a world heavyweight champion.

For Cus D'Amato, the mentor of Floyd Patterson and the light-heavyweight world champion José Torres, Tyson was more than maybe his last boxing project. He was a gift of renewal, a chance to restate all his beliefs in a business that had left him sour and bitter after a series of battles with the ruling International Boxing Club, which he deemed deeply corrupt. He was also extremely reluctant to pay taxes to a government he considered far too right wing.

D'Amato was a bona fide eccentric, but few men had formed a more mystical attachment to the challenge of making a world heavyweight champion. In Tyson he saw the means to repeat his performance with Patterson, strike back at the boxing establishment he had come to detest and, on the way, also give his new protégé his first taste of a stable, well-lit home in the town of Catskill in upstate New York.

When Tyson's mother died, D'Amato became his legal guardian. His companion, Camille Ewald, cooked the boy's food and tended his clothes while D'Amato relentlessly tutored him in the techniques and the psychology of the ring. It was education on a massive scale, and not all of it was as adhesive as the driven old fight man would have hoped.

If Tyson was required to adapt his life to an entirely new order, D'Amato had to make his own compromises, some of which were particularly hard on a man who as a devout young Catholic had contemplated the priesthood. At times, it seemed that the old man's passion for once again creating a world champion had turned him into something of a Doctor Faustus making his deal with, if not the Devil, a young man not always mindful of the proprieties observed in the quiet, tree-lined boulevards of Catskill.

One of the most serious of the inevitable flashpoints came when another protégé of D'Amato, the tough, able young trainer Teddy Atlas, took a gun to Tyson and warned him that if he ever again sexually harassed a young girl – in this case, Atlas's 12-year-old niece – he would do more than fire a warning shot. For D'Amato the issue was straightforward enough. He had to choose between a promising trainer – himself a worldly graduate of the streets of New York who would go on to earn a fine reputation – and someone, every instinct told him, who was strong enough, talented enough, to become heavyweight champion. Atlas did not survive the first round. He was fired on the spot.

Atlas argued passionately that a man he respected so much had to make a stand, had to grasp that the shaping of mere ability was one thing, the moulding of character and the necessary discipline implicit in the make-up of a true champion was another much more formidable task. Unfortunately for Atlas, and some would also say for Tyson in the long run of his life, his argument found no purchase in the old man's obsession to once again claim ownership of a world heavyweight champion.

That passing convulsion – along with the much more devastating, and lasting, effect of D'Amato's death – had been absorbed by Tyson when I rode with him to Queens. There were experiences, he said, that are always part of you. Some of him, he knew, would never cease to reside in Brownsville, never forget the cachet and the swagger of his street heroes.

D'Amato had died four months before I rode with his protégé to Queens. He was attended by a tearful Tyson at the local hospital where he was taken with pneumonia. Just 18 days later the fighter went into the ring at the Las Vegas Hilton against the WBC world heavyweight champion, Trevor Berbick.

Berbick – a Canadian by way of Port Antonio, Jamaica – had gained the title earlier in the year with an impressive unanimous decision over Pinklon Thomas. The new champion, who had administered a brusquely formal defeat to Tyson's hero Muhammad Ali in his last professional fight, had shown considerable quality against Thomas, who had disposed of such notables as Mike Weaver and Tim Witherspoon.

It meant that Tyson's rampage of 27 victories and 24 knockouts in 18 months – 'Keep him fighting, keep his mind on the job,' had been the old man's injunction – was moving on to another level, one on which his brutal power and fighting instincts would face their most testing examination.

Berbick was destroyed in two rounds. The rampage, which had included 12 round-one stoppages in his first 19 fights, was proved to be as authentic as an avalanche. The image of a ring monster – augmented grimly by his assertion after the defeat of a hapless Jesse Ferguson that he regretted his failure to drive his opponent's nose-bone into his brain – was now in train.

D'Amato's calculation about the potential of his protégé had been exact, and no doubt he would have relished the verdict of the experienced British fight observer Donald Saunders, who told readers of the *Daily Telegraph*, 'The noble and manly art of boxing can at least cease worrying about its immediate future now that it has discovered a heavyweight champion to stand alongside Dempsey, Tunney, Louis, Marciano and Ali.'

Nobility in the manly art? That was a huge claim to be made on behalf of a ferociously wound-up man-child for whom a boxing ring already seemed arguably his safest place.

It was certainly true that Tyson had offered some arresting evidence that in his black shorts and sockless boots he might indeed represent the kind of primitive force that had so swiftly carried his predecessors Jack Dempsey and Rocky Marciano into legend. Also, it was a fact that when he wasn't tending his pet pigeons in a coop in the garden of D'Amato's big wood-framed house in Catskill, he was beginning to immerse himself in the lore of boxing – and identifying himself with some of its greatest heroes.

'I read about Dempsey and Marciano, Armstrong and Louis and Jack Johnson,' he told me, 'and I see myself following in their footsteps. Cus never stopped telling me that I must pattern myself on such men – that I had the power and the ability to follow them. And it has been like someone opening the curtains and letting some light shine in. No, it isn't always so clear, I've brought a lot of crazy shit with me from the streets, and it is not always so easy to clean it away. But everyone needs something to shoot at, to be able to say, "Man, I can do something, hey, look at me . . . look at the stuff I have right here."'

But nobility? The ability to release more than the atavistic power that had so consistently welled up in him at the sound of the first bell – and had brought him two Junior Olympic titles in fight time that could be measured by how long it took him to draw a bead on the kid who shook and quavered before him?

Eight seconds was the record – and one to convince D'Amato that in his last days he had revived the dream he had lived with Patterson three decades earlier. That, too, had been something of a psychological reclamation, and one always vulnerable to the self-doubts of a fighter that reached a nadir with Patterson's crushing defeats by Sonny Liston. But then you could never imagine Patterson speaking coldly of ramming someone's nose-bone into his brain. Or shrugging with resignation when a gun was pointed at his head after the bothering of a prepubescent schoolgirl. Or breaking training because of some dark but irresistible yearning for the old dangerous streets that might have been a million miles from the Norman Rockwell picture that was Catskill.

By the time I rode in his limousine, Tyson had already exploded across the face of boxing. No one knew where the shrapnel would fall – or upon whom. Not his new managers Jimmy Jacobs, a man of great sophistication, and Bill Cayton. Not Kevin Rooney, Atlas's replacement who shared kisses on the lips with his fighter in the ring before his challenge as a trainer, and enforcer of discipline, became nightmarish and he was fired. Not, certainly, his promoter Don King, whose instinct was that in all the furies of Tyson's nature there would always be gold.

After visiting Brownsville, I drove to Catskill to see Tyson work out in the gym above the police station, which had a notice board reassuringly light on stories of horror. He was attentive to the urgings of Rooney, and the overwhelming impression was of bristling power. He stalked his sparring partners, cocking his head in a menacing motion that almost invariably signalled a burst of slugging power.

In two months, Tyson would be seeking to extend his heavyweight empire by adding the WBA crown of James 'Bonecrusher' Smith to the WBC prize surrendered by Berbick. The promise was also that by the end of the year he would be the youngest undisputed heavyweight champion of the world since Patterson achieved the distinction by beating Archie Moore.

Patterson preceded Tyson from the streets of Brooklyn and into the care of Cus D'Amato, by way of another upstate reformatory school. But if in some ways their stories had unfolded along the same track, against the same odds, their natures were separated as widely as the banks of the Hudson River, which flowed past their unlikely haven on its way to New York City.

The disparity could not have been more obvious when I found Patterson in his farmhouse on the drive back to New York. He was hopeful for his young successor, spoke of his great natural talent and power, but, yes, he saw problems – of discipline, of a proper understanding of the good luck that had come to Tyson, and the control of himself and his situation required if it was not to drain away.

'My background is similar in some ways,' Patterson said. 'We were a big family in one of the poorest parts of the city. I was the youngest of 11 children, and I got in trouble with the police for thieving. But when I had my success in the Olympics, when I beat Archie Moore and then regained the world title after losing to Ingemar Johansson, I swore to myself that I would never stop working, never throw away the gifts I had been given.

'Does Mike Tyson have this feeling now – does he realise what it will take to stay at the top of a business that is so hard and unforgiving and, sooner or later, finds all your weaknesses? Will he keep his head, recognise the people who are good for him and all those who are looking to help themselves at his expense? This is the test he faces now. His ability is there for everyone to see. But that is only the start of it. What is important is how you handle your first success, how you build your life.' And, he might have added, how you fight to get strong again at the shattered places.

Few, if any, in boxing had known as profoundly as Patterson the demands of such a challenge. Two defeats by Liston, two by Ali – the second one his last professional fight at the age of 37 – brought him to points of such terrible introspection he wore a false beard and dark glasses before going into the street. His first marriage ended because he couldn't accept the idea that he would leave the ring a beaten man.

And before he died at the age of 71 in 2006, a victim of Alzheimer's disease and prostate cancer, he produced a haunting epitaph for his days in the ring. He said, 'It is easy to do anything in victory. It is in defeat that a man reveals himself. When you have millions of dollars you have millions of friends. Boxing is like being in love with a woman. She can be unfaithful, she can be mean, she can be cruel, but it doesn't matter. If you love her, you want her, even though she can do you all kinds of harm. It's the same with me and boxing. It can do me all kinds of harm but I still love it.'

Around about the time Floyd Patterson was seeing me to his door, and past the pictures of the best of his career and life, including one featuring a Swedish marathon run with his fierce rival and great friend Ingo Johansson, it was impossible to banish an image of Mike Tyson at the start of his career. An image of a young man who couldn't disguise his hurts, who made you wonder if he would ever heal them, even with the help of so many millions of new friends.

Chapter Nine

Las Vegas, April 1987

Some fights are never over, whatever the ringside adjudication. They go on down through the years, harbouring old regrets, spawning fresh anger. That we had a prime example of this rancour-filled phenomenon was clear from the moment Sugar Ray Leonard's arm was raised in victory over Marvin Hagler.

It would always be Hagler's belief that Leonard didn't beat him but stole from him; that with the world middleweight title he took from him all he had fought for since he retreated with his family from their burning tenement building in Newark in the riotous summer of 1967. Hagler moved to New England. When he exhausted the opposition around Boston, he made further progress in Philadelphia, one of boxing's toughest theatres of action. And if some would always claim Leonard triumphed with masterful ring-craft and heroic nerve, it was an argument that would never budge Hagler from his view that he had been cheated. If some hailed Leonard as a hero, the master of his era, Hagler saw only a thief making off into the night.

The debate would still flare three decades later. It would engage Leonard quite as fiercely as the inconsolable Hagler.

Hugh McIlvanney, who was one of those at ringside most convinced that the winner had, for all his virtuosity, conjured a dazzling mirage rather than an authentic victory, many years later expressed his opinion at the end of a long TV interview with Leonard. McIlvanney had reason to congratulate himself that he had waited until the last possible moment to make his point. 'He was very angry,' he recalled. 'I didn't fear for my safety but I knew how deeply he was displeased. He turned to the man who had arranged the interview and said, "You've had me talking so long with a man who thought Hagler beat me?"'

Leonard would have been even more indignant had he found time in his post-fight euphoria to read the writer's verdict published in the *Sunday Times* and *Sports Illustrated*. 'What Ray Leonard pulled off in his split decision over Hagler was an epic illusion,' wrote McIlvanney. 'He had said beforehand that the way to beat Hagler was to give him a distorted picture. But this shrewdest of fighters knew it was even more important to distort the picture for the judges. His plan was to "steal" rounds with a few flashy and carefully timed flurries and make the rest of each three-minute session as unproductive as possible for Hagler by circling briskly away from the latter's persistent pursuit. When he made his sporadic attacking flourishes he was happy to exaggerate hand speed at the expense of power and neither he nor two of the scorers seemed bothered by the fact that many of the punches landed on the champion's gloves and arms.'

I also believed that Hagler had carried the fight, if by a finer margin. However, the weight of harder opinion was heavy. Budd Schulberg and the distinguished British referee Harry Gibbs were also both convinced that Leonard had indeed stolen the fight.

Ironically, Gibbs had been rejected as a judge by a Hagler camp still smarting from their experiences in London when their man provoked an ugly riot by beating the home favourite, Tony Sibson. It was a huge mistake. After reviewing the film back home in England, Gibbs was adamant that Hagler had significantly outscored Leonard. Schulberg's theory was that Leonard had benefited from a 'compounded optical illusion. The result was that by simply being more competitive than expected it meant that he appeared more effective and to be doing more than he actually was.'

What no one could deny was that if Leonard was a thief, nobody had ever gone about his larceny with more panache or determination. He was not a prince of thieves but a king. It was a performance that entranced the most colourful of sports columnists, Jim Murray of the *Los Angeles Times*, and for admirers of both the authority and eloquence of McIlvanney and the whimsy of Murray it was a division of opinion that said much, if not all, about the divergences of scoring at ringside.

Murray was famous for both his humour and his exotic imagery. Plagued by chronic eye problems, he once filled a Vegas salon with laughter when Don King, who so often had been a victim of the writer's barbs, welcomed him back to the boxing scene after a successful operation. 'It's great to see you, Jim Murray,' bellowed King. 'Don,' responded Murray, 'I have to tell you it's great to see anyone, even you.' When Sebastian Coe retained his Olympic 1500 metres title in Murray's home town in 1984, the columnist likened him to an athletic version of a young Lord Byron wreathed in laurels.

He was equally lyrical about the performance of Leonard, saying that the fight wasn't even close and that Hagler had been made to look like someone chasing a bus in snowshoes. Only one of the three judges, the Mexican José Juan Guerra, could have read that assessment in the Caesars Palace coffee shop the following morning without believing it had been filed from some distant, quirky planet. Guerra scored it, grotesquely, 118–110 for Leonard at the end of the 12 rounds. Lou Filippo gave it to Hagler 115–113, with Dave Moretti going in favour of the challenger by the same margin.

Hagler was at first stunned and broken. Later, he raged, 'I didn't lose my title. They took it away from me. They took away everything I had worked for all those years. Leonard came to me at the end and said, "You've won, man, you beat me." But I thought – let's wait, this is Las Vegas, the big betting town. They did this to me before with Antuofermo eight years ago. Leonard fought like a girl. I really thought they should have deducted points for all the holding and the grabbing. His punches meant nothing. I fought my heart out. I kept my belt. I can't believe they took it away from me. A champion shouldn't lose on split decisions.'

I found it hard not to sympathise with the pain of Hagler as I pushed away my copy of the *LA Times* on the early morning breakfast table. If he hadn't deserved to keep his title, if he hadn't done enough to separate the illusion of Leonard's performance from its reality – and despite the starkness of Murray's verdict, a majority at ringside decided he had – certainly he did not warrant such harsh dismissal to the foot-hills of a trade he had dominated for so long.

It was in the ninth round that all the flair of Leonard, and, maybe, the artifices, appeared to have reached the point of exhaustion. Hagler had been growing in authority in the middle rounds and now he was driving Leonard into a corner with a ramrod jab and heavy combinations. The challenger was dwindling; all his instincts, his cavalier flourishes, his bewitching footwork, were overtaken by a much more basic ambition. It was to survive.

Throughout the fight there had been passages when Hagler exerted the greater strength, the heavier, more consistent punching, but in the ninth he took Leonard to his limits. It was the single most powerful and unambiguous statement of the night. It was by no means the work of someone wearing snowshoes.

Murray's most valid point was probably that the fight had come six years too late. But then whose fault was that?

It was certainly not Hagler's. After Leonard's resurrection in the second Durán fight, and the elaborate build-up to the showdown with Hearns, Hagler was not so much the elephant as the rhino in the room. His eagerness to charge at Leonard was so overt it seemed almost to fill the auditorium in Baltimore to which he had been summoned in November 1982.

Leonard, having been medically cleared after an operation for a detached retina following his third-round defeat of Bruce Finch in his first defence of the title unified by his victory over Hearns, issued the invitation. As Leonard stood beside the master of ceremonies, Howard Cosell, Hagler waited impatiently for the announcement of a fight date. Instead, he had to listen to a stream of tributes to Leonard before a hammer smashed down on his best hopes.

Leonard was announcing not a new battle, and one that was likely to be the most demanding of his career, but his retirement. Hagler had come to Baltimore to share Leonard's spotlight, the aura of his victories over Durán and Hearns, only to find that he was just another face in a very large crowd. He flew back to Boston with an anger those closest to him suspected would never quieten. What he didn't know, though, was that Leonard would hate quite so much being away from the ring.

I encountered him during the build-up to the Hagler–Durán fight, almost precisely a year after his abdication in Baltimore. He was brooding on the fringe of a throng gathered to watch first Durán, then Hagler work out before the TV cameras in the Caesars Pavilion. I asked him how it felt to be an onlooker.

He said, 'It is hard, you know – harder than I thought it would be. I thought I could move on more easily, say that one part of my life was over and another was beginning. But, no, it's not as easy as that. I've talked to many retired athletes, football and basketball players, and so many of them say the same thing – you miss that feeling of being at the heart of some drama, you want to hear the crowd calling your name again, you want to hear that roar when you go into the ring. I suppose it is something that becomes part of you down the years.

'Today I watch Marvin Hagler and Roberto Durán and I envy them so much I want to be in their shoes. I want to be the person being asked the questions. I don't want to be just part of the crowd.'

However, he would waver another four years before stepping in with Hagler. He would have corrective eye surgery, fight the journeyman Kevin Howard deep in Hagler country in Worcester, Mass, where he was knocked down for the first time in his career and was so disgusted with his own performance he said that this time he was walking away without the possibility of a return. 'It's over, it's finished,' he snapped.

And then he went with a friend, Michael J. Fox, the Canadian actor, to see Hagler wage particularly ferocious war with the heavy-hitting Ugandan John Mugabi, a collision so merciless that both fighters received hospital treatment. At the end of the fight Leonard turned to Fox and said, 'You know, I think I could take Hagler.' Fox's first reaction was that his friend, fuelled by a ringside beer, was speaking whimsically. Less than a month later, however, Leonard went public in an interview with a Washington TV station. He said he was ready to return to the ring once again and that he had a solitary target. It was Marvin Hagler.

'I know exactly what it takes to beat the man,' he declared. At the time Hagler was relaxing on a yacht in the Caribbean, and it would be two months – for the excited, remotivated Leonard, two very long months – before he gave any reaction. When it came, Hagler might have been exacting a little revenge for his bitter disappointment in Baltimore half a decade earlier. He said that he had begun to debate the possibility of retiring and he was far from sure that he would return to the ring despite the huge lure, financial and historic, so suddenly created by Leonard.

Negotiations were concluded swiftly enough and the fight was announced at the Waldorf-Astoria in New York with huge fanfare. This gave five months of build-up for the 'Super Fight' which, inevitably, would be at Caesars Palace.

Ferdie Pacheco felt bound to say that Leonard was risking not only his eyesight but maybe also his life, but the fighter's only agonising was over the fine-tuning of his strategy. He yielded a much greater share of the fight income to Hagler – he would receive a mere $12 million against his opponent's final haul of around $20 million – in exchange for the choice of gloves (10-ounces), the number of rounds (12) and the largest possible ring space (20 square feet) in which to exploit his superior speed and ring strategy. This left Hagler with an extremely basic imperative. It was to produce the kind of bludgeoning power that two years earlier had left Tommy Hearns glassy-eyed and with legs of straw.

Hagler had to make another desert storm while Leonard, some would always contend, had the even more demanding challenge of creating that mirage. In the sports books of the Vegas casinos, the odds were emphatic. A Hagler storm was favoured at 3-1.

When the fight was over, when the challenge had been met, Leonard did not reveal the depth of his doubts when he came into the ring, and still less did he offer a breath of confirmation that when the bell rang for the last time he conceded the night to Hagler.

Yet if Leonard has always been adamant that he knew he had the means to beat Hagler, if not stop him, there was no question that his usual buoyancy was subdued, if not completely absent, when referee Richard Steele brought the fighters to the centre of the ring.

Hagler was not as extravagantly aggressive as he was during the preliminaries with Hearns but if you had to pick a winner on first appearances it would have been him. He barely looked at Leonard before Steele drew them together. By comparison, Leonard did not seem to be savouring the moment. If he was contemplating exclusively uncharted glory, it didn't show. He appeared edgy, intense, but then there was surely reason enough. No fighter had ever come back from so far so quickly. He hadn't fought for three years and then, by his own standards, extremely poorly.

But then, we didn't have to wait long for a reminder of Leonard's extraordinary capacity to remake a world that appeared to be collapsing around him. Hagler, as he had against Hearns, came striding across the ring but with nothing like the co-ordinated force of that first, unforgettable assault two years earlier.

There was a good reason for this. If Leonard's face was a mask of thinly concealed apprehension, his movement did not speak of a lack of composure. He retreated but in the most orderly, point-scoring fashion.

A mark of the uncertainty provoked in Hagler was his frequent switches from southpaw to orthodox. He resembled someone running through his keyring, confused that a familiar lock refused to open. Leonard jabbed with electric flourishes, then rolled away, rejoicing in the dimensions of the ring and, when Hagler managed to reduce them, the challenger slid into a clinch.

The crowd roared at the end of the first round, whether it was in exhilaration or relief that its hero was not only unscathed but flourishing, you couldn't be sure.

Schulberg's compound illusion theory had perhaps already danced into place. Hagler's first significant contact came early in the second when he landed a sharp left hook to Leonard's head, but if the recipient registered the impact with a grimace the effect was only to increase his vigilance. When Hagler moved back into orthodox mode, Leonard was ready to absorb a flurry of hard rights. He took the battering with his arms, clinched again before skipping away with the flash of a jab and a quickly thrown right. The round ended with a burst of action, including hooks from both men, but the result for Hagler was disappointingly inconclusive.

Again, Leonard's flight before his power had been far more calculated than cowed. For his pursuer, already, it was a most dangerous retreat. Leonard had said before the fight that he did not imagine he would knock out Hagler. But, most certainly, he added, he had worked out a way to beat him.

The growing roar of the crowd said that the plan appeared to be feasible, at times spectacularly so when Leonard wrong-footed the champion with balletic grace, but in the third Hagler, settling, it seemed, into his southpaw stance, was landing more significant punches. His jab worked more effectively as he set up multiple hooks and some hard combinations. Leonard was hardly passive – he continued to hit on the run – but if he had clearly won the first two rounds this one carried the dawning threat of attrition: it was the heavy thud of Hagler attrition, which was proven to be the most wearing kind.

Leonard's response was audacious, beautifully fashioned as he emblazoned the fourth round with all the best of his technique. He flagged a bold, long straight right – and delivered, to the delight of the crowd. Angry, Hagler pursued him but Leonard was elusive and taunting, shaking his head in disdain after extricating himself from a failed bombardment.

If the fight was to be decided on composure alone, this was vital work by Leonard but, of course, he had completed just a third of his challenge, and if the fourth was cause for fresh optimism, the fifth was quite the opposite.

Hagler landed heavy punches, closed Leonard down much more effectively, and when the challenger rallied briefly at the end of the round it was at no cost to the powerful impression that Hagler had begun to exert himself. He hurt Leonard in a way that could never be obscured by smoke or mirrors, tons of dry ice, and not even the genius of Leonard to sometimes make laughter in the dark.

But then in the sixth there was another remarkable resurrection, more evidence of the nerve and the resilience Leonard had made the staples of his challenge. His defiance, his movement brimmed again; and despite the maintained weight and persistence of Hagler's punching (always more emphatic and precise) Leonard did enough, it turned out, to take the round – or, as his opponent might say, pilfer it with uncommon style. Particularly memorable was the work that he produced with his back to the ropes and with Hagler wading into him.

Most of what followed was of the same pattern: Hagler's aggression, Leonard's ultimately unbroken ability to survive huge physical pressure and come back with something of his own, something stylish and eye-catching enough to at least postpone the belief that his eventual defeat had become inevitable. Some would always contend that Leonard's triumph in the sixth was his last true one; that the second half of the fight was nothing so much as an extraordinary exercise in damage control.

The supreme example of this was the ninth, when Hagler pounded on him so strongly it is still possible, all these years later, to remember how you came to rise from your seat, like all around you, in the certainty that you were about to see a conclusion to the most extraordinary action.

But then no one told Leonard. He may have looked broken, he may, to those of us still ignorant of the full extent of the resolution he had brought to the ring, been on the point of submission, but he fought on and out of the corner we thought had become his prison.

He could still make his version of a pirouette. He could still ingratiate himself in the minds of at least two of the judges with his late flourishes in rounds in which the tide had flowed so strongly with Hagler. Purists would always claim that Leonard had indeed come to cast a spell, conjure an illusion; that he threw 'arm' punches which, anyway, Hagler mostly blocked, and that if he had astonishing nerve it was, in this context, that of a confidence trickster. Surely, in the last professional analysis, it would not be enough.

But, yes, it was; enough to win the middleweight championship of the world, to dispossess Marvelous Marvin Hagler of that which he had come to prize most highly down all the years since that flight as a boy from burning Newark. And what a savage dividing line it was. Leonard was remade in a world without which, he had come to realise, he could not properly exist. And Hagler, whatever his protests, was destroyed.

Certainly it was true that within six months of his defeat Hagler felt it necessary to publicly deny claims that his life – and his self-regard – had imploded. Initially he did so on a Boston TV station whose sports broadcaster, John Dennis, had said that the former champion had become involved in 'widespread abuse of alcohol and cocaine'. He added, 'Those closest to Marvin Hagler say it was that decision on 6 April that started him on the downward spiral. Almost immediately on his return to Boston, they say Marvin's despair over the loss steered him towards alcohol and cocaine.' The following day Hagler told the same audience, 'I want to reassure the public I have no problem with drugs or alcohol.' He suggested that problems in his family life, and the impending breakdown of his first marriage, had been the catalyst for the reports.

However, he would soon feel the need for a more extended and deeper rebuttal of the charge that his life was breaking up, that he had become, in the pain of a shocking and unjust defeat, adrift from all his old moorings of pride and achievement. He told *Sports Illustrated*'s William Nack, 'You know some day you are going to lose but what I wanted to do was retire as the undisputed middleweight champion of the world. With all my belts. They didn't beat me. They took them from me. They took. That's what they did. They took. So that's the bitterness. I think time will help. That's all I'm asking. That's all I'm looking for. That's all I want, peace and time.'

He also assured Nack that he felt that already the worst may have passed, that he could reassure himself on certain points, saying, 'I felt I fought a very good fight. I trained for three months. I sacrificed like hell for that fight. I think what happens to me when I don't knock a guy out and he's left standing, everybody thinks, "The guy did great. He survived." That's what Leonard did. He didn't come out there to try to win the title. Leonard came there to look pretty and just to show he wasn't scared and to get in the ring with me. But, hey, he didn't come out to try to knock me out. He knew he couldn't do it.'

Leonard, as was to be expected, was quick to remind Hagler and the world that a knockout was not the point of the exercise. He had gone to beat Hagler within the rules of boxing, he had seen and exploited the way to reduce him with his speed and flair and ineffable self-belief. He hadn't gone to floor Hagler but to scale him down, to say that his own talent was of a different and superior kind. He announced, 'I went against history and now they'll have to rewrite the books. They talked about logic, that the fight was not supposed to be. Someone said before the fight, "Two things will not happen this year. Oliver North [the presidential security adviser who authored the Iran–Contra scandal] will not be back in the White House and Sugar Ray Leonard will not beat Marvin Hagler. I think they better check the White House – and I think they understand now that everything I did worked.'

Hagler never fought again and retired officially 18 months after his defeat. Unlike Leonard, he would never be tempted back into the ring. He made movies in Italy, became a hero in a new country he found congenial and appreciative of his achievements, and was remarried, to an Italian woman, after parting with his first wife Bertha, who had wearied and rebelled under the pressure brought by her husband's unforgiving and, she believed, ultimately treacherous and destructive trade. The fears that he would descend into a vortex of pain and recrimination and mind-altering drugs were proved to be groundless.

He made a graceful retirement, even if he could never completely heal the wound that had gone down to the bone.

Leonard announced another retirement but if he fooled anyone it was only himself. Five more times he was drawn back to the ring, the last occasion when he was close to his 41st birthday. He won two more titles, the light-heavyweight and super-middleweight crowns, when he pummelled a guileless young Canadian, Donny Lalonde. He boxed a draw with Tommy Hearns, but it was a tepid version of their first great battle, and then he easily defeated Roberto Durán on points on a cold desert night when the fighters huddled under blankets between rounds that never began to recall a tumultuous past.

Leonard's ring alchemy was running down now and all that was left to him in the ring were two defeats: one a terrible beating in Madison Square Garden, by the younger, stronger Terry Norris; and a last, inglorious exit in Atlantic City at the hands of Héctor Camacho.

So, who in the end was the winner: the exuberant, boastful Leonard or the soul-scarred Hagler? The truth is still complicated, perhaps even more so than when we rode out of town 30 years ago. Then we were merely wrestling with the result of a single, intriguing fight. What we couldn't see so clearly was that it was one that would never be quite over for the men who fought it.

Chapter Ten

Las Vegas, August 1987

The wind that stirred in the trees around the gym above the police station in Catskill, New York, now seemed to be announcing the violent potential of Mike Tyson. He had become the most arresting force in boxing. Indeed, as I collected my bag at the airport alongside the hookers and the dealers leading the latest influx of what might politely be described as the fight crowd, it was easy to believe the transfer of power was all but done.

Tyson had brought a new, anarchic thrust and, yes, the story of boxing had changed and moved on so quickly, so profoundly, that decency seemed to call for a moment's reflection, if not a minute's silence. Time enough, certainly, to reflect that, whatever the new era would bring, the time of Sugar Ray Leonard, Roberto Durán, Tommy Hearns and Marvin Hagler had been glorious in all its furies and dramas. It had carried us to heights unimagined when Ali was finally driven from the ring here seven years ago but, yes, we knew it had passed, irrevocably. They had fought the best of their fights, carried us with them to the extremes of their will and their talent and now they could do no more than pick what they could from the residues of their respective greatness.

Any lover of the fights, the real ones that forced men into every resource at their disposal and reminded all who watched them why this was the most ancient and durable of sports, would surely grant them that and say, 'You gave us your best, now take from the rest.' But, also, understand that you no longer occupy that place which Muhammad Ali identified as the centre of the world.

There would, though, be one last sturdy remnant of their greatness still apparent when we left ringside on the warm desert night that saw Tyson beat Tony Tucker to become the youngest undisputed heavyweight champion in history.

It was the fact that – however bitterly and long Hagler resented the vagaries of boxing justice, or Sugar Ray Leonard flashed his indignation over doubts surrounding his victory against him here in April, or Roberto Durán regretted what happened in New Orleans or Tommy Hearns pondered what might have been – they still had one reason at least to feel united in a warrior satisfaction.

They would never have to ask the question that we were about to see written all over the face of the young fighter who had consigned them to boxing history. They would never have to wonder if there was ever a time when the world did not see them as their own men. Such a claim would certainly have sounded pitiful on the lips of Tyson after the bizarre humiliation of a ceremony he had to endure after his final step to mastery of the heavyweights.

He had not been at his best while beating the International Boxing Federation heavyweight champion Tony Tucker at the Las Vegas Hilton, no more than in March when in the same ring he separated James 'Bonecrusher' Smith from the World Boxing Association crown. But, on both occasions, he won unanimous decisions by the most comfortable margins. Now here he was, the latest heir of Ali. And what was his reward? It was, apart from a $2.5 million purse that he was expected to dispose of at wanton speed, a public ordeal of quite exquisite embarrassment.

If Tyson's promoter, Don King, had put a ring through Tyson's nose and attached a rope as he led him into the Hilton ballroom, it would have been merely another notch of humiliation. King, cooing his pleasure over the latest rich field of wealth to come to harvest, called it a 'coronation'. But of a new warrior king? No, it resembled more the coming out of a prince of fools. Tyson had a diamond-studded crown on his head, a silk cape around his shoulders and a sceptre in his hand. But it was the expression he wore on his face that would be unforgettable. It was part scowl, part grimace and mostly it said it was possible to conquer the world and still be alone.

Six weeks earlier Tyson had attended a rap concert in Los Angles. It was one of those occasions supposedly designed to break the pressure that had been building over two years of relentless fighting and the earning of around $11 million. The night of rap, though, proved less relaxing than one of his one-round knockouts. It left him in the hands of the Los Angeles police and flashed still another warning that his life beyond the ring was already building into his most formidable challenge. He was accused of pestering a female parking attendant and then striking one of the lot supervisors who went to her aid. The result was a charge of assault with a deadly weapon, which Tyson denied. He said he merely slapped his victim with an open palm. Nevertheless, he settled out of court for $105,000. The amount was miniscule against his new, vast earning potential but the implication was huge, and soon compounded by reports that he had jumped training camp.

The first belief was that he had blazed down the Barstow highway to Los Angeles and the arms of the TV actress Robin Givens, with whom he had become besotted. Such an escape route from the fight camp would not have been inappropriate considering this was the road on which the hero of Hunter S. Thompson's 1971 novel *Fear and Loathing in Las Vegas* had fended off the drug-induced imaginary monster bats that bombarded his open-topped sports car. The novel's subtitle, after all, was '*A Savage Journey to the Heart of the American Dream*'.

As it would happen, the dramas of the Givens' affair – and their brief and deeply dysfunctional marriage – would take some time to play out, quite grotesquely and partly on nationwide television, and Tyson's friend Rory Holloway appeared at a press conference to explain that a four-day refuge had in fact been sought back home in New York State.

Holloway, wearing the jewellery and the top-of-the-line Rolex that was some of the early generosity Tyson would heap upon him right up to the moment he pronounced him a traitor, said that the trip was to release some of the tensions building in the camp – pressures that would soon see the fighter and trainer Kevin Rooney part company. Tyson had, said Holloway, merely 'hung out' for a few nights in the bars and nightclubs of Albany, and now he was back on the fight scene, refreshed and ready to destroy Tucker.

Tyson beat Tucker, who claimed to be fighting with a less than fully repaired broken right hand, handily enough, but it was not the volcanic eruption that boxing had been awaiting with at least a touch of ghoulish relish.

It was my third visit to Vegas in five months to see Tyson's annexation of the heavyweight titles, and if he was again plainly a remarkable natural force at 21, he was still some way from an overwhelming sum of all his variously intimidating parts.

There would, soon enough, be much more explosive examples of his withering effect on opponents undermined before they entered the ring. But in March against Bonecrusher Smith the goal of a final step against Tucker in the heavyweight unification did not galvanise him in the way that was expected. Or that had been promised in some vigorous, unbroken and brutal work by Tyson (removed from the distractions of the Vegas Strip) in Johnny Tocco's sweaty gym.

It didn't help the spectacle that Smith, six inches taller than Tyson and 13 years his senior, never began to make good on his promise to reproduce the aggression that had brought him the WBA title, against most expectations, with a first-round stoppage of the talented Tim Witherspoon. Smith, an amiable North Carolinian who became the first heavyweight champion to boast of a college degree (in business administration), put Witherspoon down three times. The verdict of the cognoscenti was that the loser, for all his good ring-craft and clever punching, had become weary of contractual battles with Don King, and the powerful punching of Smith proved one discouragement too many.

The emboldened Smith came into town talking a big fight, saying, 'Tyson was impressive against Trevor Berbick but Berbick isn't the puncher I am. When Tyson fights me, it's going to be a great fight – a bang-bang fight.' Instead, it was a bang-grapple fight, with Tyson banging and Smith grappling for almost all the 12 rounds. Tyson dismissed the Smith rhetoric quite drily: 'Everyone says they're going to come and take it to me, until the bout starts,' he said. 'But I'm the one who doesn't get intimidated or shaken easily.'

That was prophetic enough and by the eighth round, referee Mills Lane was deducting a second point from Smith for excessive holding. The crowd by this stage was booing in frustration, and at ringside there was for me the dawning dread of a long night stretching to a desert dawn back in the hotel, the spectre of a flickering computer screen, relays of room-service coffee, a fast-filling ashtray and the daunting task of enlivening a night shorn of the anticipated drama.

I had come to write of a ferocious, unfolding legend, but that hope dwindled while gathering in the fighters' reactions to Tyson's victory by unanimous decision, a formality that Smith challenged only in the last round with a heavy right hand.

Smith was still bullish in his disappointment, declaring, 'I wanted to break his concentration. I did the best I could. He can punch. He has a devastating left hook but he couldn't knock out the Bonecrusher. I nailed him in the last round, finally caught him. I buckled his knees, but the fight was nearly over then.'

Tyson was dismissive, saying, 'When I was trying to put the punches together he grabbed. This hurts boxing. This is show business, people expect a performance. I won every round and it was an easy fight. In the last round he hit me with a good shot but it didn't hurt me, it just took my legs away. He didn't want to fight, he didn't want to win.'

In May, Tyson was no less pragmatic after his sixth-round TKO of Pinklon Thomas while defending his WBC and WBA titles, the decisive action coming just when a ripple of boos signalled anticipation of some more of the tedium of the Smith fight. Indeed, but for a ferocious, almost conclusive first-round onslaught from Tyson, and his power in the sixth, it was true to say there had been more spectacle in the final pre-fight press conference.

The lavish affair in the Hilton theatre disintegrated into a scene of upturned tables and widespread fisticuffs, and as the television cameras rolled swiftly the promoter King made no attempt to restore order. As he stood apart, I remarked that he did not seem distressed that boxing might not be portrayed at its most dignified on that night's news broadcasts. 'Brother,' he said, 'my heart is jumping for joy.'

With King setting so much of boxing's new agenda – and barely going a month without some fresh legal challenge from a big-name fighter swearing that he had been robbed as crudely as any back-street mugging victim – boxing had plainly recovered some of the rowdy momentum that so many feared was lost with the end of Ali.

King had ridden on the back of men like Ali, Frazier, Foreman and Holmes to his notoriety and his fortune – and a pardon from the governor of Ohio following his manslaughter conviction over the death of a rival back in his days as a numbers racketeer on the streets of Cleveland. And now he had Tyson and, potentially, a mother lode of astonishing profit.

No semblance of such financial optimism had been apparent in the Tucker camp, and least of all in the hotel room of his father and trainer, Bob, a few days before the fight. He was a mournful, at times near-incoherent figure when he gave a rambling, shocking account of how his son's fight earnings had been eroded before Tyson threw his first hook. Whatever the depredations of King, Tyson would have plenty left from his $2.5 million fight fee to invade the luxury car showrooms and jewellery shops and designer boutiques of the Vegas Strip and Rodeo Drive in Los Angeles. Tucker, though, would, after taxes, have only a fraction of his notional wages of $1.9 million.

Sheepishly, Tucker Senior conceded that his son came into the ring not so much an intelligent craftsman heavyweight . . . but a walking mortgage. Later it would be revealed that the father's financial uneasiness had much to do with his insistence that his son went into the ring on schedule despite injuring his right hand while sparring. Still, the details squeezed out of Bob Tucker were horrifying enough.

Three months earlier his son had taken his career opportunity well when beating James 'Buster' Douglas for the IBF title. The belt had been surrendered by Michael Spinks when he elected to fight Gerry Cooney for much more than was on the table to defend against Tucker. Unfortunately, the new champion's reward was to fight more for a small army of investors than himself. Those waiting to collect when Tucker left the ring beaten, bruised and exhausted numbered seven. Cedric Kushner, his former promoter, headed the queue and pocketed $350,000. The same amount went to Josephine Abercrombie and Jeff Levine, who had underwritten Kushner's investment. There were two silent 'partners' in Tucker Inc, Dennis Rappaport and Alan Kornberg, and they received $252,000. It would emerge that Rappaport had threatened to derail the fight if his demand for $540,000 was not met. In the end he decided to settle for what he could get. Bob Tucker's share was $228,000 and former manager Emanuel Steward was the final beneficiary with a cheque for $120,000. This left the man who had to go into the ring with $600,000 and some tricky negotiations with the tax authorities. He also had a deepening cocaine problem.

It said much for Tony Tucker's resilience that not only did he survive 12 rounds against Tyson, he would go on to get the better of the cocaine and eventually return to the ring, not least impressively going 12 honourable rounds in 1993 with the formidable world champion Lennox Lewis. Given all his circumstances, it also had to be said that he acquitted himself with much fighting character against Tyson. Indeed, he had reason to speculate what might have happened if there had been more time for his injured hand to heal. The first round had one of those moments that carry the potential to change the course of a fighter's life – and sometimes even the pecking order of history. Tucker produced it as Tyson came barrelling in, throwing short (necessarily against a much taller opponent), viciously intended hooks. It was a left uppercut of great force and perfect timing. Tyson was lifted off his feet, and when he landed he wore an expression of considerable concern. He also retreated some way across the ring. Tucker pursued him, landing a series of strong right hands, mostly on Tyson's head.

The second round was, though, essentially the end of the fight, or at least of Tucker's ambition not only to survive but to take control. Later, he explained the dwindling of his horizons. He said, 'In the second round, I hurt my right hand. I had already hurt it sparring a week earlier. I was afraid if I used it again it would get broke. But then I had to use it to keep Tyson off me.'

Tyson came out of the fight with a series of major questions to answer. No one doubted his extraordinary power, his ability and willingness to get inside invariably taller men with longer reaches, but in swift succession Smith, Thomas and Tucker had shown there was a way to reduce the effectiveness of his outright aggression. With accomplished performers like Tyrell Biggs, Larry Holmes and Michael Spinks waiting down the road, this was an issue that need to be resolved. It added weight to speculation that Kevin Rooney might soon be supplanted in the corner by one of the great boxing teachers, perhaps even Eddie Futch.

What was not in doubt was that when Tucker elected to last the course, to contain his immensely strong opponent as best he could in the clinches, Tyson had again displayed the kind of power and appetite for the action that would make any attempt to fight him on his own terms almost certainly futile. He was too strong to be countered by such desperate measures. His progress to victory against Tucker, apart from the first-round explosion, was quite inevitable. Two of the judges made him the winner by five rounds, a third gave it to him by eight.

Tyson was not euphoric before his clownish coronation in the Hilton ballroom. 'I was thinking that because he was intimidated – and he was freezing at times – I would get him with a good right hand, but I guess I didn't have it altogether tonight, and the fact that he was intimidated made it tough. As long as you make mistakes, can I tell you, you have no means to be happy; I'm a perfectionist, I want to be perfect and I was trying to use my jab more. I was just a little confused because there were times he held so much I just couldn't fight my fight. I just continued jabbing.'

Tyson conceded that he felt Tucker's force in the first round. 'Yes,' he allowed, 'he is a very hard puncher, but after he hit me it was history. It went away.'

Tucker's departure from town was inevitably sad and lonely. He was a bruised, disconsolate figure virtually unnoticed in the crowd retreating through the airport. He had some hard days ahead, fighting the seductions of cocaine and the sense that his great opportunity had come and gone. But then it was also true that, however brutally boxing withdraws its favours, there are always some who get stronger at the battered places. Tucker would elect himself to their number when he beat the drugs, and earned his well-merited challenge to Lennox Lewis in another, no less demanding epoch.

Also true was that 20 years would pass before he gave full expression to the pain and frustration he carried with his baggage through Las Vegas airport. He said in 2008, 'I knew Tyson couldn't beat me but then my right hand was broken when I fought him. A couple of days before I was sparring against a guy named Young Joe Louis. This guy was doing a lot of bad talking about me. I heard this from my sparring partners. So I chose to spar against him first because I was going to put him down. I was hitting him real good when I heard a pop in my hand. When I went back to the corner I knew I had hurt it bad.

'The doctor said I had a small hand fracture. They said I would need therapy and not to use it for ten days. I had to fight Tyson in less than that. I went in determined, though I was very apprehensive to attack Tyson due to the hand. I hit him with a right uppercut early and my hand just shattered. It was the worst pain ever. I was supposed to beat this guy, but how could I with one hand? With two hands, I would have knocked Mike Tyson out. I regret that I fought Tyson not fully healthy. If I would have postponed the fight, I may have been blackballed. I wouldn't sign with Don King back then, and he was running things.'

Indeed, he was, and for me there was an enduring image of that reality as I rode out to the airport, past the desert scrub and the cacti and the casino billboards. It was of King leading Mike Tyson across the Hilton ballroom, his chest heaving with excitement and his smile glowing.

Tucker had taken a thousand regrets to the airport. It was too soon for him to grasp something that one day might bring a little consolation: that his conqueror, despite his crown and sceptre, already had reasons to begin counting his own.

Chapter Eleven

Tokyo, March 1988

Earlier in the week, before his formal destruction of the talented but grievously underprepared Tony Tubbs, Mike Tyson was awakened from a seamless and much-needed sleep. He sat up in his bed in the skyscraper suite of his luxury hotel and saw his trainer, Kevin Rooney, staring at a large television screen with an expression of considerable concern. 'What the fuck was that?' asked Tyson, rubbing his eyes. 'It was an earthquake, Mike,' said Rooney. Wordlessly, Tyson slammed his head back on the pillow and returned to sleep.

The eruption was powerful enough to raise large tracts of flimsy housing on the edge of the city and claim some lives. Tyson was safe enough in his quake-proof lodgings, though even he might have been briefly alarmed, as I was, by the sight stretching along the length of a richly carpeted corridor as knowing Japanese guests stood to attention between the sturdy door jambs of their rooms. However, Tyson might also have reflected that his own life was in danger of descending into violent uncertainties.

There was truth in this, even if in the ring the trajectory of his career was beginning to fulfil some of the most confident predictions of unprecedented mayhem. The frustrations suffered in the laboured defeats of James Smith, Pinklon Thomas and Tony Tucker had already been consigned to the past with vicious relish. Five months earlier he had brought a chill to the blood with his sadistic revenge on a Tyrell Biggs who he believed had patronised him cruelly when they were US Olympic teammates. And then, just two months ago in the same Atlantic City ring, he flattened the fine old champion Larry Holmes with a right hand so brutal some experienced observers feared for a few moments that it might prove fatal.

The trouble was that there was a coherence in his ring ferocity too often absent on the other side of the ropes. Some of his mood swings here would have dismayed Cus D'Amato and the man who had come closest to filling the emotional vacuum left by the old fight man's death, the sophisticated Jimmy Jacobs. And here was the core of the emerging problem. When Tyson raised the bed-sheets against the earthquake, he might, however subliminally, have also been shutting out some of the pressures that had been building around him in recent months.

His affair with Robin Givens had become, from his perspective, her marriage of convenience and financial opportunity and, increasingly, his humiliation. It was one that would be paraded, quite excruciatingly, across national television on the Barbara Walters' show.

He was fêted in Tokyo but the arrival of his new wife and ever-present mother-in-law Ruth was hardly the signal for an onset of serenity, even though they were careful to make sure he had his medication for what they believed was a case of chronic manic depression.

Most disturbing of all was the news from America that Jacobs, the man who had seemed best equipped to hold Tyson back from an early precipice, was now losing a long fight against leukemia. His death two days after victory over Tubbs would awaken in Tyson all the fears rooted in his boyhood in Brownsville. It would deepen his sense that whatever he achieved as heavyweight champion of the world, he would always be destined to be alone; alone with his fears and his appetites.

A small irony was that when Tyson looked down from his hotel window he could see a beautifully manicured garden of reflection, a place made for busy guests to take a few moments of repose. One of my more spiritual colleagues, Sri Sen, the boxing correspondent of *The Times* who would, when the turmoil of the fight world had become part of his past, write a haunting novel drawn from his boyhood in India, had already sought the tranquillity of the garden. Unfortunately he had shed his sense of direction in the mazy, tree-lined avenues, and when I passed I could hear his confused mutterings. From my raised position on the adjoining street, I guided him back to the entrance, where we laughed that he had managed to get lost in a place expressly designed so that a man might briefly find himself. More soberly, we agreed it could have been created with the troubled Tyson in mind.

I went back to early forebodings over Tyson's fate, including the vivid memory of returning to my room late one night at the Las Vegas Hilton. I was the sole occupant of the lift when the doors swung open and Tyson entered, alone and, it seemed, occupying a world entirely of his own. His expression discouraged casual pleasantries. His eyes swept across me, unseeingly, and then they fixed on somewhere beyond our narrow confines. He seemed so apart, so separate that he might have been out in the desert, scuffling in the shrub, shouting his anger in the moonlight.

That anger was never far from Tyson in Atlantic City when he put the hated Biggs on the rack for one second less than seven rounds. It was less a fight than an exercise in elaborate, sustained torture. He loathed Biggs not only for what he believed he had done to him but also for who, and what, he was.

He was much taller than Tyson, had an elegance of manner, a style with girls that was easy and confident, and when they were together in the squad preparing for the Los Angeles Olympics he was openly disdainful of the lisping youth from Brooklyn. Tyson was not only disregarded but, it seemed to him, almost dehumanised. It was bad enough that Biggs openly mocked his clumsy uncertainties, worse was how he freely predicted that Tyson wouldn't make the Olympic team, and certainly not in the super-heavyweight class he coveted – and in which Biggs would win gold in Los Angeles.

Tyson, seething in his frustration, was left behind when the team plane flew off to California. He had been moved to the heavyweight class, where he was beaten in the Olympic trials by Henry Tillman. As a professional, he would also avenge that slight, but in a quite different manner to his treatment of Biggs. There was no fistic equivalent of pulling the wings off a fly, just swift, contemptuous annihilation. He destroyed Tillman in less than a round.

He teased and taunted Biggs for those seven rounds and then, with a horrifying relish, reported that in the ring his opponent had cried out like a girl, made the gestures of a woman. It was a dark projection into some of the worst of the days that lay ahead. If his life was a film, there were surely already signs that the spool was running too fast, too dangerously.

Biggs had his admirers and they included the vaunted Angelo Dundee. Indeed, Muhammad Ali's guru called a major upset despite the odds that made Tyson a huge 12-1 favourite the day before the fight. Dundee said, 'Biggs will do a lot better than anyone expects. If he reverts to his style as an amateur you're going to have a 15-round fight and Tyson will get outpointed.' HBO commentator Larry Merchant, a former New York boxing writer of great distinction who could never be accused of gratuitous hype, agreed. 'Tyrell Biggs,' he said, 'is the only man on this planet capable of beating Mike Tyson.' The odds promptly fell to 8-1 but the central reality remained unscathed. Tyson was anticipating his time in the ring with the relish of a hungry man about to be served with the most tender of steaks. Yes, he might have said, I'll take it rare.

Biggs hardly helped himself in those hours before a fight that would effectively ruin his career and, as in the case of Tucker, send him into a downward spiral that included cocaine and a critical loss of the confidence that so many had believed would carry him to the world heavyweight title. He talked a big fight and, most perilous of all, he woke up some of the Tyson demons when he declared on the eve of the fight, 'He's never fought anyone like me, someone with a strong jab who can box and is not going in there just to survive. Do you think I'm going to walk into the roundhouse punches of a guy who's 5 feet 8 inches? Any expert who says I'm not ready for Tyson is no expert. I've gone through hell in 15 fights. I don't know this Tyson the way you guys talk about him. I know Tyson from way back when.'

Gone through hell? Biggs didn't yet know half of the meaning of that phrase. Tyson punished him relentlessly, round after round, but never so hard as to bring a swift end to his pain, his anguish, his hopelessness. Later, Tyson was candid about the pleasure he had taken right up to the moment Biggs broke down in the last seconds of the seventh round. His recall was disturbing in its malevolence and its glee. He declared, 'In my mind I knew it was for 15 rounds and I was prepared to put the pressure on him constantly for 15 rounds. You know, I was having a great time. I felt good. I was in the best condition of my life and I did what I was supposed to do. I knew when I came to this fight I was the best fighter in the world and that not a man alive can beat me. I was hitting him with body punches and I hurt him.

'He was actually crying in there, making woman gestures, and crying, "ooh-uh-uh." I knew he was breaking down. I was very calm and I was thinking of Roberto Durán, how he used to cut down the ring and just wear them down. I had that frame of mind when I was in the ring. I wasn't even thinking about the fact that Biggs had a cut. I was thinking about hitting him to the body, softening him up.' Nothing so merciful, certainly, as a blasting version of a boxing coup de grâce, a pistol to the head, an end to the fight, a cessation of the pain.

It wasn't a victory speech. It was the unveiling of a persona that took us beyond street mischief, the ski mask and the rough taunting of defenceless victims. It was colder than that. The boy who had shyly gone onto the high-school stage in Queens, who had grimaced beneath the absurd confection of Don King's crown in the fake Vegas coronation, had come to another phase of his journey. He had announced himself the Baddest Man on the Planet, and there was no doubt his public enjoyment of what he had done to Biggs – his talk of girlish screams, how he had come to own him, even allegedly made him his anguished 'girlfriend' – showed considerable potential in the role he had laid down for himself.

Three months later he revealed a different but no less intimidating side of his fighting nature. He ransacked the former champion Larry Holmes, who at 38 was 17 years his senior and had been out of the ring for 21 months since his second and most bitterly disputed loss to Michael Spinks while trying to regain his world title.

After that fight Holmes gathered the media in his hotel suite and talked long and bitterly of the corruptions of boxing, the dubious judging, the ever-changing alliances, and, more than anything, his determination to return to his mansion and heart-shaped swimming pool back in hometown Easton, Pennsylvania. But even as he rasped out his anger and his distress there were many in the room who nodded their sympathy while thinking, 'Yes, but for how long, Larry?'

Nearly two years was longer than they thought because they knew that of all his discoveries in life, the one he found most engaging was his ability to earn millions of dollars by doing that which came to him most naturally. Indeed, he would fight on close to his 53rd birthday, his last performance a unanimous decision over Eric Esch, the preposterous phenomenon of a less stern boxing age better known as 'Butterbean'.

For Holmes, Butterbean was – as to the Mike Tyson of January 1988 – a deposit of fat on a plate finally to be discarded. He was the last gift of a trade that had made Holmes rich beyond any of his imaginings. When Don King, with whom Holmes would have an enduring love–hate relationship – he loved the money he could conjure, hated the eternal battle to get all of it that he believed was his due – came on the phone to propose the Tyson fight, he heard again the tinkle of millions rather than the most menacing threat he would ever encounter in a boxing ring.

For Tyson, it was the first of a new seven-bout deal negotiated by King with HBO. It was worth a basic $26.5 million. When he came into the ring you could see that he had put aside the role of the torturer he had played with such blood-curdling plausibility in the company of Biggs. The rack and the nail-pulling implements had been put aside. Instead of his now-traditional basic black trunks and sockless black boots he might have donned the mask of the executioner. He lacked only a long-handled axe.

That might have helped penetrate the watchful defence of Holmes in the first two rounds, but as Tyson stalked the old champion, throwing big punches from wide angles – and Holmes countered with a long outstretched left arm and an eagerness to clinch – there was inevitably that sense of a formal execution. In the third, Holmes offered a little more offence, threw a jab or two and brought a ripple of applause from those in the crowd who remembered him at his best when he performed a brief dance.

Certainly Tyson was somewhat underwhelmed, saying later, 'The people were more excited than I was. The crowd got pumped up and Larry let his ego get involved. I said to myself, "Now he's going to get it." Even as a champion he would sometimes make the mistake of keeping his left hand too low and that made him susceptible to a right hand.'

It was indeed easy for Tyson in the fourth. His right hand found its target with a shuddering power and accuracy. Holmes went down three times. He had never been knocked out before, but when Tyson sent him to the canvas for the third time, with a punch that seemed to shake the foundations of the Boardwalk convention centre of Atlantic City, referee Joe Cortez ignored the formality of a count. He reported, 'I just felt I didn't have to bother counting. I pulled out his mouthpiece and just got out of the way so the doctor could look him over. Larry was all right. He rose to a sitting position and told everybody, "I'm OK, I'm OK."'

He was in far better shape than many at ringside could have hoped – and not least the most knowledgeable of British fight men Mickey Duff, who said with much relief as Holmes got back to his feet, 'For a moment I thought Tyson might just have killed him.'

Holmes was not in good enough shape to appear at the post-fight press conference but he did fulfil his HBO obligations, speaking briefly with Merchant, who reported, 'Larry was very generous in his praise of Tyson. He said he was a much sharper puncher than he had thought, adding, "Yes, he's better than I thought, a lot better. People can talk about Spinks all they like but Tyson is the true champion."'

Holmes, perhaps remembering the night he had gone to pay homage to his victim, Ali, in his suite in Las Vegas in 1980, left Merchant with a note of sad if not bitter resignation. He said, 'They always get you and some day they will get him.'

For the trainer and American TV pundit Gil Clancy, the latter development was some distance into a no doubt tumultuous future. He said, 'I thought Larry fought a smart fight for three rounds. I don't think Tyson knocked out a completely shot Larry Holmes. He's got that tremendous punch and he nailed Holmes. I think he has run out of opponents. I think he is that good.'

In Tokyo, whatever the extent of his private turmoil, Tyson was certainly managing to project the image of a classic warrior, someone naturally able to touch something deep in the psyche and the imagination of his Japanese hosts. An impressive witness to this was the great ring battler Masahiko 'Fighting' Harada, a folk hero after winning the flyweight and bantamweight world titles. He said, 'Tyson's appeal in Japan has to do with his spirit. Sports fans here are fascinated by the fact that while he is relatively short for a heavyweight he fights with great energy, great intensity and always defeats taller opponents – as I did.'

Tyson, unquestionably, found some release and pride in the feeling that he had arrived in a place that had so quickly recognised that, whatever his past, or his gaucheries, he had a quality that could touch the heart of a warrior nation. He said one day, with a hint of wonder in his voice, 'Man, these people seem to love to me. Maybe I've found a new home. It's crazy.'

Each morning when he ran in the streets crowds cheered, taxi drivers tooted their horns. It was not Muhammad Ali walking down Seventh Avenue but it was a statement about the aura Tyson was bringing to the world heavyweight title.

It engulfed Tony Tubbs. He was receiving $500,000 against Tyson's $10 million, and one reason for the chasm between them was explicit even before Tyson smashed his way to a second-round TKO. It was made plain at the weigh-in, where Tubbs came in at 238, 3 pounds over the mark that would have given him a $50,000 bonus on his basic fee. It would have been a statement of intent in the Tokyo Dome, which had sold 80 per cent of available tickets on the first day – and would have more than 50,000 present on fight night – but Tubbs merely shrugged when his weight was announced. He had been here before. A talented fighter, with good hand speed and understanding of how to use the ring, he won the WBA world title in 1985 when he beat the highly rated Greg Page. Six months later he was an ex-champion, beaten by Tim Witherspoon. He was 244 pounds on that occasion.

His poor showing on the Toyko scales was the story of a career that, like so many in boxing, had foundered on the gap between natural-born talent and the character to properly exploit it. A few weeks before he was due into the ring, he was talking blithely of his chance to restate his superior ability. He said, 'I know physically I'm in shape. Two hundred and thirty pounds (16 stone 6 pounds) is my weight – 228, 229 is a plus, but I'll be 230 and hard when I fight Tyson. You'll be seeing the new Tony Tubbs. When I step in they are going to say, "Wow, look at that cat." And you know, the thing about it is, once I start putting the moves down on Tyson I'm gonna change. You know what? This might not be as hard as you all think it's going to be because Mike Tyson is only good for what he can hit. I know that right now I'm one of the best heavyweights there is in the world. I can box better than any of them and I ain't taking no back seat to none of them. I'm not even taking a back seat to Mike Tyson.'

The Japanese promoters, supported by the view of Don King's matchmaker Al Braverman, had believed that Tubbs' quick hands and intelligent ring-craft would carry the fight into the later rounds. Tyson's newly acquired cult following would have value for money, but the hope was groundless.

Indeed, the optimism rivalled that of the American visitor who, wishing to return to a nightclub where he had enjoyed a riotous time 24 hours earlier, handed a book of matches he had picked up there to a taxi driver and pointed to what he thought was the name of the establishment. It was, sadly, the address of the match factory. Some hours later he awoke in the back of a taxi that had been parked, meter running, for some hours at the factory gates, not far from the top of Mount Fuji.

The sight of Tubbs coming into the ring was not a lot more exciting than the night-owl compatriot's end of journey. The extra pounds showed and, if his hands moved as quickly as promised, his feet might have been wrapped in balls and chains. By the second round, Tubbs had lost the snap in his jabs and combinations, he was anxious to clinch at every opportunity, and his rhetoric had already hit the canvas where he would soon be joining it. The best of his punches landed on Tyson without consequence and the champion made no attempt to conceal his contempt. He was in stalking, ruthless mode. At every opportunity, he punished an ill-prepared body. Towards the end of the second round, Tubbs could no longer take the last of his clinching, counter-punching options. With his back against the ropes, he gasped at the weight of Tyson's attack on his soft mid-section and then the fight was over. A vicious left hook landed above Tubbs' right eye.

Tubbs attempted a few small, grotesque steps away from the danger, then subsided. The hook had left a cut above his eye that sent blood streaming down his face, and as the referee started the formality of a count Tubbs' people, the despairing ones who couldn't persuade him to lose those extra pounds, came charging into the ring. The reality was that if Tubbs had worked more seriously in the gym, Tyson – as he had against Biggs and Holmes – would still have further augmented his fearsome image. It had come down to a matter of degree.

Tubbs, maybe, was reluctant to see this truth. He said, 'Tyson is the world champion and he came out with his lefts in the second round. I will be back. I got caught with a lucky punch.'

The man with the microphone, Larry Merchant, was under-whelmed by Tubbs' fanciful version of events, saying, 'If you thought whale-hunting was outlawed in Japan, we just saw that Mike Tyson hasn't heard about it.'

The champion was no less dismissive. He said, 'It's true he has very, very fast hands, but that's about it. He's a very easy target to hit. I was very surprised he held his hands so high. So, I went for his body to bring his hands down. I thought I was wearing him down. I landed some good shots. I did what I was supposed to do to a guy supposedly out of shape. I got rid of him quickly. If he had lasted six or seven rounds I would have been criticised. It's his prerogative to come into the ring the way he wants.'

This was a Tyson plainly comfortable in his fighting skin. It was in the other areas of his existence where a more crucial challenge lay. Tokyo had fallen for him but even this uncomplicated triumph, a warm salute to a man of extraordinary combative instincts, hadn't brought more than passing comfort.

He touched on this as he said *sayonara* to his new and adoring public. He said, 'Wherever I fight is my home. I'm only here to do a job. Sometimes I feel like I left Earth and moved to another planet. I wanted to be heavyweight champion but I never wanted to be a super-superstar. This is scary, to be a bigger star in another country than you are in your own. Yes, it scares me. The Japanese all want to touch my hair all the time. But if they touch my hair, fair is fair, I touch their hair back.'

In a little more than 24 hours he would be back home in New York, but then what was home now for Mike Tyson was a place that could feel as strange and as lonely as any faraway location. He had scarcely touched the ground at Kennedy Airport when he was overwhelmed by the news of the death of Jimmy Jacobs in Mount Sinai Hospital in Manhattan.

Once again, an underpinning of a perilous life had been jolted away. Even this raw pain would be complicated by his discovery that in the legal machinations that would install Jacobs' partner Bill Cayton – a man with whom Tyson had felt no empathy – as his new and sole manager, his protector Jacobs had attempted to make all the future fight earnings a substantial part of his own legacy.

For the moment, though, Tyson would have enough to do dealing with the loss of another figure in whom he had invested great trust and hope. His marriage to Robin Givens, almost every indicator said, did not seem likely to even begin to fill the new void. It was, no doubt, another reason why he sat alone in the funeral chapel in Los Angeles, and sobbed uncontrollably at the last rites of Jimmy Jacobs. And, perhaps, the latest evidence that he was destined always to be alone.

Chapter Twelve

Seoul, March 1988

Not all the psychological dramas in and around the boxing ring were the monopoly of Mike Tyson, even if they were not so plain before your eyes. Some, I discovered here, take a whole lifetime to play out and when they are over they are still as mysterious as when they first took shape. This at least would be my conclusion when I looked back on what was in some ways the most extraordinary episode in all my time around ringside.

I was walking in the shadow of the steep hill at the top of which is the radio mast that dominates the city skyline. It was hard work after the late nights and tricky deadlines of the Tyson fight in Tokyo but my companion invited me to speculate on how much more challenging it would be if we were being raked by intense enemy fire, if this were not a sightseeing constitutional but an effort to clear away elements of the North Korean and Red Chinese armies in the 'Forgotten War' waged here three and a half decades ago.

It was a Sunday and we had spent most of the day in and around the city. We had been to teahouses and beautiful parks and temples (and a barber shop where we scrupulously avoided that part of the tariff concerned with services not readily available at similar establishments back home) and no doubt a digestive or two would be taken in one of the more inviting Country and Western taverns still favoured by homesick GIs in the neon-lit Itaewon district. The digestives would be vital, we could tell ourselves, after a dinner of *bulgogi* and *kimchi*. If you're unfamiliar with Korean cuisine, you need to know that the beef dish *bulgogi* is not for nothing also known as 'fire meat'. *Kimchi* is a vegetable dish fermented in a brine of ginger, garlic, scallions and chilli pepper while laying several feet beneath the ground. My companion had warned that even some Koreans wonder why, having buried it, anyone ever had the nerve or the intestinal fortitude to dig it up.

My companion was not one of the scores of day-hire city guides who each morning touted for business in the lobbies of the big hotels. He was a man I had grown to know, and to love, since I first stepped onto the raucous caravan of the big-fight scene more than ten years earlier. It was Pat Putnam of *Sports Illustrated*, who would be described by the fine New York boxing reporter Michael Katz as 'maybe the best fight writer since Joe (*The Sweet Science*) Liebling'.

One of my first experiences of his kindness came when he invited me to a lunchtime drink as I hurried past the Galleria bar in Caesars Palace. I explained that I didn't have time, I had come into Vegas late and, in a few hours, had to produce a piece on Sugar Ray Leonard. My deadline was looming and I didn't have a whole lot to go on. His response was that in that case I should take his room key and look up a background interview with Leonard that he had put into his computer that morning.

Now, after covering the Tyson–Tubbs fight, we had joined a small group of American and British journalists in a stopover in Seoul, where the summer Olympics and the disgrace of the deposed 100 metre gold medallist Ben Johnson would unfold later in the year. We had looked at the Olympic installations and, one by one, were catching planes home. Putnam and I would be the last to leave. He asked me if I was free to spend a day in his company and when I said yes, I would be delighted, his face showed a surprising degree of relief.

He said that for him it would be a difficult day, one of rediscovery of old emotions and deeply buried feelings and some unhealed wounds. There would be places he would see that he expected to trigger reactions about which, at this point, he could not be so sure. He would, he suspected, be opening many doors that he had kept firmly closed for much of his adult life. In these circumstances, he said, it would be good to be accompanied by someone familiar, from a different, much more agreeable phase of his working experience.

I told him that, of course, I knew of his Korean experience: the hard fight up here from the port of Inchon with the US Marines, river crossings made under fire, the violently shifting battles of Seoul, one of which ended with his unit being overrun and his serving more than a year in a North Korean POW camp. Of course, I had heard fragments of his story from him in the Galleria and the Flame Bar in Las Vegas and in the Irish pub on the Boardwalk in Atlantic City, and in other places on the road, and always there had been the sense that quite a lot was being left unsaid.

He had never provided detailed accounts, just fleeting mentions of that time in his life which had coloured all the days that followed; and often his accounts had been accompanied by disparaging references to anyone of Oriental origin. These had been jarring coming from the pursed lips of a man of kind, often liberal instincts, a most generous colleague and a writer who had consistently and brilliantly shone a light on some of the murkier corners of the fight business.

Maybe I would be able to provide a little ballast on a day of inevitable emotional turmoil.

So, it had gone. He located, a little uncertainly at times, some of the landmarks of his ordeal and speculated about the possibility of others. Was that the ravine, now occupied by a row of small houses and pocket gardens, where he was pinned down for maybe the longest day of his life? Was that the street corner where a comrade attempted, unsuccessfully, to throw back a hand grenade that had come fizzing through the rubble? Did he help winkle out snipers operating in the eaves of a rebuilt pagoda?

I happened to be particularly susceptible to these memories Putnam was disinterring after so many years. For me it was a strange and affecting privilege, a window into a man's life – and, perhaps, a piece of history to place in a certain perspective all the spectacle and heroics we saw routinely on the sports fields and the boxing rings.

As a boy, I was deeply moved by the newsreels of the Korean War, euphemistically described as 'police action', that each week rolled across the screen of the local picture house. I remembered vividly the images of endless lines of refugees winding through the scarred and frozen landscape, and so much of the action: hillsides filled with the invading People's Army charging in their 'human waves'; the blasting of heavy artillery; and flashes of the magnificent rearguard action by the 650 men of the 1st Battalion of the Gloucestershire regiment, the Glorious Glosters, on the banks of the Imjin River. Most of the Glosters were killed, badly injured or taken prisoner, and one survivor reported that the force of the Chinese, estimated at 10,000, broke against them like a 'swollen wave' hitting the shore. There were also the pictures of street fighting in Seoul, and these came back to life as Putnam ruminated and reflected and lapsed into spells of impenetrable silence.

A visit to Panmunjom, where the Armistice was signed in 1953 in a building that still stands eerily unchanged as a relic of the Cold War, was especially evocative. We walked down a long, steep border tunnel at the end of which a solitary North Korean soldier stood sentinel for his stone-age land. Up on a terrace above the demilitarised zone, we looked north to mountains bathed in a mystical glow, which defied the idea that behind them the world had regressed to the most basic survival and tyranny and one that would be frozen until the end of the twentieth century and so many years beyond.

It was a day I would always place among my most memorable. This would be true, however troublingly and confusingly, when 20 years had passed – three of them after Pat Putnam's death – and I learned, along with the rest of the world and an army of his admirers, that he never served in the US Marines, was never a prisoner of war and that on this day in this place, which was supposedly the kernel of his life experience, he was as much a stranger as I was.

How could it be? Why would this man of superb professional achievement, this ace dissector of illusion and every conceivable folly and deceit in the theatre of the square ring, have lived so doggedly in such an elaborate and relentlessly tailored lie? He was among those of us who sniggered when the promoter Bob Arum was challenged on what he claimed to be a statement of irrefutable fact, was told that he had said something quite different the day before, and responded with a shiny smile and the declaration, 'Yesterday I was lying, today I'm telling the truth.'

Pat Putnam never had such a day of epiphany, as we would see from the sparse death notice published in the Albany, New York, *Times Union* of 29 November 2006. It read,

> Patrick F. Putnam, 75, of Squire Boulevard, died Sunday at Ellis Hospital. Mr Putnam was born in Schenectady to the late John W. and Agnes Nolan Putnam and lived in the Capital District most of his life. Mr Putnam was a Marine Corps veteran. He was a writer for *Sports Illustrated* for 27 years, retiring in 1995. He was a communicant of St John the Evangelist Church in Schenectady and was involved in Guilderland Babe Ruth Baseball. He was predeceased by a brother, Peter H. Putnam . . .

If there is any clue at all on the origins of the fantasy of Pat Putnam, it may lie in one omission in that death notice, which led with the bogus statement that twisted and corrupted the record of a life otherwise lived with great distinction and wit and the most instinctive generosity. What the death notice could have mentioned, without the possibility of contradiction, was that Pat Patnum's brother Peter did serve in Korea and was discharged honourably and with battle ribbons. Could it have been that however brilliantly he wrote, however many great boxing events he analysed with such fine and hugely respected judgement – more than 50 times his work was celebrated on the cover of one of the world's most prestigious sports magazines – Pat Putnam always believed he was in the shadow of a sibling who knew the taste of real battle? And that if you spend so much of your time assessing the kind of combativeness that for him made such compelling subjects in Muhammad Ali and Sugar Ray Leonard, Roberto Durán and Mike Tyson, you feel an ache to be something more than a mere chronicler of exceptional personal courage?

This was certainly included in the speculation of his shell-shocked friends and colleagues, men like his closest companion on the road, Ed Schuyler of Associated Press, who when the news broke said he felt as though part of him had been amputated. Putnam and Schuyler were more than friends, they were a firm, inseparable on the road – and if the job was sometimes demanding and dislocating, the press corps was never so fractious that it was immune to the warmth of their company and the quality of their one-liners.

In that last department Schuyler was particularly adept; his high point perhaps coming at a gathering in New York presided over by Don King and invaded by the wild and controversial heavyweight Mitch Green. The word was that a vengeful Green was pursuing a grievance against King while armed with a gun. Schuyler cut through the alarm when he snapped, 'Throw him some gloves . . . that usually quietens him down.' One of Putnam's sharpest moments came when a press conference was told by Sugar Ray Leonard's management that there should be no questions concerning the fighter's recovery from an operation for a detached retina. Putnam promptly stood up, raised a hand and said, 'Ray, how many fingers am I raising?'

The irony of Putnam's exposure would be that it flowed directly from the degree of the stature he built over the years with his impeccably accurate reporting, one of the earlier results being his scoop that Cassius Marcellus Clay was about to change his name to Muhammad Ali. In each of the three years after his death the Boxing Writers Association of America would make a special award for perseverance by a young fighter, and it would be given in the name of Putnam. The trophy would refer to his military service and, in the third year, this attracted the attention of a website devoted to verifying claims of a military past. The Marine Corps told the website they knew nothing of Pat Putnam.

'He had us all fooled,' the BWAA president and Philadelphia fight writer Bernard Fernandez would announce. 'His tales were totally bogus.'

How do you defend the indefensible? You cannot, not in your heart, but if you come to care for someone enough you will make the attempt, as another great character of the business, George Kimball, would do. Kimball, given his background – as the son of a US Army colonel – might have been among the more outraged when Putnam's long deceit was exposed. As a leading Boston sportswriter and boxing author, he had made his own large contribution to the hard-drinking, boisterous ambience of the men who covered the fights. One of his party props was his glass eye, which at suitably dramatic moments he would place on the bar and chuckle at the startled reaction of newcomers. As an undergraduate at the University of Kansas he ran for sheriff under the campaign banner, 'This County needs a two-fisted sheriff.' The incumbent, who had a withered arm, responded feistily, and successfully enough, saying, 'More importantly, I have two eyes.'

Kimball revered the meaning of Pat Putnam's career and would, with the fine and no less colourful Ohio columnist Tom Archdeacon, raise a glass of ouzo to his continued happy retirement on the Greek island to which the three of us retreated by ferry at the end of the Olympics of 2004. Inevitably, we rehashed some of Putnam's tales and I augmented his legend a little more with an account of the day we shared in Seoul.

When Putnam's 'alternative universe' was exposed four years later, Kimball did rather more. He wrote perhaps the most difficult piece of his career. He said,

It now appears Pat Putnam will take his place in sporting lore alongside the likes of former Blue Jays manager Tim Johnson and erstwhile Notre Dame coach George O'Leary whose falsification of their resumes brought them into disrepute and cost them their jobs. But then since the BWAA couldn't take Putnam's name off the award fast enough, maybe it should be noted we're talking about an organisation that routinely bestows awards named for crooked politicians and boxing officials of dubious ethics.

There is no doubt Pat made the claims he is accused of. He made them in my presence and like so many others I was taken in. I had no reason (or instinct) to doubt them but there is an important distinction to be made here. Pat's wartime adventures may have been tall tales but he never attempted to make them part of his official resume.

They weren't included in his biographies at the *Miami Herald* or *Sports Illustrated* or at SweetScience.com for which he wrote after retiring from *SI*. He never publicly represented himself as either a veteran or a POW. He never attempted to join groups representing either. He didn't ask to be buried with military honours and he certainly didn't ask the BWAA to label him a war hero. He didn't tell these tales to his children. "Never ever, ever," said his daughter Colleen Putnam, who was surprised by the accounts of his Korean experiences that emerged at the time of his death.

In short, if Putnam is going to be posthumously convicted of anything it should be of slinging bullshit in a bar. If that was a hanging offence, we would all be in trouble.

It was a gallant defence. I would read it heart-sore and bewildered so many years after that meandering day in Seoul.

Putnam must have known, at least it is hard not to think so, that there would come an audit of his life that would find, among all the plaudits, at least one case of fraud. That it happened after his death was, I supposed, a kind of mercy. So, too, was the certainty of so many who knew him and lived beside him that the only man he ever hurt purposely was himself.

Chapter Thirteen

Atlantic City, June 1988

Despite the tumult of his private life, and that public sobbing in the cemetery chapel in Los Angeles, Mike Tyson arrived here all of one ferocious fighting piece. He found a way to jettison the chaos a little more with each stride he took from the dressing room up to the ring.

It had become an epic of pain transference, from himself to the next victim staring bug-eyed in his apprehension.

However, it was also true that some aficionados were saying that his development as a boxer, a strategist, was not so impressive. His style was still primitive, too reliant on sheer power, and maybe, sooner or later, would prove short of vital cunning and variety. Certainly, it was right that the old warmth of his relationship with trainer Kevin Rooney had continued to decline and, indeed, would shortly come to an end. Rooney was not one of the great boxing teachers but for a while his rapport with Tyson was plainly a positive factor, and the fact that it became so frayed was another sign of the fighter's disaffection with his life and his surroundings. Nevertheless, his fearsome aura remained a huge asset. He had made seven world-title defences in less than two years; five had ended inside the distance and the last three had been profound examples of his power to intimidate. He resolved to torture Tyrell Biggs. He did it. He elected to club away the last of Larry Holmes's power. He did it, with murderous intent. Tony Tubbs was put away inside two rounds. This was no doubt why his opponent here, the unbeaten and still lineal heavyweight champion of the world, Michael Spinks, confessed to me that he had never before felt quite so much pre-fight dread.

'It is true,' Spinks told me, 'I always go through a crisis before every fight. The scale of it is not always the same but it is usual for me to have some terrible moments. Sometimes I wake in the night covered in sweat and with a great fear of what might happen to me in the ring. I find myself wrapping my arms around myself, moaning and weeping and wondering why I put myself through this. And then I come to the fight and I know what has to be done.

'You have to look back and see how you handled it before, how you have shown that you can do it . . . that the bad time in the night disappears when you hear the sound of the first bell. But then there is always a little doubt nagging at you. Will these fears go when I step into the ring with Tyson? I believe so, I know my ability, what I have done on the way here, but then who's going to believe me if I say, "He's just another fighter who has come along the way"?

'I do not say that now, you cannot say that when you see what he has done. But I can say that I will stand on my record, draw strength from what I have achieved so far.'

The challenge of Spinks, Olympic champion, the man who had twice beaten Larry Holmes and who had not lost the world title in the ring, was a considerable one, but it said much for Tyson's state of mind that it was scarcely mentioned when he met a group of reporters in his hotel suite. He was much more preoccupied by a report that he had physically abused his wife, Robin Givens, a charge to be reiterated in a forthcoming biography of him by his erstwhile friend and fellow Cus D'Amato protégé, José Torres.

Torres would report that on one occasion Tyson hit Givens so hard she bounced around the room. Tyson giggled when that specific allegation matter was raised. 'Can you imagine the effect of me hitting a little-bitty girl like her with my fist? Man, it would have separated her head from her shoulders. Her head would have been rolling around the room.' His mocking laughter lowered the temperature in the suite.

The flak was coming in hard and from many directions. There was a report of assaults against two women in a New York nightclub, and of police being called to his mansion in New Jersey when Givens and her mother, Ruth, reported that he was throwing furniture through windows. Equally alarming, he would be fined for driving while under the influence of illegal substances after crashing his BMW into a tree outside the D'Amato house in Catskill. This incident was accompanied by reports that he had failed in a suicide attempt. There was other turbulence, though mercifully less physical. Tyson was taking legal action against his manager, Bill Cayton, forcing him down from a third to 20 per cent of his fight income, which on this occasion would come to a record-shattering $22 million.

Clearly, there were the makings of a perfect storm. The immediate question was whether it would arrive before he came into the ring with Spinks. Whether it did or not, though, one assumption was reasonable enough: that, in strictly fighting terms, Spinks did represent the last serious challenge to Tyson's hold on the heavyweight title. Spinks, assuming his nerve held, certainly had the technique to exploit any Tyson failure to produce the most telling of his aggression.

Spinks had elected himself to the front rank of fighters and this status would have been assured even had he not moved from light-heavyweight to beat Holmes for the lineal heavyweight title in 1985. That triumph brought him two distinctions. He was the first light-heavyweight to go undefeated in that division – and the first to move up to claim the most prestigious prize in boxing. *The Ring* magazine ranked him one of the great light-heavyweights, behind Ezzard Charles and Archie Moore, but ahead of such luminaries as Tommy Loughran, Bob Foster, Harold Johnson, Maxie Rosenbloom and Billy Conn. Though he shared with his brother Leon the double distinction of being both an Olympic and a world heavyweight champion, his consistency and fighting discipline was of a much superior order to that of his sibling.

Now he had to do it at least one more time. He had to stand up to Mike Tyson; he had to bury each of his fears, every one of his doubts. The christening of the fight was a reminder of quite what was at stake. 'Once and for All' it was labelled and, indeed, the winner would take it all. He would remain undefeated, he would stand on his own.

Certainly Tyson, for all his distractions, didn't need telling how important the fight was. If his mentor, Cus D'Amato, had failed to concentrate his young mind entirely on the challenge of the ring, he had been more successful in conveying the meaning of the great fights and those who shaped them.

Michael Spinks spent less time than Tyson in front of grainy boxing film, but he was proud of his place in history. He had beaten Larry Holmes, if somewhat controversially (especially the second time), the man who beat Muhammad Ali, and no journey into the mists of boxing history would unearth any greater mystique than that in the business the great Joe Liebling described as the 'laying on of hands'.

Spinks came in a 4-1 underdog but, despite his admission that he had never felt such pressure going into the ring before, I had persuaded myself that he was capable of one of the great upsets. My calculation was that Spinks was intelligent enough to exploit the limitations of Tyson's ring-craft – and that if he could establish an early foothold in the fight, if he could show his much younger opponent that he would have to do more than bang away in the certainty of another swift success, he might just sow potentially crucial doubt.

It was a theory that didn't survive the first appearance of the fighters in the ring. Tyson bristled with bad intentions as he tore through the ropes. Spinks might have been stepping onto a scaffold. You could taste his fear. He could not disguise it.

Spinks revealed good physical condition when he took off his robe. At 15 stone 2 pounds he had never been heavier coming into the ring, but the trim of him made it clear that this was about the need to counter Tyson's force in the clinching and grappling and not an indication of slackness in the gym or on the road. The huge worry, apart from the haunted look in his eyes, was that in all the fine definition of an athletic body there was not a droplet of sweat. Spinks' eyes swept the sweat-sheened Tyson and turned away. It was as though he had already seen enough.

When referee Frank Cappuccino called the fighters to the centre of the ring, Tyson stared down Spinks. It was a show of the meanest intent for which Spinks had nothing to thank his promoter, Butch Lewis. As Tyson was leaving his dressing room for the ring, Lewis claimed that there was a suspicious bulge on the wrist of one of his gloves. He was wrong, he saw only a fold of the glove over Tyson's wrist, but he was not to be easily dismissed. There was a delay, and an investigation finally resolved when Spinks' trainer, Eddie Futch, dismissed the problem; and, as Lewis left the dressing room, Tyson turned to his trainer, Rooney, and said of Spinks in a chilling whisper, 'I'm gonna hurt this guy.'

Spinks lasted just 91 seconds, and his ordeal might have been briefer by a third if he had not, somehow, got back on his feet after a right hook to the body ripped through his defence. Already the fight-plan laid down by the great Futch had been exposed as intelligent theory blown apart by awesome reality.

Futch announced before the fight, 'We're not matching strength for strength. That's his game. We have other things to do. We have skills and knowledge of the ring, an ability to change the pace, the direction of attack.'

The source was unimpeachable but on this occasion the view was hopelessly flawed. If Spinks had worked on his greatest strengths, as he undoubtedly had, it was clear instantly that he had been involved in futile labour. His defensive strategy was filled with desperation. He wrapped his arms around Tyson in a way that conjured again his account of grappling with his fears in the night.

Later, Tyson went to the heart of the Spinks problem. At the first bell, he had thrown himself at Spinks and landed a hook high on his head. It was not a perfectly thrown punch, more an earnest indication of his worst intentions, and he reported, 'I noticed the fear come into his eyes right then.'

After going down on one knee after the hook to the body, he recovered from the first knockdown of his career at the count of four in a mandatory eight and, as he wobbled on shaky legs, the referee asked him, 'Are you all right?' Spinks said that he was. But he was speaking from his own lost planet. It was one from which he would never find his way back to the ring.

The Ring magazine voted the seconds Tyson required to destroy much of the meaning of a superb career as the Round of the Year. If Spinks could take anything, apart from $12 million, it was that Tyson would never again, as he had not done before, display such brutal certainty.

Many years later, in an autobiography of shocking frankness, Tyson was still relishing the scale of his mastery of Spinks. He would recall, 'I was totally confident going into the Spinks fight. But I still didn't get the respect I deserved from people in the street who had been following his boxing accomplishments longer than mine. I'd be walking around in New York or LA before the fight and a guy would come up to me and say, "Spinks is going to knock you out, nigga. He's going to whoop your ass." "Are you on drugs?" I said. "You have to be an extraterrestrial to believe that shit."

'Spinks entered the ring first. I decided to work on his mind a little bit, so I entered the ring to the sound of funeral music. I walked slowly up to the ring. I looked at the audience as though I wanted to kill them. I just wanted to create this whole ominous atmosphere of fear. Spinks wouldn't look at me during the ring instructions.'

Tyson said that he was certain he would win the moment he saw the expression in Spinks' eyes, and it was a conviction that deepened when he saw him go down from a punch that he didn't regard as especially solid – nothing to compare, certainly, with the blows to the body that had been knocking down sparring partners each day in the final stage of preparation.

Although Tyson was fêted at a post-fight party attended by such as Bruce Willis and Sylvester Stallone, and flattered to note that the great novelist Norman Mailer, the heavyweight chronicler of Ali, had been at ringside, his mood was sombre. One moment he was declaring that he could beat any man in the world, the next he was saying that he might have fought his last fight. He was engaged by the observation of Mailer that, 'Tyson looked drawn, not worried but used up in a small part of himself, as if a problem still existed that he had not been able to solve.' Tyson's reaction was that of a man who had been found out. He said, 'Norman was right but I had more than one problem.'

The truth was best known by Tyson himself. Away from the ring, he was falling. Some years later, in another besieged phase of Tyson's life, Teddy Atlas would define acutely the fascination he had created in the mind of America. He said, 'People have a compulsive interest in Mike Tyson because he inhabits a world they cannot imagine knowing themselves. To have him as their neighbour would be their ultimate nightmare. He would make their blood run cold. But to view him from a safe distance, to see him come into the ring with such bad intentions, to read about his scrapes and all the madness, well, that's a different story. It is one they just cannot get enough of.'

What was clear soon enough was that the dynamics of Tyson's descent from the pinnacle of his victory over Spinks were in place; Mailer had seen it, others had a powerful sense of its likelihood and, within two years, on cue, it was with us.

They would be two years of litigation, declining performance, and his longest break from the ring since his professional debut – a one minute 47 second rampage against a bewildered Hector Mercedes in Albany, New York, in March 1985. His previously longest break was three and a half months, and when he got into the ring with Frank Bruno at the Hilton Hotel in Las Vegas the assured venom he generated against Spinks eight months earlier was disturbingly elusive. After the fight, he admitted, 'The truth is I wasn't really fit. I'm lucky Frank Bruno wasn't able to take advantage.'

The fight was originally fixed for Bruno's hometown, London, in September, as part of Tyson's cycle of mega-million income. But that was before Tyson was beset by a series of distractions that would push back the date six months.

Less than a month after the Spinks fight, with Don King positioning himself for his most profitable kill, Tyson agreed a new contract with his manager, Bill Cayton. King privately speculated that the deal would prove about as durable as a snowflake in the Sahara. One of Tyson's demands was that he had a complete break from the fight scene of six to eight weeks, which would be time enough for him to attend to the bonfire of his marriage to Robin Givens. He also had to recover from crashing his car into the tree in Catskill and breaking his hand in a street fight with the inflammatory Mitch Green. The Bruno fight was first delayed until late October then switched from London for a February date in Vegas. This was because of Tyson's need to 'keep close to his lawyers'. Tyson would eventually receive a knocked-down

$7 million fight fee and Bruno $3.6 million. The Hilton lost on the fight which, in all the circumstances, was no great surprise.

For Bruno, preparations were relatively serene, just so long as he managed not to dwell on the fact that they would conclude with his obligation to share a boxing ring with Mike Tyson. His famous bonhomie was at one point most threatened by my taking lunch in the restaurant of his spa hotel in the Arizona desert. He demanded that I be ejected by the hotel's security staff and promptly banned me from a forthcoming press conference. 'I don't like what you have written about me, Mr *Daily Express*,' he boomed, but in a touching display of support American reporters said they would boycott the occasion in my absence. The press conference went on, but was most remarkable for the elaborate, comic show of deafness produced by Bruno when I asked a question.

He resented – and why wouldn't he, I was bound to reflect, as the man stepping into the ring with such a ferocious opponent? – my belief that he had ridden on the back of his vast popularity with the British public to the rewards of a fight for which he was simply not equipped. My charge was, as it turned out, almost as heavy-handed as anything Tyson would throw at him in the ring. It was also, like many of the champion's punches, wide of the mark.

Bruno, with much courage, not only survived an opening onslaught of much ferocity, if not the deadly precision, inflicted on Spinks, but returned to his feet to produce a moment among the worst of Tyson's reign thus far.

In the frenetic opening seconds, Tyson appeared to be challenging the 88-year-old world heavyweight title record of Jim Jeffries, who stopped Jack Finnegan in 55 seconds. A right to the jaw knocked Bruno down but he was not cowed when he came back from a standing count of eight. He landed a decent left hook and the effect was a wild but uncoordinated response from Tyson.

Suddenly, the task before Aaron Snowell and Jay Bright, the new men in Tyson's corner with the departure of Kevin Rooney, was more demanding than they could ever have imagined while watching the destruction of Spinks. Tyson was jumping wildly into his hooks and missing, and then, with the round almost over, something quite extraordinary happened. Bruno had Tyson in trouble.

Bruno landed a right that stunned Tyson, not least in its impertinence, and before he could regather himself he was hit by an even more significant blow. It was a left hook that wobbled the champion and sent him into retreat. We would never know what might have happened – or, incidentally, how much humility would have been required of me at the next Bruno conference – if the bell for the end of the round had not sounded so quickly.

As it was, Tyson managed to regenerate enough disabling power to wear down Bruno. Referee Richard Steele called a halt with five seconds left in the fifth round. Tyson was $7 million richer, still unbeaten, but he had mislaid the deadly force on display against Spinks.

In five months Tyson and his new trainers would insist it had been recovered in the first-round stoppage of the respected Carl 'the Truth' Williams, but not everybody was convinced. Some argued that referee Randy Neumann might have given Williams the benefit of the doubt when Tyson put him down with a hook and the fighters' heads collided.

Williams claimed that he was wronged in two ways. First, he could have continued; secondly, he had good reason to argue for a 'no-contest' after the accidental contact of heads. Neumann's explanation was detailed and persuasive, however. He said, 'I had a ten-second judgement to make and Williams could not answer a very simple question. That, plus the look in his eyes, told me he was not in very good shape. Yes, he was holding his hands up but I was looking for more of a response than that. He closed his eyes for a couple of seconds and then I got a blank stare. I asked him, "Are you all right?" and didn't get an answer. I had 38 fights, I'd been there too. When you get up from a knockdown, you gotta be ready to fight, not just be an erect figure. Most fighters will go out of their way to show they're ready to continue. He didn't do that.'

Tyson spoke bullishly, suggesting his image had been fully restored in the brief action. There had to be the suspicion that he was anticipating the many headlines that would be cast along the lines of the one in the LA Times: 'Another easy one for Tyson: The Truth hurts as Bout is stopped after 93 seconds.'

Tyson said, 'There is nobody that can beat me. I love doing this. No man is invincible but I will take all comers to find out. Can I tell you something? I would love to fight Evander Holyfield. Right now, tonight. How about if we go down in the cellar right now and the one who comes back up the stairs with the key is the champion?'

This was maybe an attempt to reconjure the brutal simplicities of his treatment of Spinks, an elemental invasion of a fine fighter who had retired officially and, he insisted, irrevocably, just a month after trailing away from the Convention Hall in Atlantic City.

Now Tyson was picking out the esteemed Holyfield as his next victim, unmindful of that old warning that sometimes you should be careful of what you wish for. This, though, would be something for him to reflect on some years down the road. Along with the fact that maybe he would never again know the kind of night on which he destroyed Michael Spinks.

Chapter Fourteen

Tokyo, February 1990

When he was last in Tokyo – which, astonishingly when you thought of all that had passed, was less than two years before – Mike Tyson observed a certain propriety. Mostly, he smiled and bowed at the right times in the right places. On a few occasions, albeit a little sheepishly, he even donned ceremonial robes. He was fêted as a warrior wherever he went in the city, and this seemed to trigger in him the stirrings of a desire to please. He might just – at least, it was pleasant to think so – have been at the beginnings of accommodating a new life and all its different demands.

Two years? The disquieting truth was it might have been in another lifetime.

He returned here wearing a full-length white fur coat and a belligerent scowl. His hardened, almost permanently abrasive mood was shockingly proclaimed beneath the chandeliers of the meeting room in the five-star hotel packed with television crews and much of Tokyo high life. It was his last official appearance before defending his undisputed heavyweight title against the lightly considered James 'Buster' Douglas, who could be supported in the betting parlours of Las Vegas at the extraordinary odds of 42-1. Tyson, unlike most of his audience, was casually dressed and pointedly disinterested. His expression was sullen as he listened to the rap leaking from large earphones clamped to his head.

Two years earlier it had been possible to see in him at least that hint of a Samurai as he met with Japanese fighters and sumo wrestlers and allowed new, fascinated young admirers to reach out and touch his hair. Now he shrugged and pouted and glowered and when he was asked, somewhat tortuously it is true, by a Japanese journalist about the qualities that made a champion, he replied, 'If you can't fight, you're fucked.'

An embarrassed woman translator produced a few guffaws with her long and inexact interpretation of Tyson's remarks but the rest of the occasion was tense and mirthless.

It was dominated by Tyson's obvious reluctance to be there – he would later confirm that he had to be dragged 'kicking and screaming', and 30 pounds overweight, onto the plane – and his refusal to discuss the Douglas fight as anything other than another piece of throwaway destruction. It was a chore he was obliged to undertake, another step along a road that was becoming as wearisome, many were beginning to say, as it was obscenely profitable.

He would receive $7 million for his casual forced labour, against Douglas's $1 million, and he was making it clear that it was an irritating interference in his new priority of 'partying and having women'. The women were coming in an endless, mostly anonymous stream and included chambermaids.

His trainers Aaron Snowell and Jay Bright were wearing expressions of dismay. When they got him to the gym, past the women flocking to his suite, they were powerless to engage his serious attention – even when, two weeks before fight time, he was flattened by his sparring partner, Greg Page. What could Snowell and Bright do? They could only recoil in the face of Tyson's distaste for the idea of working seriously – and nurse their wounds after Teddy Atlas, fired by Cus D'Amato after that attempt of his to impose discipline on the teenaged Tyson at the point of a gun – delivered the withering verdict: 'Those two guys couldn't train a fish to swim.'

For Don King, who had scheduled Tyson's next fight for Atlantic City in June against the undefeated Evander Holyfield for a guaranteed pay night of $22 million, any alarm would have been much more acute if it hadn't been so widely assumed that Douglas would fold under the first weight of Tyson's aggression.

This confidence that the big – and not untalented – man from Columbus, Ohio, would surrender quickly, shamelessly, went utterly unchallenged. Despite the widespread belief that Tyson was not only unfocused but uncontrollable, the odds against Douglas did not shorten by a single point.

Four days before the fight, however, Dave Anderson of the *New York Times* had filed a warning that might just have provoked at least a flicker of apprehension in King. He wrote, 'Considering his competition, the only person who can beat Tyson is Tyson himself. By not training. By not caring. By not surrounding himself with experienced corner men. Chances are Tyson will quickly swat James Buster Douglas into submission. Even so, reports in Tokyo of Tyson's training are enough to question if the champion is sabotaging his own reign.'

The Page knockdown in the gym was especially concerning, along with another report that in the next session work was abandoned by a distraught Snowell in the face of Tyson's lack of interest. Had the recently ferocious champion really come to care so little for the prize that he once said conditioned all his hopes – and his thoughts? Had the exhortations of Old Cus simply faded away and the worst fears of Floyd Patterson taken on the weight of prophecy?

Everything we were hearing – and seeing – day by day was an invitation to put a little more fuel on the doubts. His sexual appetite, which he had categorised as routine and joyless, had apparently become Olympian. But however wretched Tyson's approach, however recklessly he behaved, King could reassure himself that James Buster Douglas's state of mind, if not his conditioning, had surely stripped away any need for serious concern. Douglas's first great trauma was seven years in the past, when he saw his younger brother Artie bleed to death from gunshot wounds, but that horror had become the opening chapter in a story guaranteed to sap the spirit of any man. No one could say precisely the extent of the psychological damage caused by the first tragedy, partly because there had been so much else that seemed sure to bring him down. Three years before the Tyson fight, his father Billy, a respected, combative middleweight in his own fighting days, said he would no longer train him. In a shattering public rejection, Billy Douglas pronounced his son a quitter. That was his angry reaction to Buster's surrender of what was widely seen as a winning position in the tenth round of the IBF heavyweight title fight with Tony Tucker on the undercard of Tyson's defence of the WBC and WBA titles against Pinklon Thomas in the spring of 1987. Douglas had controlled the fight with his long and confident jab and poised and varied work off it. But when Tucker landed a strong right hand, Douglas promptly capsized under a flurry of punches. Douglas Senior walked away from ringside mouthing the word 'betrayal'.

Since then Douglas had scored six straight wins, including unanimous decisions over two men who in their time would take fleeting hold of a part of the heavyweight title, Oliver McCall and Trevor Berbick, but the stigma of the Tucker defeat was not easily banished, and especially when placed against the intimidating power and trail of destruction created by Tyson.

Nor did it help that the tide of sadness, and personal crisis, lapping around Douglas remained quite relentless. His wife, Bertha, walked out of the family in the summer before Tokyo, leaving him with two dogs and a drinking habit that had led to his prosecution for driving under the influence. When Bertha walked out, he announced that he had found God, but in his personal life there seemed to be little reason to celebrate his discovery.

And then, shortly before he boarded the flight here, his beloved mother, Lula Pearl, died suddenly from a stroke. His new trainer, and Lula's brother, J. D. McCauley, managed, perhaps out of long practice, a defiantly hopeful note. 'She was his centrepiece,' he said. 'I think, if anything, James will turn it into a positive. I really believe that.' But then even as his uncle was saying it, Douglas learned that Doris Jefferson, the mother of his 11-year-old son Lamar, had been diagnosed with leukemia.

Gamely, Douglas had at least paid lip service to the prediction of his trainer and most steadfast ally. He recalled his mother's impact on him as a nervous, fretful schoolboy, saying, 'I came home one day crying because some kid said he was going to get me. She told me to quit crying and either stand up to that kid or fight her.' He then added, 'Something great must be about to happen to James Douglas because something out there is definitely trying to deter me.'

Something great was indeed about to happen to James Buster Douglas, and it would have stood well enough in the Tokyo Dome had it been marked merely by the kind of respectable resistance notably lacking in the performances of Michael Spinks and the previously respected Carl Williams when they faced Tyson. It was the poise that Douglas brought into the ring that was most startling in its promise of what might follow. He wasn't supposed to come in like that. He had not for a second been cast in that way. He was supposed to be another forlorn representative of the Tyson-oppressed heavyweight classes. Spinks had been unable to conceal his dread. Bruno had crossed himself and wore a look of great foreboding. What Bruno achieved, and it was more than most expected, came from a great pool of apprehension. Williams had a less intimidated expression but it lacked the straight-on, clear-eyed quality of Douglas's gaze. It was as if Douglas was saying, as he strode confidently around the ring, 'Do your worst, Baddest Man on the Planet, but do not think you hold any terror for me. I too have been in bad places. I know about the streets and all the cruel things that happen in them: I've seen my brother's life blood run away, I've lost people that I could not contemplate living without, I've made many mistakes, but here I am, I have done my work and I know what I must try to do.' Tyson, as always, poured out his aggression, stepping into the ring with a face that said his work would again be quick and brutal. He scowled across at Douglas but, unlike Spinks, the man from Ohio did not avert his eyes.

Fighting was never going to be Douglas's sport in those days when he ran fearfully home to his mother. Tall and athletic, he was a basketball natural, and you were reminded of this as, at 6 feet 4 inches, he towered above the squat Tyson as they listened to the instructions of Mexican referee Octavio Meyran.

Douglas went to two colleges on basketball scholarships but his classic ticket from the ghetto was revoked at the second one, in Erie, Pennsylvania, when he failed to meet the modest academic demands made on potentially star student athletes. He turned to boxing under the care of his father and won his first five fights before losing to David Bey, which was no disgrace in that his conqueror had an impressive record as an amateur and would go on to challenge Larry Holmes for his world title, creating some serious problems before being stopped in the tenth.

Now, in Tokyo, Douglas was obliged to take what might well be his last chance. Plainly, he had run a gauntlet to challenge the will of any man. Yet whatever the result of the fight, there was at the very least a surge of belief that he would go beyond that first statement of resolve when he came into the ring. You could see it in the certainty of his jab, the snap of his right hand, his unhesitating pursuit of the smaller man.

He was certainly belying the blurted, pre-fight concession by his manager and former college counsellor, John Johnson, that maybe he would have been better suited to firing the basketball. 'His problem as a fighter is that he is too nice,' said Johnson. 'He can be kind of passive. I just can't see what he is going to do against Tyson. I guess we'll see.' In the countdown, Douglas may have encouraged his manager's vagueness when saying, 'I'll just hit him, I guess. It seems that nobody ever hits him hard enough to gain his respect. Yes, I think his opponents have been afraid of him.'

Not Douglas, though; not for a second in the first two rounds. His punching was quick and well directed and was telling Tyson that all his assumptions had to be put away. The street bully was being given something to suck on, something that wasn't sweet or at all familiar. Rattled, Tyson wound himself into one of his churning assaults and then stepped back when Douglas beat him to the punch with his long right hand.

In Tyson's corner the tyro big-time trainers, Aaron Snowell and Jay Bright, were facing the greatest demand of their brief professional lives, and their expressions were already saying that it might well be beyond them.

The second round was a replica of the first, Douglas going forward, saying that if he went down he would not be on the back foot when it happened. The second ended as it began, with Douglas so much the more assertive it was almost as though his manager's charge of passivity was sounding in his head like the ringing of a church bell on the day of atonement. He closed with a right uppercut, which snaked through Tyson's defence so easily a gasp ran through the big stadium.

Tyson had more presence, more weight in the third, and disturbed Douglas's confidence and momentum with a punishing shot to the body. But it was only for the moment, and by the fifth Douglas was again in control, shaking Tyson with another hard right and once more posing more questions than the champion had ever imagined he might have to answer while attempting to annex in its entirety the charm of Japanese womanhood. An additional problem for Tyson was that his left eye was beginning to swell and close, a development that had his corner men floundering in pursuit of makeshift remedies in a manner guaranteed to scandalise any experienced fight man, and not least the discharged Rooney.

Douglas was dominant again in the eighth right up to the moment, six seconds from the bell, when Tyson – caged by his opponent's movement and more fluent technique, and unable to muster the ferocity of those two-handed assaults that had left such a trail of destruction on the road to this ring – produced something from deep inside his fighting will. Douglas, perhaps lulled too quickly into the belief that he had established an unshakeable control, didn't see it coming. It was a right uppercut, one of those Tyson punches that seem to well up from deep in some atavistic mist. Inevitably, Douglas went down. Not, though, without a gesture that would be, for me at least, the most pertinent fact in the controversy that for a little while would cloud all that we had seen to that point. Douglas slapped his left glove on the canvas, as someone suffering no more than acute embarrassment over his own carelessness might.

It was significant in that all else Douglas had produced – and would continue to do so right up to the dramatic denouement two rounds later – would be attacked, principally by Don King, because of referee Meyran's mishandling of the count. He did not synchronise his beat with that of the time-keeper (he started two seconds behind) and King would lead the argument that Douglas was saved by a long count, that ten seconds had elapsed between the knockdown and his readiness to resume the fight.

The reality, which after torturous hours would be justly reinstated, was that at no point had Douglas taken his eyes off the referee. Plainly, he had not been separated from his senses or his ability to fight on, and with splendid, composed productivity.

Douglas, incensed by his own lapse, was immense in the ninth round. Tyson, his left eye almost completely closed, was battered against the ropes. The rock-like, grounded strength had been reduced to the gyrations of a pummelled rag doll. Douglas hit Tyson with four unanswered punches and the champion tottered back to his corner. Back in Vegas there were, no doubt, serial optimists already in mourning that they did not go for the whimsy of Douglas at 42-1.

In the tenth the last of the doubts disappeared in the tide of Douglas's reasserted superiority. The wrecker Tyson was demonstrably wasted, by a brave and accomplished opponent and his own folly, his own terrible overweening arrogance. He was pitiful at the end. When he crashed to the canvas he was parted from his gum shield and his response was that of an anguished, abused child reaching for the comfort of his dummy. He found it and somehow managed to get half of it back into his mouth but it still protruded, a pathetic symbol of the extent of his humiliation and the collapse of his fighting faculties.

Tyson was the most conspicuous victim but the expression of his pain and shock was more measured than that of the desperate King, who was planning to follow his man's inevitable victory here with a world tour of unprecedented plunder, including that $22 million pay night for Tyson in Atlantic City against the unbeaten Evander Holyfield, and perhaps the richest reward of all in a proposed date with the reincarnated George Foreman at the court of the Sultan of Brunei.

King's itinerary had been turned into smouldering ashes as we went from ringside to our hotel rooms and the business of writing up arguably the biggest upset in boxing history. But then, of course, the promoter was hardly a man to be easily confounded by even the most unpromising circumstances – and still less by the force of natural justice. Long before our reports were completed, we were summoned by King to hear a statement of the 'utmost importance'. With Tyson slouched behind dark glasses, King announced, 'The tapes of the fight clearly show two knockouts took place but the first obliterates the second. Buster Douglas was knocked out and the referee did not do his job and panicked. As the promoter of both fighters I'm only seeking fair play.'

King made his statement of impartiality with the precision and solemnity of a Supreme Court judge, but beyond any disguise was the fact that, from the moment Tyson went down under that last fusillade of punches, he had been working as hard and as ruthlessly as at any time since he hustled in the streets of Cleveland. He had succeeded in persuading the ruling bodies to delay ratification of Douglas's victory, and finally he dragged in the hapless referee for what he hoped might just be a decisive confession.

Abjectly, Meyran held up his hands and said, 'I don't know why I started my count when I did and made my mistake. Yes, he was down longer than ten seconds.' He didn't concede that Douglas had followed his beat with close and completely focused attention. Tyson listened to it all with what seemed to be a great weariness. Eventually he roused himself to say, 'I thought I knocked him out. I thought he was counted out.'

José Sulaimán, president of the WBC, confessed to being deeply confused, and all that he could state with anything like conviction was that a rematch was 'absolutely mandatory'.

But it wasn't. King's fight against justice was failing, and there was a clear sense of this by the time I left for home. It was a shocking setback for the man who thought he had boxing in the tightest of grips, and he would feel it most acutely when James Buster Douglas returned to the ring as the undisputed champion of the world. It would be in Las Vegas against Evander Holyfield, and King would have no financial interest.

If Mike Tyson felt excessive pain, if the removal of his titles had left him as diminished in his own eyes as it had in those of the world, he was not saying. Instead, he wrapped himself in his white fur coat, battened down the dark glasses and offered a few battered but not ignoble truths about his ultimately unforgiving business. He said, 'Greater fighters than I have lost.' And, 'The easiest part is winning. The hardest part is coming back.'

It was probably just as well that no one, and maybe least of all himself, could begin to imagine how hazardous that journey would prove to be.

Chapter Fifteen

Las Vegas, October 1990

James Buster Douglas should have come to Vegas dressed in glory. He should have been an heir of James J. Braddock, the 'Cinderella Man', who reminded boxing of its ability to make unlikely heroes. He should have been cheered as he walked down Las Vegas Boulevard or headed into the desert for his morning run. Morning run? Lunch-counter shuffle was more like it.

The 42-1 conqueror of Mike Tyson remade a broken life so spectacularly six months earlier in Tokyo that even here, in a city that lived by chance and speculation, his story had the potential to carry a quite awesome weight. Unfortunately, so too did he.

The deflating truth was that Douglas had come here desperately unprepared to meet Evander Holyfield in his first defence of the title. According to Holyfield's senior trainer, Lou Duva, Douglas was 'the only man to put on weight in a sauna'. And maybe the first undisputed heavyweight champion of the world to throw away the great prize as casually as he might have discarded a fast-food wrapping.

The owner of the Mirage casino hotel, Steve Wynn, was so alarmed by his first sighting of Douglas, to whom he was obliged to pay more than $24 million whatever the quality of his performance, that he put a private sauna at the champion's disposal. He was quickly alarmed all over again by the fact that on one of his first visits Douglas sent out for $98 worth of room service.

Duva, a short man with an ex-fighter's battered profile but a combative temperament still pristine, could not stop chortling. Whenever he encountered a member of the press corps, he shouted, 'Roll him in and carry him out.'

The unbeaten Holyfield was sleekly, beautifully honed. He had believed he would be fighting Mike Tyson in a contest that would have been pitched to the heavyweight ages. He had been at ringside in Tokyo, intent, absorbed by every second of the action that brought Douglas's stunning triumph. He was impressed by Douglas, noted that when he came into the ring he had the bearing of a man who had not come to lay down, to take his beating and limp away with his money. Holyfield said at ringside, 'At last it looks like Tyson is fighting someone who isn't scared near to death.'

His pre-fight appraisal of the Douglas who appeared here in Las Vegas is not on the record but the scorn pouring from his camp was eloquent enough.

Holyfield had trained ferociously in Reno before coming down to Vegas shining in his fitness and serious purpose. Details of his preparation would have been impressive in any context. In the one created by Douglas's sweaty gorging, they spoke of a man pounding his way to the peak of Mount Olympus. He had been answering to the promptings of three trainers: Duva, the father of Holyfield's promoter Dan; Ronnie Shields, an impressive young corner man in the first stages of building a notable reputation; and, most significantly, George 'the Professor' Benton.

Benton, a fine middleweight in his own fighting days who operated on the principle of 'win this fight, look good in the next one', carried the most imposing credentials. He learned his most important lessons from Eddie Futch and had been at ringside for the third Ali–Frazier fight.

After analysing Douglas–Tyson, Benton had identified the clearest point of weakness in the new champion: that he was least impressive when an opponent denied him space and time. Benton told Holyfield, 'Douglas only punches when nothing is coming at him. He has a tremendous jab. And the way you beat a jabber is by jabbing. Evander, I want that left hand of yours growing out of his face.' When Duva offered a small glimpse of the battle orders to a group of reporters, he said that the fight would be split into three four-round sections: part one, jabbing; part two, all-out assault. Someone asked, 'And part three?' Duva snapped, 'There ain't going to be no need for a part three.'

If Douglas had word that his opponent was striking such levels of fitness – and finesse and power in sparring – it did not seem to arrest the self-indulgence that had seen him put on up to 50 pounds in the months since his victory in Tokyo. He had been particularly receptive to his grandmother's signature dish of chicken necks and beans, and when he was asked what it was that made him gain weight so relentlessly he gave a small, resigned shrug and said, 'Second and third helpings.' The power of reflection, the character to make his stand so superbly against Tyson, now appeared to have been buried beneath a stack of dirty plates.

Shock and disgust over Douglas's condition was officially instated at the weigh-in. Holyfield not only glowed with fitness, he might also have been passing an audition for the role of a maturing Adonis. There were cries of admiration when Holyfield stood on the scales. They were almost as loud as the groans when Douglas stepped down and gave another shrug as his weight was announced at 17 stone 8 pounds, which was more than a stone heavier than when he went in against Tyson.

The 'fight', inevitably, was brief but in the wretchedness of Douglas's performance it went beyond the measurement of time. Douglas was counted out at one minute ten seconds of the third round, but even at that early stage it was not so much a brutal conclusion as a deliverance. From what, precisely? Mostly it was the rage of indignation. Douglas both massively enriched and impoverished himself at the same time. No one – not Ali nor Leonard nor even the once monstrously threatening Tyson – had been paid as much as Douglas on this night when he had so shamelessly laid down. He did not attempt at any stage to take the fight to Holyfield as he had to Tyson. This was partly due to the brimming authority of Holyfield. He had come forward with a jab that was the piston Benton had demanded, and Douglas had neither the time nor the inclination to interfere with his progress. As early as the first round the word 'scandal' was on almost every lip.

When the end came, it was almost comic in its simplicity. Douglas telegraphed an uppercut at such distance he might have been in a McDonald's line-up back home in Ohio. Holyfield could not believe his good fortune that such an opening should be offered so guilelessly. He took his opportunity so perfectly he could have been back in the gym in Reno ending the shift of another hapless sparring partner. As the bulk of Douglas lurched to his left, Holyfield moved into position to throw the right cross. It crashed against Douglas's jaw, and before he hit the canvas there was no doubt that the parody of a fight was over. Douglas made no attempt to save anything of his name. He lay under the desert moon with an eerie detachment, a resignation that was described by referee Mills Lane with barely concealed contempt. Lane said, 'I don't know whether he could have got up but he sure never tried. I looked into his eyes and his eyes looked good to me.'

He used them not to register concern, still less defiance, but to languidly inspect his gloves for blood after wiping them across his face. In his own time, he got to his feet and walked away. No fighter ever did it with more money in his pocket and less honour on his record.

Eddie Futch, the most demanding and intelligent of trainers, but inherently a compassionate man, was at ringside and his verdict was measured and, perhaps because of that, ultimately damning. He said, 'He allowed himself to get into such a poor condition, he had nothing. His judgement of distance, his timing, well, he had no snap. He landed just one good punch in three rounds. The things he did, rubbing his face and looking at his gloves to see if there was blood – I'm sure he was aware of what was going on. In my opinion, he could have got up in time. But he chose not to do so, so maybe he had his own reasons.'

Whatever they were, Douglas kept them to himself on the walk back to the dressing room, a place as mirthless as a crypt. And then he flew home to Columbus, no longer a champion, no longer the man who had had the courage to stand and fight and put behind him the most demoralising days of his life. That was the Douglas of Tokyo; the man of Las Vegas, physically huge, morally diminished, had lost all of that bravely recovered ground, and more.

At home his orgy of eating and drinking would pick up still more momentum. His once-athletic body, a beacon for high-school basketball scouts, mushroomed grotesquely. His eyes were foggy and unfocused. His blood sugar count soared to 800, his weight to more than 400 pounds, and it seemed that a forlornly unpromising fight to find some meaning in the rest of his life was over when he descended into a diabetic coma.

They saved him at the hospital, bringing him around with drips and around-the-clock care, but to what purpose? Could he ultimately save himself? It would take hard months and years to get anything like an answer, but when it came it was more positive than could have been anticipated by anyone checking his vital signs at that hospital bedside.

Douglas would never pretend that he had ever found again the exhilaration that came when Mike Tyson folded beneath his fists, but his achievement was one that sometimes even the bravest of men find beyond them. It was to regain the will to continue to make a life, to put together something to hold against the bleakest, most discouraging times. We would have needed to spend a while in Buster Douglas's oversized shoes to know quite the effort of determination required for him to make his way back to a boxing gym. To turn his gaze away from the fast-food joints and beer parlours where he had pursued his lonely, near-fatal attempt to find some gratification. To pick up the strands of life with his previously disaffected wife and their four children. And, most challengingly of all, to again put on boxing gloves, which he had last used to check his face for blood.

He would reflect sadly, but valuably, on the bad days that brought him so near to death, saying, 'I was drinking and eating whatever I wanted. I just didn't give a darn. It was never about money – I was financially secure after the Holyfield fight – it was just the way everything didn't go as I planned after I won that title, and then there was the readjustment to get over that. But I kept wallowing in self-pity. The lowest point was when I went into the coma. I put on all that weight and almost passed away. But I got a second chance and I came through.

'I woke up after being in the coma for three days and I decided right there that it was time to get back on the horse and start riding again instead of sitting around and moping and feeling bad about myself.'

He didn't ride back to glory on a white charger. But he did do the next best thing. He found reasons to put one day on top of another, to move away from a terrible sense that his life was over. Most remarkably he went back to the ring and, though his opponents were not formidable and Hollywood was not alerted to a real-life *Rocky* story, he would win six straight victories. The run would end with a one-round knockout by Lou Savarese in front of a raucous gambling crowd at a resort in the Connecticut hills. On that occasion he did twice rise to his feet before the decisive blows. It meant that there would be no return to a world-title ring, no reviving of his old status. But then nor would he be carried out of a career that knew one supreme moment of triumph. He fought twice more and won on both occasions which, despite the obscure venues – Burlington, Iowa and Boise, Idaho – and opponents, was something for him to take away.

He returned to the gym to train boxers, including his two sons, and he would say, 'I'm doing something I know, something I enjoy. It is better than sitting around eating and drinking and thinking about the things that went wrong. Maybe I didn't put a proper value on life, understand that you only get one of them. But it is different now. I have things to look forward to, people I want to be around.'

The man who destroyed him so briskly in Las Vegas would never be required to share his victim's speculations, and regrets, on how different his life might have unfolded had he been more energetic in pursing all of its possibilities. There would be much turbulence down the road for Evander Holyfield, and his own share of regrets – inevitably, perhaps, for a man who went through three failed marriages, fathered 11 children with six different women, and after career earnings estimated at more than $500 million would, in 2012, be described as 'flat broke'. But none of it would be created by any inertia of the spirit.

Or any questioning of his own value. While Douglas was limping home from Las Vegas, and heading for the darkest phase of his life, Holyfield was unashamedly declaring himself the new lord of the boxing universe. No, he would not grant Mike Tyson an immediate chance to win back his title. Tyson could wait – while he, outrageously but fascinatingly, announced that his next opponent in six months' time in Atlantic City would be a man who would come into the ring 14 years older and 11 pounds heavier than had Buster Douglas.

What was this? It was hard not to believe it was a blatantly cynical, even absurd abuse of a gullible public; another example of boxing surrendering all of its values to the supreme imperative of turning a profit. Piquantly, it could in retrospect be said to be an ambush partly sponsored by a casino owner experiencing certain financial pressures, who would later turn his hand to politics and land the presidency of the United States. Yet it also has to be said it would have felt more an outrage if the ancient who shared Douglas's passion for fast food wasn't named George Foreman.

But how, really, could it happen, 16 years after Foreman's submission to Muhammad Ali in that fabled jungle clearing and 14 years after his career had apparently come to an end, at the age of 28, with defeat by the accomplished Jimmy Young? It could happen because of one of the most remarkable reinventions in the history of sport.

Starting with Steve Zouski, who was even slower than his huge and elderly opponent, four years earlier, Foreman came in against Holyfield with 24 straight victories, only one of which had gone the distance. Not all of his victims were 'tomato cans'. Well, not the last one, anyway. That was Gerry Cooney, the former white hope who was Michael Spinks' last opponent before his doomed fight against Mike Tyson.

Foreman had looked at boxing from the distance of another life, where money was so much harder to conjure than in the ring, and seen that if he worked hard enough, and hyped himself with sufficient panache – and humour – he could still exploit a once-fearsome reputation. So he had refashioned himself as 'the Punchin' Preacher', an amiable presence in the street and on the TV screen, whose transformation from a grim, bullying figure was particularly stunning for Colin Hart of the *Sun*.

The future doyen of the British press corps felt his blood run cold when, at the peak of Foreman's first career, he lit a cigarette at a poolside press conference. Before taking his first drag, he found himself in Foreman's ferocious glare. 'I put out the cigarette at some speed. I'd never seen such instant menace in a single expression.'

Now, Foreman was spreading the word of the Lord – and inventing his own fast-food grill device, which he marketed with the gusto of an old snake-oil salesman. He also still fought well enough to make himself a viable opponent, in the eyes of Holyfield's promoters and the casino owner Donald Trump, for the latest mega-dollar fight.

It would be a better, more intriguing fight than anyone could have imagined when the deal was signed, and 26 years later it would provide a delicious backward glance at some of the business style of the man sworn in as the 45th US president. Trump won the live site promotion rights with an $11 million offer, broken down into one million on contract, $2.5 million on 1 February 1991 and $7.5 million from the gate, which was based on most tickets going on sale at $800 and $1,000.

However, with the start of the Gulf War Trump won the provision that the fight could be delayed or abandoned in the event of an act of God or war, which might prevent the attendance of many travellers, especially high-rolling Muslims from the Middle East loaded with oil money. In these circumstances the future president wanted to scale down his outlay to roughly half the original offer, a move that provoked from fight promoter Dan Duva the threat of relocating the fight to Las Vegas.

This was routine fight haggling, you might think, but also perhaps worth a wry snigger in the future when Trump's own restrictions on easy travel into the homeland from Muslim countries came into such controversial force. Duva was dismissive, a source close to him saying that the war provision concerned the possibility of 'tanks rolling down the boardwalk, not whether a war was an inconvenience to Donald Trump'. A compromise was reached when Trump produced his second payment of $2.5 million and then managed to reduce his guarantee on the gate. This was not before, though, it was suggested in banking circles that Trump, having hovered close to bankruptcy the previous year, had come under pressure from some of his creditors when they saw how much money he was investing in the fight. One banking source was quoted as saying, 'What really happened was that his creditors took a look at the deal and got edgy. They made him try for a better deal.'

As it turned out, Trump had the 'Real Deal' in Holyfield, and a surprisingly rewarding one in Foreman. While Holyfield submitted to his customary ordeal by sweat and pain, Foreman trundled down the Boardwalk, delivered slow but crunching blows into stationary punch-bags and only marginally more mobile sparring partners, and made a series of amiable, self-deprecating jokes. One of them was, 'My wife gets big chains and at night she puts them around the refrigerator. They are so strong, I can't break them.'

Rather disingenuously, this former young predator of some mean streets in his hometown of Houston, Texas, also said that he wasn't fighting for money. 'You've got to have a different focus,' he said. 'If you just fight for money, you get hurt. If you focus on the title, you'll just naturally make money doing it.' He added, 'I like Evander Holyfield. He's a nice young man. None of the punches I throw at him will be in anger.'

Before the fight the disparities between the combatants could be measured in various ways. One of the more striking was the combined age of Foreman, his assistant trainer, Archie Moore, and his esteemed cut-man, Angelo Dundee, who had been on the opposite side in Kinshasa 16 years earlier when Muhammad Ali scored the victory that shook the world. It was a prodigious 187 years. The 77-year-old Moore had been the oldest man ever to fight for the world heavyweight title. He was within a month of his 43rd birthday when Floyd Patterson knocked him out in 1956. Though Dundee was a mere, spry 68, Team Foreman still might have done their early training in a retirement home in Florida without attracting too much attention.

However, if the sparring was sedate – even arthritic by the extraordinary standards set by Holyfield under Benton – it did carry the practicality of the ages. If Foreman's assets had been reduced by the years, those he had left he could still use with a rough and brutal wisdom. Principally, he could still throw a quick jab with the force of a battering ram and follow up with legally dubious but damaging assaults involving his huge forearms and a hard, clubbing and accurate right hand. Benton had urged Holyfield to work close, to have Foreman concentrate on protecting his head against his opponent's heavy jab and the kind of right-hand cross that ushered James Buster Douglas into such premature reflection.

Holyfield dominated the first round, made Foreman look as ponderous as everyone had expected. There was an early sense that soon there would be a cry of 'Timber!' as Foreman crashed to the canvas, but this was wrong, and in the second round he made the point with shuddering force. The big, deceptively swift jab jolted back Holyfield's head and Foreman followed up with two hard rights guaranteed to make anyone think. Holyfield's reaction was to follow the Benton dictum of close, fast work but again he was thrown off course, this time by a forearm to the throat. Referee Rudy Battle would be required to closely monitor the propriety of some of Foreman's most damaging work and in the 11th round he deduced a point for a low blow.

By this time the scorecards had become academic, Holyfield leading comfortably on all three. But the threat of Foreman was maintained through the fight. It was generated by an almost eerily still precision of intent as Holyfield swarmed about him, jabbing, hooking, working so hard to drain the last of the resistance.

The champion started this process most earnestly after the alarms of the second round. He discouraged Foreman's jab with some telling right-hand counterpunches to the head and, by the end of the third, Foreman had the look of a man who had produced his best and was, maybe, beginning to feel the wearying tug of an ebb tide.

In the fifth, though, there was no doubt that Foreman had reannounced himself as something other than an old bulbous statue about to topple. Under pressure on the ropes, and perhaps speculating that he might be heading for a bad place, Foreman suddenly produced a left hook that rocked Holyfield, then another. Foreman moved on Holyfield, not quickly but with the measured tread appropriate to his situation. He landed a series of weighty punches but could not find the sweet blow to the jaw that might have brought the most sensational result.

In the seventh it seemed he was again within one solid punch of an upset to put alongside his own demise in Zaire. His trainer Charlie Shipes was certainly filled with a heady boldness. Before the bell for the seventh, he shouted into Foreman's ear, 'The miracle is going your way, George. You just got to get closer.'

For Foreman it was a call to action that thundered down the years, bringing back to his mind his most destructive moments, including the time he waylaid Joe Frazier in Kingston, Jamaica, with one of the most brutal, sustained assaults heavyweight boxing had ever seen. He could not reproduce such concentrated force but, for a 42-year-old who had been so long assigned to the past, he continued to occupy the most extraordinary level of commitment and hope. He landed a strong right to the head, which forced Holyfield into retreat, then maintained an attack that was counted at 27 uninterrupted punches and four bullish pushes. Here, with Shipes and the venerable Moore yelling excitedly from the corner, might have been one of the most improbable moments in the history of the heavyweights.

But if Holyfield was harassed, surprised, at all worried that all the work in Reno and here, all the dreams of a personal empire presided over from his Atlanta mansion, was in jeopardy, he was still Holyfield, still a born fighter to the tips of his fast-moving toes. He staged a rampage of his own – a good left hook to Foreman's head and 18 unanswered punches – but if this was impressive work, fighting grace under pressure, it did not lift the siege. At the end of it he was spent and needed the respite of a clinch. Foreman, having absorbed the blows, shoved Holyfield away and moved forward, not quickly it was true but with resolve, a bit like a tank battered but still on its tracks.

At the end of the ninth, though, he had his most serious crisis. He sent out a languid, weary jab and Holyfield punished him with a sharp right to the chin. Scenting a kill, Holyfield delivered 11 unanswered punches and when the bell sounded the referee felt it necessary to ask Foreman, 'You OK, George?' And George found the energy to nod.

The rest was attrition and it lasted until the dwindling seconds of the last round, when both fighters entered what looked, perhaps fancifully from a distance, not a desperate clinch but a warrior embrace, a mutual understanding that both men had something to take from this battle: Holyfield the certainty that his title had been retained; Foreman the knowledge that he had stepped, magnificently, beyond the image of an old huckster chancing his meaty arm.

The reading of the scorecards was a formality, a confirmation of what we had seen and what the fighters knew. Holyfield won by a margin of five rounds on one card, seven on the other two. Foreman, his arm draping Holyfield, anticipated the verdict, saying, 'Thank you for giving me the opportunity. You won.'

He said it, though, as a man who knew that he had also gained something that would enrich – and underpin – so much of the rest of his life, and in a way that James Buster Douglas could only pine for through more years than he would care to count.

It was the respect that naturally goes out to a man who has confirmed, beyond all doubt, the integrity of his fighting heart. And, you had to ask, what was the lure of the ring without that?

Chapter Sixteen

Indianapolis, February 1992

Each day in the Marion County Superior Court down the street from the restaurant where we were eating steaks while waiting for word of the jury, it had become a little more evident that all of Don King's men could not put together again the life and the mega earnings of Mike Tyson. And when the call came that the jury was in, and we rushed down to the courtroom to see Tyson impassive, and King distraught, we did not have to wonder too hard how it was that the verdict on the charge of rape was guilty.

The broader fault lines had been visible enough for quite some time, and certainly before Tyson's disaster in Tokyo. The breaking down had come as inevitably as the seasons, and the truth was that there had been no warming spring for the 25-year-old heading for prison, just a rush from a wintery coldness of the spirit to a burning, self-destructive summer. Tyson had kindled his own conflagration. When he was invited to the Miss Black America Beauty Pageant in Indianapolis his mood was unashamedly predatory. He saw, he desired and he took.

Partly it was King's fault that it had gone so badly in the two weeks of the trial. Tyson had been a bristling, hostile presence in the courtroom. He wore his anger as though it were a suit of armour. If there was a case for him, and an argument to make about the inherent dangers of his situation – even the unlikely possibility that he had been, in all his celebrity and indiscretion and boundless wealth, as much prey as hunter – it was not made.

King's choice of defence lawyer, Vincent Fuller, was each day confirmed a little more profoundly as bizarre. Tyson, surly and unresponsive to any attempt to soften his brutal image, had required the knowing, deft skill of an Alan Dershowitz and the emotional pyrotechnics of a street-smart Johnnie Cochran, legal celebrities who two years later would help shape O. J. Simpson's sensational acquittal in his murder trial in Los Angeles.

Dershowitz, the eminent Harvard law professor, was eventually recruited but by then the damage had been done. Dershowitz argued an appeal confidently, basing his case on evidence that would have benefited his client but was never called. One of the three appeal judges agreed that a miscarriage of justice had occurred but the other two confirmed the verdict.

Tyson seethed. He had a courtroom lawyer, at vast expense, who seemed utterly out of place in the raw exchanges and heightened sensitivities of a rape trial. Fuller was a man in a perfectly cut grey business suit, for whom the street and its rough affairs seemed like a place he passed through as expeditiously as possible on his way to some Wall Street consultation. The prosecutor, Greg Garrison, a local star attuned to the nuances of Midwest life, and prejudice, at times had the air of a man who could not believe his good luck at drawing such an ungrounded adversary.

In a place like Indianapolis, Fuller needed to make some show of bonding with his client from one of Brooklyn's most hopeless ghettoes. The requirement was to humanise Tyson, to humour him into an understanding of the part he had to play. He had, at the very least, to be coaxed into a degree of amiability, of convincing humility. Fuller could not do it, but then nor was Tyson apparently capable of meeting the challenge of effectively fighting for his freedom.

He conveyed a contempt for the court as much as the charge of beauty contestant Desiree Washington, Miss Black Rhode Island, that he raped her in a hotel room in the city. He said that he had had consensual sex, as if it was a most casually routine event, a right that he had come to assume for himself, something endlessly on offer to put alongside the habit of diamond merchants and designer shops and luxury car showrooms of allowing him to make his purchases behind doors temporarily closed to the rest of the public.

On Fuller's behalf it needs to be noted that 20 years on Tyson would reveal a state of mind that probably pushed the prevention of his conviction and imprisonment beyond the powers of even the most brilliant courtroom advocacy. If O. J. Simpson had superb legal assistance, it was also true he never forgot in the courtroom in Santa Monica who he was and what he was supposed to represent to the American people, black or white.

Tyson would recall in his autobiography a sense of doom that had been building for some time, saying, 'I knew from the start of the trial that I was in trouble. I wasn't being tried in Los Angeles or New York, we were in Indianapolis, Indiana, historically one of the strongholds of the Ku Klux Klan. My judge, Patricia Gifford, was a former sex-crimes prosecutor and was known as "the Hanging Judge". I had been found guilty by a jury of my peers, two of whom were black.

'But in my mind, I had no peers. I was the youngest heavyweight champion in the history of boxing. I was a titan, the reincarnation of Alexander the Great. My style was impetus, my defences impregnable and I was ferocious. It's amazing how a low self-esteem and a huge ego can give you illusions of grandeur. But after the trial this god among men had to get his black ass back into court for his sentencing.'

Six years was the sentence, three of which would be served. He received the news with sullen resignation. No longer a titan, no longer another Alexander the Great, no longer fêted or persuaded that he could get quite whatever he wanted, when he wanted it, he was led away a common felon required for the rest of his life to sign the register of sex offenders.

We couldn't know then, as we packed our bags and turned our thoughts to the men who would fill the vacuum created by the court-room convulsion, that there would still be many lurid and poignant chapters to be written in the story of Mike Tyson. He had not come and gone like some primeval eruption in polite society. For me, certainly, there was an overwhelming sense that since I first met him on that Manhattan sidewalk five years earlier, I had been watching a ferociously but insuperably wounded young man charging towards his own worst self-fulfilling prophecy.

The streets, he had suggested so many times, always won, always claimed their dues, and now, as I headed to the airport and he to the slammer, so many of the old, bleaker images came back into play.

I saw him again, gauche and lisping, on that high-school stage in Queens, speaking of how many of his young street companions were imprisoned or wasted or dead. I heard him talk of the titans of his boyhood, not some neighbourhood high-school basketball star, but the bejewelled pimps and the dealers. I went back, in my mind's eye, to the battered, abandoned boulevards of Brownsville and speculated on how many miles he had covered, how many dollars he had splurged, on his journey back to where he would one day describe as hell. I thought of the scary, lost apparition in the Vegas lift, and the bewildered, tortured expression he had worn when Don King planted a crown on his head after he had unified the world heavyweight titles.

I thought of how vulnerable the most ferocious fighter most of us had even seen had been to the worst of his experience. Had I been prescient enough, I might also have seen in one of Tyson's most outspoken supporters some of the wider coarsening of American life. However, this would have involved the huge, even unthinkable, leap of viewing Donald Trump not as merely a somewhat crass example of a new and self-regarding entrepreneurial class, but a potential president of the United States, a successor to George Washington and Thomas Jefferson. Then, I might have lingered a little longer over the extraordinary perspective displayed by Trump in the days after the trial.

He said, 'It's my opinion that to a large extent, Mike Tyson was railroaded in this case. You have a young woman who was in his room, in his hotel, late in the evening at her own will. You have a young woman who was dancing for the beauty contest, dancing with a big smile on her face, who looked as happy as can be.'

And then 14 years on, soon after Tyson's autobiographical confession that back in the day his life was conditioned by the pleasures of drug abuse and a great production line of instant sexual gratification, the winning presidential candidate would trumpet in Indiana, of all places, his pleasure at his endorsement by, yes, Mike Tyson. On this occasion, he would say, 'Mike Tyson endorsed me. I love it. He sent out a tweet, Mike, Iron Mike. You know all the tough guys endorse me. I like that, OK. But Mike said, "I love Trump, I endorse Trump." And that's the end. I'm sure he doesn't know about your economic situation in Indiana. But when I get endorsed by the tough ones, I like it, because, you know what? We need toughness now.'

Mike Tyson had toughness, all right, and you couldn't dispute that on the way to the airport. Nor could you forget, as the prison gates were shutting behind him and almost immediately he was having a week tagged on to his sentence for hitting a prison guard, how he had come to his fate still exhibiting a most durable talent to make destruction in the ring.

Between his shocking defeat by Douglas in Tokyo and his day of sentencing in Indianapolis – and despite the clearest evidence that his life outside the ring had run out of control – he fought four times. He showed, despite his abandonment of any pretensions to the life of a professional athlete, no notable signs of physical decline. When he came into the ring his presence was still enough to chill the blood. He still, plainly, had the means to prosecute his bad intentions.

Four months after the Tokyo débâcle he faced Henry Tillman, the Olympic heavyweight champion of 1984 who had also brought him much pain in those days of striving for a place on the American team under the scorn of Tyrell Biggs. The fight was at Caesars Palace in Las Vegas, and the high rollers got what they paid for: some authentic mayhem. Tillman, who had beaten Tyson twice in the amateurs, was ransacked in two minutes 47 seconds of round one. Tyson was in his optimum aggressive mode, and Tillman left the ring groggily shaking his head and, perhaps, regretting old impertinences.

Alex Stewart fared even worse six months later in Atlantic City, going down three times before being shepherded to his corner after just two minutes 27 seconds.

If Tyson was doing all he could to destroy his career outside of the ring, inside it he was still reminding the world of quite how much earning power he was putting at risk. In the wake of the Stewart victory, however, there was one indicator that at least some in the promotion of boxing were no longer prepared to grant him his old unconditional status as the young and untouchable god of boxing. James Buster Douglas had done serious damage to that status, as we saw clearly after Home Box Office, who held Tyson's pay-per-view contract, were given a straight choice between their insightful presenter Larry Merchant and Tyson.

HBO received an ultimatum from Don King. If Merchant – who criticised the poor competitive level of the Stewart fight and said it had done little to reinstate Tyson in the eyes of the public – was not fired, Tyson would refuse his new deal with the company. HBO said they would not sacrifice Merchant and Tyson promptly signed with Showtime.

Perhaps, though, Merchant had sunk home his point. Tyson's next opponent, the Canadian-Jamaican Donovan 'Razor' Ruddock, was of a quite different and superior order to Stewart. They met at the Mirage in Vegas, and the fight was memorable for the intensity of both men's efforts as much as referee Richard Steele's controversial decision to award Tyson a TKO near the end of the seventh round. It might have been a hugely significant result for Tyson, coming a little more than a year after losing the title. Unlike the pummelling of Tillman and Stewart, it required him to go more deeply into his reserves of aggression. Anything less would have seen him subside again beneath the force of a big opponent willing to stand and trade the heaviest of punching.

Across the Strip, Frank Sinatra was making still another series of farewell performances at the Riviera, sipping iced tea from a whiskey glass, lighting a cigarette or two, and, despite finding some of the notes of the past beyond him, evoking some of his old glory. But, as he would admit, he was offering no more than a remnant of his talent, a surviving panache and a still-flawless diction, which made the $100 tip for the waiter who put you so close to the stage in the show lounge an investment not in mere passing entertainment but a memory for the ages.

From Tyson, though, we saw something more current, more about what he might just still make of the present if, by some mighty act of will, he stepped back from the chasm he seemed intent on making for himself. His dissipation, plainly, had still to take away the core of his power.

Both men had come to fight most seriously, and though Ruddock threw the kind of punches that would put him on boxing's all-time list of heavy-hitters, beside the likes of Liston and Foreman, Marciano, Dempsey and Shavers, it was those of Tyson that had the most dramatic, immediate effect. He put Ruddock down in the second and third rounds but with no accompanying sense that he was on the point of another formal destruction. Indeed, when Ruddock got to his feet on both occasions he did not look like a man contemplating surrender. He whaled back at Tyson and the crowd were drawn to their feet. At the end of the sixth round – always a critical point for the fast-burning Tyson, even in the first rush of youth – it was Ruddock who was landing the stronger punches, and an uppercut was thrown so perfectly it left his opponent visibly stunned.

Tyson's reaction in the seventh was fierce. He staggered Ruddock with big hooks and crosses. His instinct, it was impossible not to believe, was to fight for all that he had left in his career and his embattled life. It was as much an atavistic roar as a counterattack and, again, the crowd were back on their feet, first to applaud the exceptional action, then to yell in protest when Steele stopped Tyson's attack by waving Ruddock to his corner. Disbelief was quickly replaced by a hard anger. Ruddock had already displayed his ability to come back from such an assault and both he and his corner were aghast at the decision to stop the fight.

Fighting broke out in the ring between the rival camps and Steele required a protective cordon as he headed out into the hostile crowd. Tyson had made an impressive restatement of his enduring ability to battle at the highest level, but then Ruddock had also shown that he too belonged at the top of his trade. Tyson colourfully conferred such status on his opponent when he shook his head and said, 'He punches like a fucking mule kick. That was the hardest I've been punched.'

Every syllable shouted rematch, and so it came, three months later. It was another hard battle, another example of Tyson's surviving ability to prove that if his personal discipline was shot, that if he was unpicking his life so carelessly, he could still be an extraordinary natural force when he returned to the ring.

Again, Ruddock was twice knocked down, but this time he got to the end of the fight and once more he provoked from Tyson some of that unrelenting power and determination that had been such a feature of his early prime. Ruddock had a broken jaw (some reports had it coming as early as the fourth round), and Tyson's price for the unanimous decision – which was never in dispute, with winning margins of six rounds on two cards and four on the other – was a perforated eardrum.

If Tyson won handily on points, he was never free from the risk of a bruising ambush by Ruddock. It was a collision that brought both men to their limits, and many years later Ruddock would speculate that they had been required to give so much they would never again be quite the same. 'We dug down very deeply,' he said, 'and sometimes in that situation you give more than you know.'

Tyson was again magnanimous, saying, 'Man, this guy is tough, he'll be champion of the world if he stays dedicated and doesn't slip up.' It was an ironic observation from a man about to have his life, and his career, disappear for some years under a mound of misadventure, and in time it was Ruddock's prediction that would survive the better. Ruddock slipped up only in that a year later, with Tyson struggling through the early rounds of his prison sentence, he agreed to a WBC heavyweight title eliminator with the impressively emerging Lennox Lewis.

Ruddock came out at London's Earl's Court throwing heavy punches, but Lewis, the Olympic heavyweight champion in Seoul four years earlier, was immense. The prize, at least in theory, was the chance to face the winner of champion Evander Holyfield's defence against Riddick Bowe, who had been beaten by Lewis in the final in Seoul. Lewis flattened Ruddock in the second round, and George Foreman's reaction lingers powerfully. He said, 'Times are a changin'. I think we may just have seen the next champion of the world. I'm not sure I would want to go in the ring with Lennox Lewis.'

Nor was Bowe, and his reluctance would foreshadow a time – one so brilliantly banished in the battles of the Leonard, Durán, Hagler and Hearns era – when some leading fighters and their people came to make the fights that best suited their career strategies and extended earning potential. Such positioning, at least to some degree, was as old as professional boxing, but in those first years after Ali, when so many gifted fighters seemed to be most impelled by an ambition to prove who was best, one great and intriguing fight followed another by clamorous demand. It was a glorious imperative.

Inevitably, you had to believe on the road out of Indianapolis that the long and potentially obliterating incarceration of Mike Tyson was a heavy blow to such a seamless, thrilling process. If his life had changed, by his own reckless hand, so too had a vital dynamic in the sport he had come to dominate so ferociously. There would be more big fights; the fierce cavalcade would move on, but with a new foreboding. It was the fear that the next great fight might just be the last.

Chapter Seventeen

Las Vegas, November 1992

Concerns that the great fights were over, that they had gone clattering and raging away down the high road of history along with Mike Tyson in his prison garb, were premature. We would know this before the end of the year. To be precise, we would know it here two rounds before the end of Riddick Bowe–Evander Holyfield I.

There was no doubt about it as we shook our heads and sucked in our breath at ringside. We had something that would not only ease the suspicion that Tyson, by denuding the sport of his wild but magnetic presence, had done as much damage to boxing as to himself; it would also glow through the ages as an unforgettable fight. And this was no less so when, in their rush for profit, the men who ruled boxing failed to see quite what a magnificent new landmark had been created. Unfortunately, too few stopped to consider how it was this stupendous collision happened. It was because two superb fighters had been properly aligned and had come to fight. It sounded simple, as basic as the original appeal of David and Goliath, but the thread of logic would be thrown into the wind soon enough. For anyone who still believed in boxing's capacity to redeem itself in the most heightened, skilled and honest action, it was a terrible, and potentially terminal, neglect of boxing's most elemental appeal.

The first round of Hagler–Hearns would always be regarded as one of the most memorable, sustained onslaughts of fighting will. So too would the tenth round produced by Bowe and Holyfield. Among heavyweights, no one – not Marciano nor Ali nor Frazier – had fought harder than Bowe or Holyfield. No one ever took a fight to a finer balance. And in the case of Bowe, it also had to be said that no one would go on to surrender so artlessly high ground magnificently won.

Holyfield's refusal to submit readily to the superior height and reach and power of a Bowe who, at 25, was five years younger was maybe the least surprising aspect of the tumultuous night at the Thomas & Mack Center.

Nobody needed to tell Holyfield – as the man who had torn the great prize from the loose and flabby grasp of James Buster Douglas – that the fight was his most serious test. When he came into the ring his intensity was remarkable. As always, he might have been a gladiator stepping out onto the sand. But on this occasion it seemed that he was aware of a new imperative, one that went beyond his warring instinct and concerned his credibility as the undisputed heavyweight champion of the world, a true successor to the likes of Joe Louis, Muhammad Ali and Joe Frazier.

Though two of his first three challengers – George Foreman and Larry Holmes – had fought with nerve and the sweep of vast experience, they were the past. For many it was impossible not to see in their selection as opponents the first worrying indicators that already the title was being turned into a citadel of safe profit.

It was also true that the man sandwiched between Foreman and Holmes – Bert Cooper, a reformed drug addict – was hardly equipped to enhance Holyfield's championship status. The drug background didn't help, nor did the fact that he was a substitute for a substitute. Tyson was the original opponent, but he had cried off with an injured thumb on top of the pressure building around his date in court. Tyson's nominated replacement was the Italian Francesco Damiani, who withdrew because of an ankle injury. The Italian's wife, mourning the loss of $750,000 worth of lira, was seriously underwhelmed and offered her own withering diagnosis: not one wounded ankle but two cold feet.

So Cooper, an ersatz Tyson with 23 knockouts in 33 fights, arrived in Holyfield's hometown, Atlanta, to make a show and maybe revive his career. He made a small gesture towards Tyson's style, coming into the ring without a robe but, unfortunately, forgetting to remove his socks, which happened to be white. However, in the third round he scored a knockdown, the first suffered by Holyfield since he was a 17-year-old amateur. Shaken and embarrassed in front of his own people, Holyfield did manage to restore himself and with a few seconds left in the seventh round referee Mills Lane stopped the fight. It would, though, take more than his next win – on points over Holmes – to placate the doubters.

Now, though, no one could argue that Holyfield was not making an authentic defence. Bowe, in the sharpest contrast to Foreman and Holmes, was in the prime of his life. He was also in possession, according to his trainer Eddie Futch, 'of more natural gifts than I have ever seen assembled in one young heavyweight'. However, there was still the fear of a flaw, and not even the wise Futch could be sure it would not surface when Holyfield, as he would so brilliantly in the tenth round, made his big stand. The apprehension was that when it mattered most Bowe might suffer a failure of resolve. In other words, he might quit. Many believed that he had done that in the Olympic final in Seoul against Lennox Lewis, when he took two standing counts of eight and did not persuade the referee – or too many knowledgeable observers, including the scouting Emanuel Steward – that he had much heart for further combat.

Indeed, the memory of that affair lingered so strongly for Futch he needed to know how much Bowe really wanted to be a big winner in sport's most demanding arena. Futch liked what he saw: 'I had loved what I had seen of his talent. For a big man, he moved beautifully. He had the balance and the grace of a real fighter, a genuine thoroughbred – and that was exciting. You can go a long time in boxing without seeing such qualities leaping out at you. But then, of course, it doesn't mean anything if the guy deep down doesn't really want to fight; if, when the going gets hard, he has any kind of inclination to turn his back. I had worked with men like Joe Frazier, Kenny Norton and Larry Holmes, and when you have that you don't want to take anything less.'

In fact, Bowe had already won some quite remarkable battles. He had emerged from the same Brownsville war zone the young Tyson, clad in his ski mask and his anger, had survived. Bowe won four New York Golden Gloves titles. He showed remarkable athleticism for someone who had grown up against a background that was often as grim as it was straitened. The 12th of 13 children, he lost a sister, murdered in the street by a drug addict for her welfare cheque, and a brother to Aids. As a boy, he had been required to step over the body of a victim of a neighbourhood crack war, a corpse that had been left on a landing of the family's apartment building for the best part of a day.

If he had failed in Seoul, he did have some victories to buoy him – enough, certainly, to persuade Futch that the investment of care and a fighting education should be made. And for a little while at least, it would shine like gold.

And never more so than in that tenth round at the Thomas & Mack Center, where Lennox Lewis had come to shout his rights. Lewis's presence had brought another notch of tension for Bowe when he came into the ring. If he had to prove anything to anybody, there was no doubt that the big, mostly amiable man born under the shadow of West Ham football ground was at the front of the queue. In the days before the fight, Bowe had confessed to the impact of his defeat by Lewis – and to the point of revealing that he was about to join the US Army before his manager, Rock Newman, had come to Brooklyn to explain in some detail quite how much he would be throwing away in the service of Uncle Sam.

'I was on my way to the recruiter,' reported Bowe, 'when Rock came to say that he had faith in me. Everybody else had given up. Since then it has been just me and Rock and Papa Smurf [his pet name for the fatherly Futch].'

Papa Smurf could hardly conceal his pleasure as the early rounds unfolded. Bowe was fighting well, with skill and poise unusual in such a big man, but it also helped that Holyfield, not for the first time, was ignoring key advice from his own acute and brilliant trainer, George Benton. Holyfield's macho tendency would never be far from the surface, as we would see soon enough in this fight, but now, critically, he was neglecting his supreme assets: his quickness about the ring, his ability to shift the point of attack in one potentially decisive moment.

Holyfield started well enough, but he was merely feeding the illusion that he could live on his own terms with the formidably strong and deceptively adept Bowe. As the fight wore on, Benton's agitation increased exponentially. He was appalled to see the ease with which Bowe picked off Holyfield as he charged in. It was as though Bowe could do anything he chose in the close exchanges. He was especially punishing with short, battering blows to the body, and then, effortlessly, he switched to two-handed attacks to Holyfield's head.

By the ninth round the priority in both corners was to keep open clear lines of vision. Holyfield's need was the greater: his right eye was closing at an alarming rate and his left was cut. Bowe's right eye had shown signs of swelling as early as the fourth round, and in the eighth his corner complained that Holyfield's thumb had caused damage to his left one. It was the nightmare of the cut-men who worked furiously between rounds but out in the ring it did nothing to stop the flow of action.

Holyfield was piling all his chances on his ability to take down Bowe with one of the big hooks that had become his most frequently used weapon. The rest of trainer Benton's strategy littered the canvas so thickly it might have been a cutting-room floor. Holyfield knew he was behind in the scoring, as did Bowe, who later recalled his mood when the bell sounded for the tenth, saying, 'I decided it was time for him to go.'

It was a bold resolution, given all the life still left in Holyfield's efforts, but for the first minute of the round it appeared that Bowe might just deliver on the promise he had made to himself. A perfectly thrown uppercut had Holyfield's head shooting upwards, and as the champion attempted to steady himself Bowe connected powerfully again, this time with a hook to the head. Holyfield fell back on the ropes then lunged into Bowe's path in attempting to stifle the stream of his punching. It was clear, though, that Bowe had brought much discipline to his bid for brutal closure. He continued to connect, to pick off Holyfield, and the tide of his superiority had been so continuous and impressive it was amazing to note that just a minute of the round had been spent.

Then it happened, stunningly, unforgettably. Lazarus, the dead man, was able not only to pick up his bed but also to use it to batter the head of Riddick Bowe. How close he came to saving his title, how fine was the measure of the challenger's resistance, only Riddick Bowe will ever truly know. What you could see clearly enough from ringside was that for a minute Bowe was required to stare into the face of appalling defeat. Holyfield, all logic insisted, had one overwhelming imperative after absorbing that minute of intense and brilliantly created pressure. He had to hang on for survival. Instead, he landed a hard right that, after a clinch dictated by Bowe's needs, was the precursor of a vicious hook, a fierce flurry of combinations and a series of uppercuts. Bowe was on the point of being overwhelmed. Desperately, he tried to renovate his jab – so immaculate up to this point – and threw a right hand that suddenly looked languid, tentative. Holyfield marched through anything Bowe could throw but what he could not do was deliver the kind of chilling right cross that had sent James Buster Douglas crashing into La La Land.

The problem for Holyfield was that Bowe wasn't Douglas, certainly not on this occasion. He had done his work, listened to the exhortations of Papa Smurf, and in the last minute of the tenth round he re-found some of the best of himself. He had recovered to the point of standing toe to toe again and when the bell sounded, with neither man prepared to take a backward step, a good and intriguing fight had become a great one. The crowd surged to its feet and, no doubt, had it been dressed in the clothes of Georgian or Victorian England it would have been fishing into its pockets for gold sovereigns to throw into the ring at the final bell.

Holyfield, astonishingly, still had a little left in the 11th, but not nearly enough, and the great fight was coming into shore gloriously. Bowe, showing impressive stamina, put Holyfield down for a mandatory count of eight, but there was no question that the champion would fail to go the distance. When the last bell sounded, both men were throwing punches. Inevitably, the decision was unanimous: two cards showed a margin of five rounds for Bowe and the other one of three. The drama was not in the scoring but the waging of the war, the undying possibility that something quite extraordinary might happen.

Later, in the suite of his manager Newman, where he ordered a stream of video reruns, Bowe looked back on the tenth and the state of mind he had carried in and out of it. He said, 'I was rumbling, that's all I know. I was trying to take him out. I wanted to prove that I could be as strong in the late rounds. In the corner before the round I said to Eddie Futch, "I think I can take him out and put him on the canvas." Eddie told me to go ahead and get him. Then, after I'd shook him I realised he was still strong and determined. He somehow made it through my barrage and after that I said, "I'm just going to box him the rest of the way."'

That he did, with great poise and a talent and strength that put within his grasp one of the great heavyweight careers. He had proved himself to the boxing world, shown that he had, along with his natural ability, a superb instinct to fight. Seoul? Surely it was a quirk, an aberration of a young man who had come into a new and fabulously rewarding life from a place no less threatening, and potentially warping, than that of the fallen Tyson. All he now had to do was carry with him the redemption he had found against Holyfield, and in the first rush of his triumph the signs could not have been more encouraging for a boxing man of Eddie Futch's quality. He had been made to believe deeply in his once-troubled protégé's prowess and, more vitally, his character.

Bowe climbed onto the ropes, picked out his Seoul conqueror Lewis and shouted, 'You're next.' Lewis responded, deadpan, 'Sign a contract.'

There, the heavyweight future was sealed for a while. Indeed, there would be new drama and intrigue. At least it was exciting to think so. For precisely a month and a day. Then Riddick Bowe arrived in Lewis's London and threw the WBC heavyweight title belt, the one once worn by Muhammad Ali, into a rubbish bin. He told his challenger that if he wanted it so badly he could retrieve it from the garbage.

It was a development that sickened the blood. It was as if the meaning of that glorious round against Holyfield, that promise of a great young fighter ready to take on the world, had been casually excised. Bowe's manager, Newman, explained that he was operating on sound business principles in making Lewis a derisory offer and compounding the insult with Bowe's literal tossing of the belt into the rubbish bin. Bowe had won himself a strong negotiating position, powerful enough, according to Newman, to offer Lewis a mere 10 per cent of the purse.

Though Lewis would be guaranteed $3 million, it was still an offer to a supplicant rather than the man who had sent a tremor through every heavyweight camp with his demolition of the hard-punching Razor Ruddock. Lewis's manager, Frank Maloney, said the terms could not be stomached, and nor could a second proposal that Lewis step aside from his claim as the WBC's number-one contender, have a warm-up fight for $2.5 million and then earn $9 million when eventually fighting Bowe.

Newman's negotiating tactics might not have been novel in their attempt to exploit the world heavyweight title but rarely had we seen a more deliberate attempt to avoid, behind the smokescreens of dealmaking, a dangerous opponent. Lewis, a man not cheaply roused outside of the ring, was enraged. His priority was to get Bowe into the ring and re-enact something along the lines of the Olympic final. He had destroyed Ruddock, far more convincingly than Tyson, and was asking only for that which he had won for himself so spectacularly in the ring. Under that pressure from his fighter, Maloney blinked, said that he would reconsider the first offer of a mere $3 million. Newman said that Maloney was too late, he had missed his chance.

Effectively, the heavyweight title had come into the possession of a former host of a Washington radio talkshow, car salesman and college basketball star. Lewis and his people could propose whatever they liked, but Newman had the title and all the options that came with it. One of them had been to toss the WBC title belt into the rubbish bin at a press conference and among others was a multi-fight $100 million deal with Home Box Office–Time Warner. He could also seek out opponents who, as serious world-title contenders, belonged in the bin that briefly housed the WBC belt.

The first was Michael Dokes, who was 34 years old and weighing 17 stone 6 pounds, several pounds more than a Bowe who had alarmed Futch with his languor in the gym before the fight. Dokes had serious prospects before acquiring a cocaine addiction – he once claimed to have built himself up for a big fight largely on Jack Daniels and drugs – but even Newman had to groan when Dokes made his way into the Madison Square Garden ring. It was a travesty of a fight – after stopping it two minutes and 19 seconds into the first round, referee Joe Santarpria offered the bleakest postscript. He said, 'I looked into his eyes and he was gone. His eyes were glassy and he was falling all over the place.' So was the legacy of the Bowe–Holyfield tenth round.

Jesse Ferguson was no better in the RFK Stadium in Washington. If Newman was going home to celebrate his good fortune and shrewd business strategy – his emergence as boxing's latest power broker – he saw quickly enough he had created a most hollow occasion. Bowe was earning $7 million and Ferguson $500,000 but, even though it was the first world heavyweight fight in the capital for 52 years, barely 5,000 paying customers made it to the big, gaunt baseball and gridiron stadium. Those who stayed away may have noted, amid the hype, that Bowe, having thrown away the WBC belt with his refusal to fight Lewis, had only the WBA title to defend, the IBF deciding that Ferguson was an unworthy challenger. They were vindicated briskly enough with Ferguson surviving a count of nine at the end of the first round and then lasting just 17 seconds into the second.

In between Dokes and Ferguson, Bowe took a world tour and hobnobbed with Pope John Paul II in Rome and Nelson Mandela in South Africa. Newman considered it a great publicity and marketing coup. Particularly valuable, he reckoned, was a picture flashed around the globe showing the world champion cradling a young boy wasted by malnutrition in Somalia, for where an emergency food airlift was arranged.

Back home in America, Eddie Futch was dismayed. His worst fears – those he chose to put aside while watching Bowe run so hard in the Nevada hills and which were so brilliantly allayed in the defeat of Holyfield – were coming back into a hard and discouraging focus. He said, 'That world tour was a bad idea. Bowe should have been in the gym fortifying himself in technique rather than parading around the world for publicity. When you hold the world heavyweight title you have a responsibility to both yourself and the sport which has given you so much.'

Futch's rival Emanuel Steward, who nurtured a generation of brilliantly competitive fighters in his Kronk gym in Detroit, hit a similar note of foreboding. He said that when he looked at Bowe he saw 'a hunger subsiding'. It was something all boxing had to regret because, he added, 'Riddick Bowe is the second most perfect fighter I've ever seen in the heavyweight division . . . after Muhammad Ali.'

Both these superb judges of boxing talent had identified the essence of Riddick Bowe's unfolding story. He had become too comfortable in his riches.

The most serious point of his decline from being so briefly a proud, upright champion came with the pleading of a defence attorney that Bowe should be spared a prison sentence because he had suffered irreparable brain damage in the ring. The plea – which was made six years after the first, great Holyfield fight – didn't work. He was sentenced to 30 months in a federal prison after being found guilty of kidnapping his estranged wife Judy and their five children at knifepoint.

He sued Rock Newman, claiming that he had been robbed of $55 million. Later he withdrew the action and apologised, saying that he had been misinformed by a former associate. Newman reported that Bowe's ring income had been more than $55 million. Now, it was said, his fortune was down to less than $30,000.

His next initiative was to become a Thai kickboxer, but it did not go well. He arrived in the ring scaling 300 pounds and was counted out after a series of kicks on the shin from a Russian named Levgen Golovin. Bowe was 45 and hopelessly out of shape.

It had certainly been a long, relentless journey down the other side of the mountain. He had fought Holyfield twice more, his fitness and ambition questionable on both occasions. He lost the first one, coming in 11 pounds heavier than when he had fought Holyfield to a standstill, and his decline was so marked that the fight would be always remembered mainly for the 'Fan Man' who descended from out of the Vegas sky on his motorised paraglider and smashed into the ropes during the seventh round.

It was arguably the most bizarre incident in the history of prize fighting but there didn't seem a whole lot to say after supplying the details demanded by the TV pictures that played and played across the world. These included the fact that the culprit, James Miller, was a known, unhinged extrovert who was briskly turned over to psychiatric care after being beaten severely by one of Bowe's entourage wielding a mobile phone of that ancient type you couldn't easily slip into your shirt pocket.

Either side of the 21-minute stoppage – which ended with the battered Fan Man being taken away on a stretcher – there were separate fights. In the first one Bowe, despite plainly lacking the sharpness he had displayed so impressively a year earlier, forged ahead on all three scorecards. Holyfield attacked with his usual élan but his punches, even the most penetrating of them, crucially lacked weight. However, if the Seventh Cavalry didn't come to his aid, the Fan Man certainly did. After dominating the last rounds, Holyfield explained, 'Yes, Bowe and I fought two different six-round fights tonight. In the first one I was just getting ready to go toe-to-toe with him when that guy dropped in. I was in a rhythm and I felt like I could outgun him. I started to get upset after we had to stop but then I realised it was the same for both of us. With that cleared from my mind I just went out and got my rhythm back.' It helped that Bowe was not much more than a bulky shadow of the masterful heavyweight champion of the world.

They fought for the third time in 17 months but they were no longer who they may still have hoped they were. Bowe won on a TKO in the eighth round but if the pay was good ($8 million for both fighters) it no longer came with the world title, Holyfield having dropped his two versions of it to Michael Moorer. More critically, Holyfield was kept in hospital after the fight because of reported heart abnormalities, a situation that provoked a retirement announcement. That was rescinded after consultations with a faith healer and a reassuring examination at the Mayo Clinic, but against Bowe Holyfield again provoked doubts about his future. He knocked Bowe down, inflicting the first of his professional life in the sixth, but suffered the first stoppage of his own career two rounds later.

There had been spectacle, certainly, but they were not the men who thrilled and enthralled the crowd at the Thomas & Mack Center in their first fight. In the fifth round George Foreman was especially affected by Holyfield's obvious fatigue. He got up from his ringside seat and shouted for the fight to be stopped. 'This man is going to end up in a pine box,' he roared. 'He has heart trouble.'

Holyfield would in time show evidence of a mended heart and some extraordinary late momentum in an already turbulent and frequently superb career. He would never come to the ring without a fierce imperative to fight. For Bowe, though, the last of the best had passed.

He appeared twice more as a professional to be taken seriously after defeating Holyfield in that third fight. Both fights were against the erratic but dangerous Polish-born Andrew Golota. Bowe got both decisions but on disqualifications, Golota repeatedly throwing low blows. In both fights Golota led on all cards. After the first one, at Madison Square Garden, there was a wholesale brawl, spreading out from the ring and all the way to the cheaper seats. Bowe's manager, Rock Newman, who had a history of unseemly behaviour at big fights (he had made his own contribution to the battering of the Fan Man) was in the forefront. Everyone said it was a scandal – and insisted on the rematch at the Convention Hall on the Atlantic City Boardwalk. After the near-replica of the first fight, which lacked only the wholesale punch-up and stomping contest, Bowe announced his retirement.

He came back eight years later, and the record of his last three fights is forlorn even in a uniquely unforgiving trade. In 2004 he fought the obscure Marcus Rhode at a casino on native Indian tribal land in Shawnee, Oklahoma. He had him down four times before the fight ended in the second round. Afterwards, Bowe, now 37, said he felt 'like a kid in a candy store'. Discouragingly for confidence in his future hopes, he also resembled one who had spent rather too long on the premises. He weighed 263 pounds.

His physical condition had deteriorated still further when he next appeared in the ring, in 2005, against a small heavyweight named Billy Zumbrun, in another casino, this time in the Californian hills. He came to camp at 20 stone (280 pounds) and when he got the verdict, on a split decision, the casino showroom was filled with boos.

Three years later he reappeared in Mannheim, Germany, reportedly having shed more than 50 pounds in training after scaling more than 21 stone. He won a unanimous decision against Gene Pukall, who had 12 defeats on his record and would never fight outside of his native Germany.

In that tenth round in Las Vegas, when he and Holyfield touched the fighting ages, you would have backed much on a different account of the life of Riddick Bowe. But that was before he revealed the weakness that Eddie Futch, the wisest of boxing men, had looked for so keenly that morning on the mountain above Reno. Before the great talent who liked to be known as 'Big Daddy' so diminished himself. And maybe nowhere more damagingly so than in his own eyes.

Chapter Eighteen

San Antonio, Texas, September 1993

Don King rarely needed much of an invitation to make a speech. He could unfurl one in the time it takes some men to order a drink, and here in the hotel lobby one morning he provided a classic example. This one was hard and indignant and was provoked by my telling him I was on my way to look around the Alamo.

'Ah, the Alamo, the great symbol of courage and patriotism for white America,' he said. 'The place where heroes are honoured. White heroes from Texas and Davy Crockett's men from Tennessee, and volunteers from foreign lands, including yours. You will see their names on the wall. But you will not see the names of the black brothers who died for the cause of a free Texas, I'll venture to tell you that. Oh, no . . .'

His ire was huge and impressive and would have lasted the week much better if at the end of it he wasn't widely seen as a prime influence in the denial of justice to another black brother, the superb WBC world welterweight champion Pernell Whitaker.

But then it is also true that Whitaker was not fighting under the flag of the Republic of Don King. That, with all its advantages – and hazards – was the role of his opponent, the already legendary Mexican Julio César Chávez.

With Mike Tyson just completing the first of three years in prison, and Riddick Bowe the new world heavyweight champion after an epic victory over Evander Holyfield, King's ascendency in the affairs of the big men was at its lowest point since his annexation of Muhammad Ali's career in the seventies. So, naturally, his greatest cause was the protection of the standing, and earning potential, of his biggest current asset. It would mean that by the end of the week his anguished rhetoric on behalf of the unrecognised Afro-American heroes of the Alamo, the brothers who died anonymously beside the likes of the fabled Colonel Travis, Davy Crockett and Jim Bowie, would represent the merest clearing of his throat.

For some time Chávez would be the bulwark of King's empire so seriously depleted by Tyson's exile behind bars in Indiana, which was made to seem worryingly indefinite by reports of his difficulty in getting through his days in the prison environment and the likelihood that his sentence would be extended by bad behaviour. While Tyson was doing his hard time, King was cosseting Chávez with the usual care he applied to the most lucrative of his earners.

The merest glance at Chávez's antecedents, and the number of Mexican supporters he had drawn to the streets of the city – days before the fight, their total already far exceeded the 2,000 crack troops brought by President General Antonio López de Santa Anna to the conquest of the old Alamo mission in 1839 – explained the promoter's devotion to his fighter. He was not a heavyweight but in all else he was custom made for the task of filling a fight hall with fervent compatriots.

For some years Chávez had been rated boxing's best pound-for-pound performer and – bringing a fine edge to this welterweight world-title contest that rekindled memories of the prime of Sugar Ray Leonard and his rivals – Pernell Whitaker had been his most persistent challenger.

Chávez brought all the macho commitment of a Roberto Durán. Whitaker was a fighter of science, of timing, of clinical counterpunching. The fight thus carried the prospect of a wonderful change of pace and emphasis from the pounding furies of the big men. Both fighters had the records of master performers, men who knew their strengths and applied them with the relentless attention needed to prove that they were indeed the best in the world.

If Chávez had a swagger about him, it could not have been harder earned. His regard among fellow Mexicans was a testament to the resolve he had brought to his life and his fighting career. When Mexicans looked at him, and roared when he came into the ring with his red headband like some reincarnation of Pancho Villa or Emiliano Zapata, they saw more than a mere sporting hero. They saw an expression of their blood and, in so many cases, the courage required to conquer the difficulties and the burdens that came at birth.

Chávez was certainly granted his share when he was born in a disused railroad car in Ciudad Obregón, Sonora. His father worked on the rail tracks to provide for Chávez and his four brothers and five sisters, and by the age of 16 Chávez himself was fighting to help provide for his family. He moved to the border town of Tijuana to launch his professional career, and he would reflect, 'I saw my mother working, ironing and washing people's clothes, and I promised her I would give her a house, a real house, some day and she would never have that job again.' It was a similar promise to the one made by the spectacular Spanish matador of the sixties, Manuel 'El Cordobés' Benítez, who told his young sister, 'I'll give you riches or I'll dress you in mourning.' Chávez, however, did not make the caveat of possible disaster and nor did he have any need.

By the end of his career his record would be an astonishing monument to his determination, his relentlessly waged, crowding power and punching, and above all his capacity to take the fight to his opponent in even the most discouraging circumstances. One by one the records would fall.

He would be a six-time world champion in three weight divisions. He would break the record for most defences of world titles (27 of them), the most world-title victories (31), and finish second in the table of knockout title defences (with 21), and the only fighter to stand above him would be Joe Louis, with two more knockouts. He had come here to San Antonio trailing more battle ribbons than the army of Santa Anna, and they were honours mostly won at considerably tighter odds.

Four months before arriving here he battered his latest challenger for the WBC light-welterweight title, Terrence Alli, to a sixth-round defeat, which carried his 13-year career to the stunning mark of 87–0. His last five wins had come inside the distance. Before the run, he had been required to go the distance against the undefeated and hugely lauded Héctor Camacho, the Puerto Rican pride of the New York's *barrios*. Chávez didn't knock out Camacho but won a unanimous decision by huge margins on each card. Camacho, an extrovert character of much skill and panache, admitted, 'The bottom line was I just couldn't keep Julio off. He was too strong, he didn't give me a breath.' However, Whitaker was a different kind of challenge. He was cagier, less overt in his confidence, but beautifully synchronised, a man who would invite you in and then ambush you behind a suddenly closed door with demoralising ease.

Many good judges believed he too should have come here undefeated, with a record of 33–0, but that possibility was ended five years earlier in Paris in extremely dubious circumstances.

Whitaker, the 1984 Olympic champion, fought the Mexican José Luis Ramírez for the WBC lightweight title and was widely considered a poised and comfortable winner. Harry Gibbs, the British referee and ring judge, certainly considered it one of the least challenging of his chores. He gave it to Whitaker by a margin of four rounds. Newton Campos of Brazil took a radically different view, scoring it 118–113 for Ramírez and provoking a large collective gasp, and the local judge, Louis Michel, gave the Mexican the nod by one round. The worry, which lingered still in San Antonio, was that Whitaker didn't win for the simple reason it would have sabotaged some considerable business for Don King and his friends at the WBC.

A deal had already been made for an all-Mexican unification bout between Chávez and Ramírez, and a Pernell win, to say the least of it, would have been an inconvenience. In all the turmoil and accusations that came in the wake of the Paris fight, maybe the most telling contribution was from Whitaker's manager, Shelly Finkel. He reported that at the weigh-in a WBC executive approached his fighter and 'shoved a piece of paper in front of his nose and told him to sign for a Chávez fight in case he won. Ramírez had already signed one. We wouldn't do it. After that, we had a fear of what would happen.'

It was an apprehension undisturbed by Whitaker's easy control of the fight, his ability to win the vital phases with the kind of ring-craft and timing that would see him twice voted Fighter of the Year by *The Ring* magazine and, in 2002, have him ranked tenth in the list of the 100 greatest fighters of the last 80 years. He would also be ushered into boxing's Hall of Fame in New York State in his first year of eligibility.

Certainly, there was no question that against Chávez he was fighting for that mythic title of the world's best pound-for-pound fighter. However, the man from Norfolk, Virginia, did not beat his chest. He wasn't, like Chávez, buoyed by a legion of zealous fans. He tended to worry about the challenges ahead, and it was interesting that his promoter, Dan Duva, kept from him the fact that a match had been made with the Mexican demigod Chávez before his last fight four months earlier, when he beat James McGirt on a unanimous decision to take the WBC and lineal welterweight title at Madison Square Garden.

Duva believed that the shadow of Chávez would have been too influential in the Garden. It would have taken Whitaker's attention away from the not-insubstantial challenge of beating McGirt, the reigning WBC welterweight champion. As it was, McGirt was not at his best. Soon after the fight he would have a major operation on a shoulder injury sustained in sparring. Whitaker produced a more than adequate performance and, given his nature and his ability, no one doubted that it was one that could almost certainly have been raised to another level had it been necessary.

So, Chávez was a fresh challenge and the requirement was, Whitaker didn't need telling, the clearest focus of his already deeply impressive career.

When the fighters came into the ring, the Alamodome was ablaze with the red, white and green flags of Mexico. The 65,000 crowd was overwhelmingly for Chávez. He whipped up his supporters, churning his fists and holding up his right one in the promise of a crushing triumph.

Inevitably, Whitaker was more reflective, and he merely shrugged when he saw and heard the extent of his opponent's following. Few fighters, after all, had needed to understand so implicitly that when the bell sounded a man was never quite so alone.

For two rounds it was – at least on the face and sound of it – all Chávez. He charged in, pressurising, throwing punches in a stream, and when one of them landed the Mexicans made thunderous noise. There was the sound of a bugle, an echo of Santa Anna's attack maybe, but Whitaker's defence was not significantly breeched. He was content to backpedal, throw a brief flurry, mostly jabs, and measure the distances between himself and his assailant.

He was more assertive in the third round – and magnificently so. He had done his measuring of space and tempo, and now you could see the confidence welling, subtly, easily. If there was any doubt in the minds of Chávez and his roaring throng that he was involved in a real fight, it was sinking faster than a tropical sun in the dusk.

Chávez had a fight on his hands, all right, and it was one that was bringing a frown to his brow. He lunged and battered but Whitaker was gone. Then he returned with a stinging jab and an artful cross. He was skipping across the ring while Chávez almost churned up the canvas. Whitaker's jab was scoring easily and there was much less certainty in Chávez's swagger when he returned to his corner.

In the fourth Whitaker was masterful. Plainly, he believed that the fight was his to shape and control and there were moments when Chávez stopped and whirled his head like a tormented fighting bull. But if Chávez was deeply frustrated, and his corner was showing increasing signs of desperation, he was not about to bend his knee. He proved this in the fifth with his most effective round, an effort of the strongest will that saw him pound Whitaker against the ropes and land one hard right lead, which, for a few moments, removed the confidence from the tilt of Whitaker's head. It was, though, less a crisis and more a pause, a time to regather all the elements that had so clearly changed the momentum of the fight.

Whitaker won the sixth, seventh and eighth rounds with great relish. He was doing what he said he would when, before the fight, he was asked about the pressure he would feel from the weight of Chávez's support and aggressive style. He said that whenever he was 'on the road' he loved to subdue a hostile crowd, reduce it to silence with the cool efficiency of his work. It was not so much a strategy as something that came from deep in his nature. He was an outsider with the knack of imposing himself on any neighbourhood, however menacing or raucous.

Chávez made his last, desperate charge in the tenth. He threw a barrage of punches, but mostly they missed, and the harder he fought, the more futile his task became. Whitaker took command of the round, moved with taunting confidence and sailed through the 11th, demonstrably a winner, a man who had faced the greatest challenge of his career with a superb mixture of nerve and skill. He made the 12th risk-free, a killing of time and threat, a last stroll to the peak of his fighting life.

That, at least, was how it should have been. It was Whitaker's brilliantly earned right. Instead, he was given a draw. It was sickening. It was an outrage. It was one of those moments when you wanted to walk away from boxing and say that such cold-eyed dishonesty was an insult to both intelligence and decency.

There was, inevitably, an impassioned inquest. *Sports Illustrated* emblazoned the word 'Robbed' across its cover and *The Ring* magazine advised against anyone who thought the fight a draw buying a copy. Whitaker's promoter was quizzed vigorously as to how it was he had yielded so much ground in the selection of judges, only one of whom gave the fight to Whitaker, by 115–113, with the other two scoring the draw.

Duva explained that the Texas boxing authority had put together a panel of five possible judges, with him and King having the right to strike out one name. He added, 'It was clear to me that the five were not among the best in the world. Early on I suggested getting Jerry Roth of Nevada, the guy who is recognised as the best. My opinion is that he was turned down [by King and the Chávez camp] because he had Meldrick Taylor ahead when he fought Chávez.' That was when Chávez's unbeaten record was preserved by referee Richard Steele when he stopped the fight with two seconds left in the final round.

Who could possibly deny that Chávez on this occasion had been even more fortunate? Duva made the point with some venom as he reported that WBC officials had expressed bewilderment over his post-fight anger. 'They said to me, "What are you complaining about? This is the perfect result. Everyone wins." This is just sickening. On the day of the fight everyone who knows me knows that I had one fear. It was that Pernell would get robbed.'

And so it happened, as brutally, as shamelessly as if he had been pounced upon by muggers while strolling by a secluded stretch of San Antonio's Riverside Walk.

Perhaps it was not surprising that Don King's rage at failures of natural justice appeared to have peaked the morning we spoke on my way to the Alamo. The lesson, I supposed, was clear enough. There were times when a brother was a brother, just so long as he didn't get in the way of a few million dollars more.

There were also moments like the one I had at ringside when the result was called and I wondered, not for the first time but with more force than usual, if riding the caravan of the big fights was, for all its excitements, an entirely appropriate way to spend a large part of an adult existence. The worry was that boxing, along with the rest of sport, wasn't always the thrilling or exact metaphor for life it was often cracked up to be. And that perhaps there should be a little more involvement in the real thing.

But then maybe not. There would be an opportunity to test the feel of life beyond the playpen of sport and, it had to be reported, it was not overwhelmingly seductive. It came while covering the funeral of Richard Nixon in Los Angeles in the spring of 1994, an assignment handed to me by the *Daily Express* as I left Las Vegas after reporting Evander Holyfield's defeat by Michael Moorer. The *Express*'s Washington correspondent, Peter Hitchens, was otherwise engaged at an execution in a Texas prison.

It was interesting to note the operating style of the White House press corps, who had their own working tent at the site of the burial in the grounds of the Nixon museum at his birthplace in a modest suburb in south Los Angeles. The tent was a sacred place from which the likes of an itinerant sportswriter were expressly barred on the working credential that I picked up at a US Marine Corps Air Station. They were a grand bunch, the White House reporters, and it was amusing to imagine quite what the lordlier of them might have made of an evening of relaxation in the gathering place of the fight writers, the Flame bar, open 24 hours beneath its bright-red neon legend a block from the Desert Inn on the Vegas Strip.

Many hours had been spent there discussing the verities of life and the big fights and on one occasion the crowd included a fighting kangaroo, which behaved so notably well it was in danger of bringing a touch of genuine decorum. Ed Schuyler Junior and Pat Putnam tended to preside, at least until dinner was taken, quite often around 2 a.m., and the company had a shifting population, depending on deadlines and the ability to continue standing up, though not always in that order.

There were many memorable exchanges, including the one that came when Schuyler and Putnam, with the help of Michael Katz, challenged Hugh McIlvanney's assertion that Paul Scofield was arguably the best living actor on film or the stage. The Americans laid their bait well, offering their own John Wayne as a serious rival, much to McIlvanney's exasperation. Aghast, he thundered, 'John Wayne! You could fire a burning arrow up his arse with no guarantee of a change of expression.'

Maybe, I reflected as I packed my bags in Los Angeles, there was a case for staying with that which you knew best. And which could still make you laugh as well as cry.

Chapter Nineteen

Indianapolis, March 1995

It was eight years since I first stood alone in the dawn waiting to see Mike Tyson with such little idea of all the time and the miles and the threshing he would demand of anyone attempting to give a coherent account of his life. It had, from the start, been not so much a life as a vortex, and now it was whirling at maximum force.

Outside the prison gates there could be no doubting that the challenge of making some sense of his furies had, at the very least, redoubled. When he came out, the frenzy was immediate and intense and involved a breathless charge across frost-laden fields. This was provoked by the cry of Wallace Matthews, the boxing writer of *Newsday*, when Tyson was ushered by Don King through the blaze of the television lights and into his stretch limousine. 'To the mosque,' shouted Matthews, as the limo forked away from the main road that led to the airport.

Tyson, a convert to Islam during his three years in prison, was heading for morning prayers at the local mosque. And there he would serve breakfast to no one less than Muhammad Ali. So, of course, we ran and stumbled in our eagerness not to miss a telling image, however carefully it had been choreographed.

Tyson played his role with becoming humility. Plainly dressed for a holy place, head bowed a little, he said he was both proud and humbled to have the great man waiting for him just beyond the gates of the prison. He had endured three hard years but he had survived and now he would make a new chapter. We were given mats and invited to pray beside him. And then, with a watery sun rising above suburban Indianapolis, we went away to write our stories.

Did we write about the new, redeemed Mike Tyson, free from the purgatory of prison, chastened by past mistakes and ready to exploit, at the age of 28, potentially the richest years of any fighter's life? No, by and large we didn't, and it was just as well. In time, when so many new convulsions had come and gone, when so much of his life remained imprisoned deep in his wounded psyche, he would give his own version of the days that followed his release from prison. They were not the days of a penitent turning towards his own hard-won vision of Mecca with uncomplicated hope. They were still, he would recall, shaped by an unbridled need for drugs and the most casual sexual gratification. They were still marked by rage. He flew, paradoxically enough given his other appetites, into one when he found that King had loaded the limo with bottles of Dom Pérignon, draped yellow ribbons on the trees around his Ohio mansion and had tables stacked with lobster, shrimp and roast pork for a mob of guests for whom he felt no affinity.

Tyson emptied the house of his unwanted visitors and in his anger fired King on the spot, a prelude to legal action that the promoter stalled with one of his routine ruses when faced with a rebellious fighter – a suitcase filled with a million dollars.

Even more substantially, King had arranged fights worth more than $200 million, but if Tyson saw vast monies at hand – despite his belief that King and his co-managers and erstwhile friends John Horne and Rory Holloway had conspired to rob him when he was behind bars – it was just one certainty in an ocean of doubts.

Looking back, he would say, 'I had no time to adjust to the world. I had so many people in my face because I had all those fights lined up. I was worse than before I went in. Everyone was saying, "Mike's the man. He's the man." But now I had a different frame of mind. I was afraid of everybody. Prison doesn't rehabilitate anyone. I don't care how much money you earn, when you get out you're still a lesser person than when you went in. I was paranoid. I thought everyone was gonna hurt me. I'd panic every time I heard an ambulance siren.

'I wasn't the same guy. Prison basically took the whole life out of me. I never again trusted anyone – not even myself around certain people. I never wanted to be in any kind of situation around women. It had been brewing over my head for so many years that I wasn't able to let it go; it even really bothers me to this day. I had these two contracts which advanced us a lot of money, so no one wanted to hear that I needed some time to get my life and my mind together. As scared as I was, though, I was also starting to get arrogant again.

'I wanted everything. I thought I was owed a lot from my time in prison. I wanted the best girls, the best cars, [to] own the best houses. I was the Count of Monte Cristo. I was a gladiator. God himself couldn't produce a better fighter. And here I was afraid of ambulance sirens.'

Really, you didn't have to wait down the years for the soul-baring of Mike Tyson to know that all was not as it might have seemed as he made his genuflections to Muhammad Ali and went down on his mat to make his prayer of thanks for salvation. Tyson may have been out of prison but clearly not much in his life had changed beyond the reinstated accessibility of huge money and instant sex. The easy generating of so much income was the result of an insatiable public curiosity. How had he emerged physically from the prison days? Would he still produce anything like the old menace when he stepped back into the ring?

Unfortunately, we would have to wait for some time to know this, certainly beyond the August night when, five months after his release, he fought somebody from Boston called Peter McNeeley at the MGM Grand in Las Vegas. It was, arguably, the most preposterous, dishonest, larcenous, meaningless fight in the history of boxing. McNeeley's father, Tom, had been a heavyweight contender who fought Floyd Patterson for the world title and played gridiron for the formidable Michigan State University, but his son brought to Vegas nothing but a risible threat – he said he was going to wrap Tyson in a 'cocoon of horror' – and an extremely light enthusiasm for the action. It was soon clear that McNeeley and his people hadn't come to fight but to exploit an undreamed, unearned opportunity and King, of course, was the author of something hard not to see as a scam – the biggest, most egregious and profitable of his entire career. The fight grossed $96 million, it smashed the pay-per-view record at $63 million, going into 1.52 million American homes, and this was just the start of the world's reacquaintance with the former Baddest Man on the Planet.

The 'fight' lasted one minute 29 seconds, but mere indignation was never likely to dent King's sense that he was once again in charge, however precariously at times, of boxing's most compelling commodity. King, after all, hadn't promoted a fight but an occasion, an opportunity for the world to re-announce its fascination with Mike Tyson. Far from breaking a brutal spell, the years in prison had only deepened the dark and thrilling force of his presence.

If it was also true that Tyson brought his own fears and uncertainties into the ring – if indeed he believed that the long days in prison could not be so easily jettisoned as unwanted baggage – that was not what those who paid $1,500 for a ringside seat witnessed. They were reminded of the old imperative to make mayhem, to destroy anyone put before him, and this, after the interruption of his career and that bad morning in Tokyo, was a reality that tempered any sore reaction to the brevity of the action and the absurd manner of its conclusion. The

Tyson Horror Show was playing again and, for the moment at least, it was scarcely in need of a supporting cast.

McNeeley charged across the ring, threw some wild punches – which Tyson easily avoided – and then, after less than ten seconds, was on the canvas. He was put there by a right hook that Tyson appeared to produce from a sound working memory – a reflex action, which announced that his chore was as formal as it was hazard-free. McNeeley took a standing count of eight from an already appalled referee, Mills Lane, and then resumed his show of bogus aggression, most notably in an exchange of punches in the corner of the ring. Only one of them counted. It was an uppercut from Tyson that returned McNeeley to the canvas. It was then that the last semblance of a serious fight descended into farce.

McNeeley's manager, Vinnie Vecchione, came into the ring and effectively stopped the fight. Lane, his outrage up another notch, waved the fight over, disqualified McNeeley and no doubt would have physically washed his hands of it had he the means.

There were shouts of protest from some of the crowd, but it was relatively muted. Most were happy enough that they could say they had seen the return of Tyson, the first instalment of another story guaranteed to bring fresh levels of fear and loathing and violent drama. McNeeley received his mother, father and girlfriend into the ring and kissed each of them. Whatever the feelings of his father, the tough old fighter who had worked his trade rather more resolutely in formidable company, he kept them to himself.

Tyson left the ring as reassured as any man who claimed he had become apprehensive of his own shadow could maybe have hoped to be. 'I forgot how much I really love this sport,' he said, before adding reflectively, 'I did all right but I have to cultivate my skills.'

Three months later in Philadelphia the restoration of his aura moved up to a more significant level when he knocked out the more talented, but light-hitting, Buster Mathis Junior, in the third round. The death shortly before the fight of Mathis's father – a notable performer who, as an amateur, had beaten Joe Frazier in the Olympic trials and gone 12 rounds with Muhammad Ali – was said to have diminished Buster's resolve and his ambition, but then Tyson was also a discouragement. Against a more serious professional, he confirmed that he was still recognisably himself, a point that was made but not so easily as in the McNeeley fiasco.

There could be no doubting that it was indeed the second coming of Mike Tyson, whatever the quality of the opposition. He still had a unique brand to market.

It was a reality that Frank Bruno – despite holding the WBC heavyweight title and crossing himself an estimated 19 times as he walked down to the ring before their meeting at the MGM Grand in Las Vegas three months after the Mathis fight – was utterly powerless to challenge. On the face of it, and certainly before seeing the extent of the apprehension he failed so profoundly to conceal before stepping through the ropes, it was reasonable to believe he had a chance.

After failing in three world-title challenges – against the extremely able Tim Witherspoon before his own huge crowd at Wembley Stadium; Tyson, when he landed that memorable left hook down the road at the Vegas Hilton; and Lennox Lewis, who he surprised and embarrassed in the early rounds on a cold night in Cardiff – Bruno had finally reached the promised land six months before his second meeting with Tyson. He had outpointed the eccentric Oliver McCall, who had so stunningly deprived Lewis of the WBC title, and was bathed in huge patriotic acclaim in the stadium where he had fallen to Witherspoon.

He was the restored national hero at Wembley, but in Las Vegas all that hubris had drained away. The idea that he had a chance, that he could again marshal the power and the purpose that had first disturbed Lewis and then overcome McCall, simply disappeared in the great maw of Tyson's menace. The curiosity provoked by his release from prison had, inevitably, slipped from its first extraordinary peak, but it had been replaced by a compelling need to know where Mike Tyson was heading. Tyson earned $30 million, and the champion Bruno was happy to accept the biggest pay night of his life at $6 million.

That was handsome reward for a work shift that lasted just 50 seconds into the third round. But how do you quantify the degree of one man's humiliation, the cost to his self-belief, the idea of himself he had carried through a career that had made him one of Britain's best loved sportsman?

Bruno was more than a world-champion boxer when he arrived in Las Vegas in March 1996. He was an institution whose amiable persona – his worn but winning one-liners, his exuberant malapropisms, along with his success in the boxing ring – had passed favourable inspection by many as the makings of a national treasure. But when he left, for all his new wealth, he was a man deeply diminished in the eyes of both his public and himself. He faced years of difficulty that included concerns over his mental health and the collapse of his marriage. He would never fight again. It was more than a defeat Tyson inflicted so roughly. It was an emotional, psychological disaster.

For Tyson – in a way the victories of McNeeley and Mathis could never have been – it was the rough, clubbing restoration of so much of his old status. He was indeed the bad, ferocious man again. Furthermore, he was a world heavyweight champion again, and if that didn't repel all the demons that continued to come to him in the night, it was still a prize of great value.

Bruno, at 17 stone 9 pounds, was 27 pounds heavier than Tyson and, as always, cut an impressive figure at the sound of the first bell. But he would have dwindled hardly less rapidly had he been winged by a wrecking ball. Tyson simply walked through him, hitting him at will and shaking him to his foundations in the first two rounds before the last, engulfing assault in the third. There was nowhere for Bruno to go except the darkest place he had ever known.

The final onslaught was an eruption of 13 uninterrupted punches. The first was a crunching body shot, the last a vicious left hook that sent Bruno crashing into the ropes. Bruno lolled on the first strand, without any kind of defence or hope. Mills Lane was again the referee and he must have mused to himself that he might more appropriately have come along in the winged collar, black crêpe and top hat of an undertaker. His shepherding of Bruno back to his corner was certainly the last word in bleak formality.

Tyson did not have a lot to say, murmuring to his handlers that they should tell the press that he had hit Bruno with the force of a mule, adding, as if no one had noticed, 'I was going for the knockout from the first round.' The scale of Bruno's defeat, his absolute failure to make any kind of stand in defence of his title, hardly needed much elaboration, and when he left the arena, his head down, he seemed more aware of this than anyone. There were no one-liners to crank up, no mock optimism. Instead, he produced a morsel of the pathos of the boxing ages, saying, 'You will find I was a little broken-hearted when it was over.'

By the sharpest contrast, Don King – assuming he could keep some kind of control over his supreme asset and continue to flip open suitcases filled with large dollar bills – had every reason to exult. He had played his cards outrageously but – when all was assessed, and from his perspective – as adroitly as ever before. Mike Tyson had been restored to the stage with maximum effect, and if there were still serious doubts about how much of his old power to inflict damage on the highest class of opponent had been retained, his ability to still intimidate was about to be reconfirmed.

You could write down the date, 7 September 1996, a year and a half after the prison gates had swung open, with total certainty. It was the end of the beginning of Mike Tyson's return to the peak of boxing. In private he might have those anxiety attacks that had him pacing the night, but there was no evidence of self-doubt when the ring lights came on.

Bruce Seldon brought along the WBC title to the MGM Grand, and if he was an underdog (22-1) he had some supporters who believed he had the fighting means, and the nerve, to perhaps do more than make a passing show.

One of them was the celebrated daredevil Evel Knievel who, from a position that demanded a considerable degree of respect, spoke to me of the mysteries of nerve and courage, how some men had it in them to meet the most demanding occasions of their lives. In this category he placed his friend Seldon. 'Bruce,' he said, 'is one of those guys who is capable of digging deep inside himself. I have spent a little time with him. Yes, I give him a chance.'

Soon enough that was reason to recall an old Don King reaction to similar reaches of hope: 'The guy has two chances, Slim and none; and I have to tell you Slim just left town.' Seldon, who had claimed the vacant title by defeating Tony Tucker and successfully defended it against Joe Hipp on the undercard of Tyson–McNeeley, had reason to catch the first plane out of town. He didn't lose, he surrendered, $5 million richer but, like the raddled Bruno, consigned for ever to the ranks of fighters who had been overwhelmed as much by their own fears as the man they faced.

The fight was over in one minute 49 seconds, and at ringside it was hard to identify a significant Tyson punch, certainly nothing to rank with the power he had laid on the unfortunate Bruno. Seldon was known as 'the Atlantic City Express' but this was the night he crashed, virtually unassisted, into the buffers. When he came into the ring his apprehension was as palpable as Bruno's and, going back, that of Michael Spinks. The smell of terror filled the hall. Seldon hit the canvas twice and, on both occasions, it seemed it was pure fear that had taken him there.

Reruns of the first knockdown were especially damning. Tyson threw a right hand that seemed, a little more blatantly on each inspection, to have done no more than graze the top of Seldon's head. No matter, he went down as though poleaxed but, remarkably, managed to rise to his feet at the count of six. The second knockdown was only marginally more convincing. Tyson threw a left hand that more than anything seemed to be about measuring his distance, and certainly Seldon appeared to have retreated successfully from its full power. But again he crashed down, and when he rose his legs performed a little dance that convinced referee Richard Steele much more than the crowd, who began shouts of, 'Fix.' Only heaven knew what Mills Lane, the circuit judge and former US Marine, would have made of it.

Seldon made an impassioned defence of his performance before leaving town. He said, 'You know how hurt I am right now? I came to fight, I came to win. I did not realise how hard he hits or how fast he is. He is a destroyer and I'm witness to that. The shot rattled my eyes and I couldn't see straight. I didn't train for 12 weeks to come here and take a dive. I'm already a millionaire. It's not about money. I'm sorry. I tried my best. He is a great fighter. He is a bad man.'

It was a statement that served well enough the idea that Tyson was indeed restored in his brutal mystique, even though it was true that the only genuine violence of the night came shockingly after the fight, when the rapper and actor Tupac Shakur took fatal gunshot wounds when a Cadillac drew up alongside the car in which he and his entourage were riding to a nightclub.

Tyson's diary was brimming with what Don King believed were much less hazardous entries, especially after persuading him that it was good business to pay the dangerous Lewis $4 million step-aside money. Instead, Tyson would, just two months after the Seldon fight, take a softer option. Or so he imagined. He would fight Evander Holyfield.

Chapter Twenty

Sacramento, May 1995

Two months after Mike Tyson was let out of prison, Lennox Lewis came up to northern California to start a sentence of his own. It had been imposed not by a court but by one moment of catastrophically failed concentration. He had broken a fundamental rule of his brutal, unforgiving trade. It was a lapse that lost him his WBC title against Oliver McCall – and required him to remake his fighting career and his life.

Lewis had to believe in himself again and, most critically, restate convincingly the claim that he might just be the last great heavyweight standing. Now, in Sacramento, so far from the glitz of Las Vegas or the aura of Madison Square Garden, he had to remake his career against a maverick fighter whose life outside the ring was marked by a chaos fuelled by drugs.

However, if Lionel Butler of Bogalusa, Louisiana, arrived here crumpled in a black leather coat and plainly far from his best condition – he would scale 18 stone 9 pounds – and almost immediately began attracting the attention of the local police department, he did have one asset and a little hope. He had a potentially ruinous right hand – some believed it to be the hardest of any heavyweight around – and the chance of a shot at the WBC title so unexpectedly annexed by the lightly regarded Oliver McCall when Lewis made his career-threatening stumble.

They were factors Lewis could not afford to discount. The McCall defeat had been much more than a thunderous wake-up call. It had made him look at himself in a way he had never done before. He came here, certainly, as a man who had seriously engaged with the meaning of the first defeat in his professional career. He had spent hard days at Big Bear Lake in the San Bernadino Mountains under his new trainer Emanuel Steward – his old one, Pepe Correa, having been dismissed after the McCall fight – and before that he had retreated to the hills above his mother's native Port Antonio in Jamaica. There, he attempted to answer some of the questions he believed held the key to the rest of his life. Touching them all was the fact that there was nothing to redeem, or excuse, his performance against McCall.

Early in the second round, having won the first comfortably enough with his long and accurate jab, he threw a casual, languid right, which the erratic, eccentric McCall, in a moment of cool deliberation utterly at odds with so much of his previous existence in and out of the ring, stepped inside so sharply, so adroitly he might have been performing a guardsman's drill. He produced the perfect counter to the point of Lewis's jaw.

Lewis went down, and though he was up again at the count of six his legs were wobbling and his eyes were glazed. Referee José García stopped the fight before wrapping his arms around him. Later, after Lewis protested that he could have fought on after smothering McCall's attempts to finish the fight, the referee said, 'I'm absolutely sure about what I did. Lennox Lewis was knocked out. To allow more punches to Lewis could have had fatal consequences. My duty is to protect the health of the boxer.'

Lewis's first reaction was to say that he had fallen to a lucky punch, a charge fiercely rejected by an Emanuel Steward about to switch camps. 'It was not a lucky punch,' said Steward. 'It was well planned.'

As Lewis disappeared from the building, surrounded by an entourage stunned by both the result and the loss of earnings, estimated as high as $30 million, he stopped for a few moments to say, 'It's too early to tell you how I really feel. This has got to sink in. I must look at myself and my situation. Right now, I still think of myself as a champion. If I no longer feel like that when I wake up, who knows what will happen?'

His brother Dennis was hardly more positive, saying, 'Right now I'd say it's 50-50 whether Lennox carries on. He has a lot of pride and he may not want to leave the memory of his career here, but he knows what he faces, he knows the politics of boxing well.'

If Lennox needed a reminder, there had been one visible enough as he was helped out of the Wembley Arena ring. It was the sight of Don King embracing the new champion, rejoicing in the fact that he had been so unexpectedly returned to the heart of heavyweight affairs six months before Tyson's release from prison. For veteran observers there was a hint of the notorious occasion when King drove to a heavyweight title fight with the great Joe Frazier in Kingston, Jamaica, then drove back from the arena with his conqueror, George Foreman.

Lewis didn't need telling that he could not expect favours from King. He had presented an unreceptive ear to the promoter's blandishments and driven a hard bargain when King won the purse bid for his first defence of the WBC title against Tony Tucker. King had taken a loss on the fight in Las Vegas, where Tucker showed that he had regressed in the six years since defending his own IBF heavyweight title against Tyson. He went down twice under Lewis's heavy punches and lost a unanimous decision. For the winner, though, there was no warm embrace from the promoter. King may have smiled in the television lights, but he did so with narrowed eyes.

Here, though, in the spring sunshine of California and a short drive from the burgeoning vines of Napa Valley, Lewis had the bearing of a man who had looked hard and long into the future and believed he could meet all of its challenges.

Stretching out in his hotel suite after some hard work under Steward's gaze, he told me, 'You could say Oliver McCall is part of my growing pains in life and, yes, you could also say he is a bit of a ghost for me. What happened at Wembley that night shocked me so much it definitely made me think about the need for some caution. I just did not believe I could be beaten. I had all the title belts in my sights and I felt that nothing could stop me becoming the undisputed champion of the world. It was my destiny, what I was born for.

'Then I made a terrible mistake – and I paid a huge price. The punch came from nowhere as far as I was concerned, and I would be lying if I said it didn't affect the way I look at fighting now. Before, I had only half the picture. I knew about my own ability, my particular strengths. But what happened that night at Wembley told me there was more to it – and I'll never forget that lesson.

'In the hills in Jamaica it was very painful, but gradually I came to terms with what had happened. Friends tried to help me, said that everything would come right, but I said I had to work everything out for myself. I didn't think any less of myself as a fighter. I still believed I could prove myself the best in the world. But most of all I had to change something in myself. I still thought I was a warrior. But now I would be a smart warrior. I would make sure I didn't give anyone else the chance I gave Oliver McCall.'

He believed the discharging of Pepe Correa was an important first step. The trainer's stint had been marked by a high degree of arrogance: he had been dismissive of both Tucker and McCall, and it was noted that before the disaster the trainer's most memorable initiative had been to throw a women's suspender belt into a McCall press conference. Nor had there been any striking development in Lewis since the victories over Tucker, Frank Bruno and Phil Jackson, the last two of which had demanded decisive eruptions of power from Lewis rather than the measured application of superior gifts and a coherent fight-plan.

Before accepting Lewis's call, Steward was scathing about his predecessor. He described Correa as a 'braggart' who had grossly exaggerated his contribution to the development of Sugar Ray Leonard.

As for Lewis, according to Steward he was a diamond whose polishing had been critically delayed. Steward said, 'When I look at Lennox Lewis I see a terrible waste. This is a man with all the tools, with ability to make any trainer worth his salt drool over. But for some time it has been clear to me he hasn't been progressing. If he had been improving we wouldn't have had such a clear target in that last fight, we wouldn't have been able to keep on saying to Oliver McCall, "Look, this is his big weakness, work on this, take advantage of it just once and you can be champion of the world." You just cannot compare the natural ability of these two fighters. I've said that Lennox has more talent than any fighter I've seen since Muhammad Ali. You cannot say more than that.

'Lennox can come back and be champion of the world. I've no doubt about it. But he would have to change a lot of things. He would have to open himself up to new training methods. He would have to hurt in the gym, hurt in the training – and he would have to take a few blows to his ego. Whether he's willing to do this at this stage of his career, when he is 29 years old, is the big question. Would I train him? I would be delighted to. But only if he met those conditions.'

Soon enough Lewis convinced Steward that he was prepared to cover the hardest terrain of his fighting life. He said that he had come down from the Jamaican hills some way to being mended at the broken places – and, by way of an early statement, he would show this against the big, unruly but also potentially dangerous Lionel Butler.

In the Arco Arena in Sacramento, a modest auditorium more familiar with the first ambitions of high-school basketball stars, Butler did not announce himself as a man who had prepared fastidiously for what might just prove a pivotal point in his own life. He wore a leather coat into the ring, stretched against his bulk, and a quizzical look on his face that might have been the beginnings of a sneer. Already, he had caused some alarm. There were daily reports of his irregular lifestyle. Police were called to his room at his motel – a mean, unwelcoming building across the freeway from Lewis's more luxurious accommodation – following a disturbance between Butler and his wife. There were rumours of guns in his room – and of a questionable white substance left on the back seat of a taxi returning him to the motel in the small hours of the morning. He might have been a refugee from the bleakest pages of *Fat City*. But then, as Lewis had been continually reminded by Steward, he could punch.

Shortly before going into the ring, Lewis made one last earnest statement of his determination to put the McCall pratfall behind him. 'I have one priority here,' he said. 'I have to prove what happened against Oliver McCall was a fluke. I have to show the progress I have made with Emanuel Steward over the last few weeks. I have to pick up on what I was doing before McCall. I have to show that I can get right to the top, whatever Don King and his friends come up with.'

Lewis avoided fresh disaster, put away an exhausted Butler at the end of the fifth round, but what he couldn't claim was that he had marched imperiously back to the peaks of his best performance. There was certainly little of the authority that first announced his potential to dominate the heavyweights, that ransacking of Donovan Ruddock two and a half years earlier. Lewis had to lift sharply the level of his jabbing after Butler scored with a heavy overhead right in the first round – a blow that brought a chill that lingered through the second and third rounds, when Butler connected with several powerful hooks.

Lewis finished strongly, putting Butler down twice and showing some of the power that had first announced him as the prospective dominant heavyweight. But his more resolute critics – who had formed an American-led cottage industry at ringside, which had as its most ignoble product the claim that he had a yellow streak running down his back – were unappeased.

The assessments squeezed into the post-fight politics had a common theme. It was that Lewis still carried the legacy of the McCall tremor. You could see the fault line. He made his concession to that possibility after first responding with some sarcasm to King's defence of Tyson's lightning reinstatement as number-one contender, and WBC president José Sulaimán's assurances that everyone would be treated with scrupulous fairness. To that promise, Lewis responded, 'I've every confidence that the WBC's word is golden.'

He discussed his performance more soberly and at rather greater length, saying, 'When you come back from defeat – and especially when it is the first of your career – you naturally have some doubts in your head, but throughout the fight I felt strong and confident and I know I can make a lot more progress under Emanuel Steward. He has already unlocked the door on some problems, and this situation between us will only get better. Whatever the politics, I do expect them to go on for some time. I know we'll reach a point together when I just cannot be ignored when anyone talks about who is the real champion of the world.

'We worked on my balance before the fight, getting inside more positively. I knew I had to be patient against an opponent like Butler. He has fast hands and a heavy punch. I had to remove the threat without taking any silly chances early on, and in the end I was happy with the way I got the job done. It was an unusual situation for me, coming off a defeat, and that can play on your mind if you let it. I wasn't going to leave myself open to any kind of sucker punch.'

Steward's demeanour was that of a zealous man moderately pleased and he claimed that he was satisfied, up to a point, saying, 'This was a good start. I give Lennox eight out of ten for tonight's effort. Next time you'll see a whole lot of improvement.'

As one of Lewis's less abashed admirers, who had seen in him not only superb athletic talent but a degree of warmth and decency not always conspicuous in his chosen trade, I was inclined to agree, if a little tentatively. Before driving with Hugh McIlvanney to the Napa Valley, where we tasted some of the most recent vintage and were invited to a wedding at a local winery, I filed my piece to London in the dawn. It concluded, 'No doubt there is much work to be done in the remaking of Lennox Lewis but this was a hazardous place, in and out of the ring, to make a start and it could all have ended almost before it began. But it did not, which means that for a little while at least the politics can wait. This was not about politics but redemption. It happened.'

A generous, premature conclusion? Maybe so. If there would be a night when Lennox Lewis could indeed hold his arms aloft and declare that he was the undisputed heavyweight champion of the world – a worthy claimant to the legacy bequeathed by such as Joe Louis and Rocky Marciano, Joe Frazier and Muhammad Ali – it would not come nearly so easily or as agreeably as that first glass of Chardonnay amid the vine groves. It would, for example, take him the best part of two years to again share a ring with his nemesis Oliver McCall. And another two before he would stand in the ring of Madison Square Garden, at the age of 33, with all the prizes of heavyweight boxing within his long reach. It would be a long campaign indeed, one marked by drama, tragicomedy, intrigue, severe tests of both nerve and talent, deep frustration and, in the ultimately poignant case of McCall, evidence of both blood-chilling cynicism and something undistinguishable from outright insanity.

First, though, was the comedy. It came less than two months after the Butler fight. Lewis fought Justin Fortune, a 5 foot 9 inch tall Australian who had been discovered, without widespread awe, working in Freddy Roach's Los Angeles gym. The fight was in Dublin, where Lewis came in the ring with the troubled look of someone fearing that he had been dragged into a joke of deeply embarrassing potential, a possibility not so easily discounted in the light of a report that shortly before embarking for Dublin, Fortune had been utterly out-sparred by a seriously over-weight Tony Tubbs.

Eight inches taller than Fortune, Lewis peered down at him with a mixture of disbelief and the foreboding that comes when you fear you have come to a party whose guest list you perhaps should have checked a little more carefully. It didn't help that Lewis, in his elab-orate determination not to make a mistake, encouraged Fortune to throw a few punches, several of which landed. However, by the fourth round Lewis acted upon the absurdity of the situation and Fortune was twice sent crashing to the canvas, the second time without hope of recovery.

Three months after the comedy, Lewis brushed forcefully against tragedy when he overwhelmed Tommy Morrison in the sixth round of their fight on the Atlantic City Boardwalk. Morrison didn't have the power to prevent one of only three defeats in a career that enjoyed moments of high promise, but he had most everything else – at least it seemed so at that stage of his sadly foreshortened life. He had looks, a degree of star appeal that had already seen him perform alongside Sylvester Stallone in a *Rocky* film, and plenty of the ol' boy charm of his fellow Arkansan, President Bill Clinton. Unfortunately, he also had – as he put it shortly before he died of Aids 18 years after the Lewis fight – a lifestyle that was 'permissive, fast and reckless'. That hardly made him unique among his fellow workers, but nor did it lessen the sadness that came with the news of his plight. As Lewis weighed the professional obligations imposed by Emanuel Steward, Morrison seemed to inhabit a world free of any shadow or doubt. He would fight and he would live and he would take each day, each challenge, as it came. His last distinction was his stoic acceptance that he had fashioned his own fate.

Some of that quality would continue to underpin Lennox Lewis's efforts to reinstate himself in the narrower confines of the ring, and it was a vital element in his next victory, which was over the hard and remorseless Ray Mercer seven months later at Madison Square Garden. It wasn't a spectacular fight, there were no knockdowns. Rather it was one of those collisions that carry you to the heart of boxing's most insistent imperative: a refusal to take a step back, an understanding that your first sign of weakness might very well be your last. Lewis won a majority decision over ten rounds but the announcement was greeted by a volley of boos. The scoring was narrow, as had been the shifting balance of the fight. One judge made it a draw and Lewis had margins of two rounds and one on the other cards.

Mercer, who won the Olympic heavyweight title in Seoul in 1998 while Lewis was taking the super-heavyweight prize with victory over Riddick Bowe, took defeat as hard as he had waged the fight, declaring, 'I don't know what the judges were watching. I don't think I lost the fight. I gave away a couple of rounds but I still think I did enough to win.'

Lewis was generous even as he disputed Mercer's claims. He said, 'I felt I was comfortably ahead but I don't take anything away from Ray Mercer. He is no slouch. Ray Mercer comes to fight all the time. He had everything to gain and nothing to lose. Ray gave Holyfield a great fight. He gives everybody a great fight.'

Maybe the most significant assessment came from Emanuel Steward. He said, 'Lennox Lewis moved up another level as a fighter tonight against someone as tough as Mercer. He showed that if he has got to go to war and gut it out he can do it. Lennox will perform a lot better than that but he won't often be required to show so much character in the ring. It was the kind of performance I can live with. It showed me that he wasn't going to run away when the going was tough.'

This was an encouraging observation for Lewis whose next fight would be the rematch against McCall. Fight? It would be many things, but a fight – no, it was never that. Indeed, in the opinion of almost everyone but McCall's promoter Don King it was something that should never have happened. And that it did, before the public gaze, was both a tragedy and an outrage.

Before he came to the ring it was evident from the briefest contact that McCall was deeply disturbed. A few days before the fight he had some of us in his hotel room. The experience was both bizarre and excruciating. It was to see a man coming in and out of what appeared to be the last of his senses.

Seven months before the fight, McCall was arrested on charges of possessing crack cocaine and marijuana. Soon after, he went into rehab. A few months later, however, he was arrested again for throwing a Christmas tree across a hotel lobby. He also spat at a policeman. He returned to rehab. That month King announced the McCall–Lewis fight. He also confirmed that McCall was in treatment but that he would be fine by fight time.

In the days before the fight, and his holding court in his hotel room, he had behaved eccentrically enough to cause still more alarm. One day he threw handfuls of dollars at a startled (but no doubt grateful) bagwoman on Las Vegas Boulevard. In his room he interrupted long, confusing monologues to make important phone calls then lapsed back into his staccato reflections, which were punctuated by sudden glares.

At fight time he had what could only be described as a public nervous breakdown.

The first three rounds were relatively routine. Lewis worked his jab according to the new regime of Steward and threw in a few stiff rights. It was at the end of the third round that everyone could see that something in McCall was seriously amiss. He refused to go to his corner, where his trainer, George Benton, wore an expression that mixed both alarm and a degree of resignation. McCall walked around the ring, distracted, immersed in some plainly troubling thoughts.

When the bell sounded for the fourth McCall continued his walkabout, now with his gloves protecting his head. He threw two punches in the round, at the end of which referee Mills Lane took his arm and led him back to his corner. There, McCall began to weep copiously as Lane and Benton tried to make sense of the situation. At one point McCall yelled, 'I want to fight, I need to fight.' However, in the 55 seconds of the fifth round that the referee permitted, McCall threw just one punch. When Lane signalled the fight was over, officially, Lewis winning on a technical knockout, McCall marched wordlessly to his dressing room.

Astonishingly, he appeared at a press conference the following day to say, 'My strategy – and I know it sounds absurd – was a kind of rope-a-dope. When I cried in the ring I was trying to get myself into an emotional state.'

Two months later, McCall was detained in a mental hospital after his wife applied for an emergency custody order. After examining McCall, a mental-health expert testified that he was mentally ill and in need of hospital care.

By then, most in boxing had accepted that what had happened in the Las Vegas ring was among the most shaming events in the entire history of boxing. That verdict was widely accepted before the sun rose on a day of fierce and angry moral accountancy. Lewis, amazingly enough, was criticised for failing to envelop McCall in a tide of relentless attack.

Almost sheepishly, he explained, 'At first when he was walking away I thought he was trying to trick me.' Mills Lane offered a little understatement, saying, 'I think the young man really needs to talk to someone in the mental-health field.' The WBC president Sulaimán, on whose watch the nightmare had unfolded, made a feeble attempt to distance himself and his organisation from the heart of the scandal when he said, 'I believe he had a nervous breakdown and maybe it was a reaction to the way he was living outside the ring.'

McCall's own trainer, George Benton, was most candid, though this did provoke the question why a man of his great reputation had not been more forthcoming before the fight. He declared, 'Lewis was in there with a lunatic. McCall was talking incoherently, but he had been doing that all week. It started a long time ago and I think it caught up with him.'

Inevitably, and with some justice, blame finally rested with Don King. Lewis's promoter Dan Duva claimed, 'Don King should not have made him available to fight. He was in no condition, mentally or physically, to fight. We tried six weeks ago to get Don to replace him.'

Still, though, looking back there is a certain twinge. It concerns the worry that it was maybe a little convenient to heap all the blame on the bogeyman of so many of boxing's misdeeds. King authored the scandal, worked it into his strategy for regained mastery of the heavyweight division, but he didn't do it in the depths of the night. He did it brazenly and without much opposition until it was too late, until Oliver McCall became an object of pity and scorn. No one came out of McCall's hotel room resolved to declare that the fight had to be stopped, that you couldn't send a man into the ring in such a pathetically fragile state of mind.

Yet if I – as just one close-up witness to the extent of McCall's confusion and agony – had felt any personal remorse, it hardly announced itself in the report I filed to London in the early hours of the morning. It started thus, 'Lennox Lewis is the WBC heavyweight champion of the world again but as he stepped into the desert night and his red stretch limousine he knew better than anyone this wasn't a resurrection. It was the professional crack-up of Oliver McCall, broken by drugs and the chaos of his desperate life. Lewis was awarded a technical knockout in the fifth round but his punches had been accessories after the fact. Defeat had come in the tortured mind of McCall, who wept, walked around the ring distractedly and refused to return to his corner. Lewis collected his title from a pugilistic madhouse.

'It was the night boxing, for reasons which scarcely bear scrutiny in a civilised society, offered up to Lewis a recovering junkie with severe mental problems. It wasn't the triumphant rise of Lennox Lewis. That might come later. It was the pitiful descent of Oliver McCall.'

It was a decline that at the time threatened to be bottomless and, indeed, McCall was 49 when he fought his last fight. It was in Legionowo, Poland, and he lost to Marcin Rekowski on a unanimous decision. At last, though, the arc of his collapse both in and out of the ring found a degree of relief. A lawyer in Florida who won him release from a six-year jail sentence following another round of drug-related charges offered him more than professional assistance. He gave him friendship and the means to win back some self-respect. It was a facility he always found elusive in boxing, which, worryingly, maybe said as much about the sport as the disorder of a deeply troubled life.

For Lewis, disentangling himself from the tragic convulsions of Oliver McCall and remaking his career and his old status as the man everyone had to beat – and on his own terms – took two more years of resolute work under the insistent, unforgiving tutelage of Emanuel Steward. His first defence of his regained WBC title took him to Lake Tahoe and the cloying embrace of the Nigerian spoiler Henry Akinwande. Frustrated by his opponent's shameless holding, Lewis had little chance to unfurl his most impressive power, and it was a relief for both him and his audience when the fight ended with Akinwande's disqualification in the fifth round.

Steward was especially incensed by the Lake Tahoe impasse, which after the McCall fiasco seemed to be still another troubling sign that heavyweight boxing in general, and Lewis's profile in particular, was in danger of becoming enmeshed in a death wish. Steward slammed his fist on a table and said that he was no longer prepared to squander time on readying Lennox Lewis, an outstanding talent, for meaningless fights. He wanted a serious opponent, someone against whom Lewis could properly reveal the growth of his technique and his nerve.

It was a hard and timely ultimatum and just three months later yielded a most spectacular result. Andrew Golota may not have been a byword for stability in the heavyweight division – indeed, there were times when his wildness in the ring dismayed all those who saw in him a huge and destructive power – but in one respect he met perfectly the requirements of both Lewis and Steward. As he had proved against Riddick Bowe in his previous two fights, in which he'd led on all cards before being disqualified, Andrew Golota came not to hold or to showboat but to fight; to fight, as powerfully and as dangerously as any heavyweight around.

Lewis was the narrowest of favourites at 6-5, but he mocked the odds as imperiously as he destroyed Golota in Atlantic City. It took him one minute 35 seconds of the first round, and the sound and the fury of it went into every corner of the fight business. Heavyweight affairs had a pulse again, *Sports Illustrated* noting the fact with a headline that said, 'Drawn and Cornered Lewis Woke Up the Heavyweight Division by Turning Out the Lights on Andrew Golota.'

It was a reality untouched by Golota's routine post-fight dramatics, this time an alarming seizure in the dressing room, which demanded resuscitation by paramedics and would lead to legal action against the doctor who administered a prescribed painkiller shortly before the fight. None of this, however, affected the meaning of Lewis's triumph. He said, 'I wanted rid of all the misfits and this was the last misfit.' Golota conceded, 'There was too much pressure. I was nervous.' Steward had some light back in his eyes, saying, 'Boxing saw some of the real Lennox Lewis tonight. Fighting like this, I believe he is out on his own.'

Five months later Lewis returned to Atlantic City to win his third defence of the title, against Shannon Briggs who, in his previous fight, had won a controversial decision that marked the end of George Foreman's career. Briggs jumped Lewis, landing some heavy blows in the first round. He swaggered back to his corner at the end of the round but by the fifth he was paying a heavy price for his impertinence. Lewis knocked him down three times before referee Frank Cappuccino ended it one minute 45 seconds into the round.

Steward wasn't happy with Lewis's early laxity but he agreed that his fighter had made another stride forward, produced a little more evidence that he had staked out new terrain.

He had served his own hard time on the long road that started in Sacramento. His prison gates, he had reason to hope, might also have swung open.

Chapter Twenty-one

Las Vegas, June 1997

Some images will never be erased and the one taken from here had a power to shock that made most everything else seen in a boxing ring seem sedate enough for the drawing room. Even by Mike Tyson's standards, it was conduct so abandoned, so primeval, he might have been disinterring the Stone Age.

It wasn't only that Tyson twice bit into Holyfield's ears, first his right and then his left – events, after all, not unprecedented in the history of boxing, though perhaps not performed with such naked savagery – more oppressive still was the feeling that all of us at ringside, the high rollers, the sensation-seekers, the hucksters and, yes, the writers too, had helped so vigorously in priming the pump of Mike Tyson's rage. Yes, surely, it was true we had come not so much to measure again what was left of his fighting power, and the superb combative instincts of the extraordinarily revived Evander Holyfield, but to see what a deeply troubled man might do when the odds facing him became insuperable.

Now we knew as we rushed to make our excoriating judgements after seeing his breakdown, his wild charges across the suddenly choked and chaotic ring, but maybe there was a moment when we might have stopped and examined our own status. Was it that of precise, sure-footed arbiters of right and wrong – or of voyeurs gifted with a sensational story to tell?

Some months later Tyson said to me, 'If somebody comes from hell, you shouldn't be too surprised if there are times when he goes back there. That's what I did. I had so much anger I couldn't control it.'

Late on the night, when the gory details had been gathered in, including the fact that a substantial part of Holyfield's right ear spat out by Tyson had been placed in an ice bucket and mislaid on the ambulance ride to hospital, the referee Mills Lane made a speech that still lingers in the mind. He came somewhat haltingly to his decision to disqualify Tyson after the second bite in the third round, but when he stood up to address a crowded room he was in no doubt as to what he had been forced to adjudicate upon.

He said that everyone in boxing, and maybe all of sport, had been called to a moment of profound reflection. Was the juggernaut of money and sensation, of cynical deal-making and the acceptance that anything might pass critical – moral – examination, if the profit was sufficiently big enough, past a point of no return? He wondered what glory, what redemption there could be in what we had seen.

It was something to think about, certainly, at least when the stories had been written and the jokes had been made. Jim Murray of the *Los Angeles Times* walked that line with his usual gusto, suggesting that boxing was now in need of pre-fight rabies shots.

And so it went, in indignation as raw as Holyfield's tattered ears, as intense as any biblical denouncement. Inevitably so, because in many areas, and not least the Tyson camp, there was an astonishing level of justification for the call of Mills Lane for some light to be shone into the dark. Tyson, initially at least, seemed bemused by the outrage all around him. Indeed, it seemed to fuel his own sense of being wronged. He said, 'My career was on the line. It was my retaliation. Holyfield should have been disqualified for using his head. That's illegal too.'

One of Tyson's co-managers, John Horne, who soon enough would be in legal dispute with his friend and sponsor, alongside Don King, was equally scornful. He yelled at reporters, 'A little nick on his ear don't mean nothing. My fighter had a three-inch cut.'

Holyfield needed eight stitches and plastic surgery and a tranquillising shot to come down from the shock, which sent him leaping into the air when the first bite came in. He said, 'I thought my ear had fell off. Blood was all over. He spat the mouthpiece out when he bit me.'

It was surreal and disturbing and it made you feel, as Lane so eloquently suggested, that you were part of an anarchic world that had come to make its own rules – restraints so light they could be shrugged away and reinvented according to almost any need.

The allocation of blame, self-appraisal, some cry for older values that had something to do with the pride and dignity and mutual respect of natural-born fighting men might, on that long night, have been the properties of another universe. In tracing the breakdown it was necessary to go back to the first fight on the night of 9 November 1996. It was then that the dangerous extremity of Tyson's situation had been put, quite thunderously, into place.

Before the fight I had a theory, but one too irresolutely held, that Holyfield might indeed confound the odds that made him a 25-1 underdog. I put it to a man whom I held – and would continue to do so – in the highest respect. It was Teddy Atlas, the knowing fight man who had tried so hard, so early, to contain the chaos of Tyson's nature. I explained that I believed Holyfield had the fighting character and the movement to batter Tyson out of the comfort zone created by his brutal subjection of hand-picked opponents.

Holyfield wouldn't bombard himself with signs of the cross on his way to the ring like Frank Bruno, he wouldn't capsize beneath phantom punches in the manner of Bruce Seldon – or come to collect his money and his Andy Warhol moment of fame in the abject way of Peter

McNeeley. No, he would do as he always did. He would come to fight to his very limits, and who really knew how the relaunched Mike Tyson would react to the most serious challenge he had faced since walking out of prison? No one fought with more passion or self-belief than Evander Holyfield.

Atlas listened and nodded from time to time and then said, 'It's a nice theory but there is one big problem. The Evander Holyfield you are talking about doesn't exist any more. He has been to the well too often, the best of him has gone. In his last fight against Bobby Czyz, who is not a true heavyweight, he looked to be struggling seriously. He looked worn out, dried up. Fighting Tyson is just a step too far.'

It was a belief deeply embedded in the Tyson camp, and some of its expression went beyond mere arrogance. Co-manager Rory Holloway brought pre-fight rhetoric to a new low when he claimed that Holyfield was at risk of leaving town not only without glory but in a coffin.

One day the press were ferried by bus to Don King's house in the Las Vegas suburbs, where we were received by a Tyson whose mood swung from the surly to a strange, almost domesticated amiability. He said that he no longer cared what the world, and especially the Fourth Estate, thought about him, wrote about him. He had children to look after, a relationship to forge with Dr Monica Turner, a graduate of the prestigious Georgetown University, and if his reflections were sometimes troubling they were now mainly concerned with explaining himself to his children.

One morning he had gone to the grave of Sonny Liston in the cemetery under the Las Vegas airport flight path. He had taken flowers and said a prayer and said that he understood how it was to be an outsider. Liston had died in mysterious circumstances – some believed from a Mafia hit – and Tyson had wanted to show his respect for a fellow loner who had been required to fight his own battles without seeking anyone's sympathy.

That was how he came into the ring that first time against Holyfield: bristling with aggression and the determination to re-announce that he was operating on his old level. He didn't need the affection or the respect of the world. He didn't need anything beyond the force of his own ability. After his slaughter of Bruno, and cuffing aside of McNeeley, Mathis and Seldon, he came into the battle not only sure of himself but also buoyed by that general feeling expressed so forcefully by Atlas over our morning coffee. Five years earlier, when the fight was originally made and Tyson was coming out from under the Tokyo pall, Holyfield had the momentum of his world-title victory. He was 30 and at a beautifully shaped prime.

Now the main question, I was reluctantly persuaded, was not would he win but would he make something of a fight. The Nevada Athletic Commission demanded that the condition of his heart be thoroughly investigated once again, and some pay-TV salesmen – concerned about the public's suspicion of another Tyson blow-out – offered a sliding tariff determined by how many rounds Holyfield survived. He had lost three of his last seven fights and, compared to Tyson, he was subdued when he entered the ring.

Subdued, that was, in the way of a coiled cobra. If he had carried signs of erosion, they fell away like so many discarded scales.

The first round was a surge of action, a testing of strength and a statement of resolve, and it was immediately apparent that neither fighter countenanced the idea of yielding an inch. Both men sought to claim the centre of the ring. They bombarded each other with punches, clinched with the force of stags locking their horns.

Tyson, at 15 stone 12 pounds, was 7 pounds heavier but his reach was inferior by 6 inches, and that very quickly seemed to be the more significant statistic. Most apparent of all was the fact that, once again, Holyfield had come to fight with everything he had. In the second round he landed a left that not only stunned Tyson but, he claimed at the end of the fight, left him strangely disorientated as he attempted to respond to Holyfield's aggression and sharpen his own attacks. Later he would claim that referee Mitch Halpern had repeatedly ignored Holyfield's unscrupulous use of his head and that became an obsession from the sixth when Holyfield's brow caused – inadvertently, it seemed to the impartial observer – a small cut above Tyson's left eye. Much more influential was a fierce Holyfield left hand that put Tyson down in the same round and announced, irreversibly, that a stunning pattern had been imposed. Suddenly you knew, and more surely than in Tokyo, that Tyson was under an investigation he was unlikely to survive.

Inevitably he produced flashes of menace, but the sea change of the sixth became a full-scale storm in the seventh. Holyfield backed Tyson up with a rhythm of punches that spoke of soaring confidence – and an absolute rejection of the idea that he had come into the fight searching desperately for the last remnants of the quality that had made him a great fighter. Tyson, in retreat almost at Holyfield's will, threw punches laden with more optimism than accurately applied power, and later Holyfield gave a clinical account of how he had taken over the fight. He said of his former Olympic teammate and sparring partner of the eighties, 'I've been watching him for years and years and when he dips and throws a left hook you either get hit or you hit him first with a right hand. You have to beat him to the punch.'

As the fight wore on, and Tyson was worn down, Holyfield almost invariably did. Desperately, Tyson made his last stand in the tenth but Holyfield, as he had in the sixth and seventh rounds, refused to surrender any of his momentum. He delivered a stream of uninterrupted punches, most notably a withering combination and a hard right to the head, and when the bell sounded Tyson had his back to the ropes and his thoughts, as much as he could unscramble them, were concerned entirely with survival. He staggered 37 seconds into the 11th round before the referee wrapped him in his arms and said it was over. Later, Tyson said he could not remember the last round, or so much of the fight. 'I got caught in something strange,' he sighed. There could be only one, brutal response. It was that he had been enveloped by a superior, better prepared fighter. One, indeed, living in a reality that had demanded something more than the mere re-furling of old and, it now seemed, time-expired menace.

Tyson claimed to be less than traumatised by his defeat. What was the worst that could happen? Monday morning would come around and the odds were that he would be offered another fight contract of around $30 million. That would cover a few packs of diapers, not to mention unlimited supplies of whatever else he deemed necessary to get through a night.

And, of course, the contract arrived as he imagined it would, even as he treated the livid bruises Holyfield had imposed. It was precisely according to his casual estimate. He would go in against Holyfield for another $30 million. But what he couldn't quite grasp was that maybe life would never again be quite so seamless, so self-fulfilling in its crazed munificence. Perhaps that was the discovery he made early in the second fight with Holyfield, one that shocked him right down to his bones and drove him, finally, into an understanding that even he would one day be required to operate within the limits of a constraining world. It was one way to explain the rage and the abandonment that carried him so wildly over the edge.

For Tyson, some consequences were immediate. He was fined $3 million – the maximum 10 per cent of his fee that the Nevada Athletic Commission could impose by law – and was banned from the ring for 12 months. In Las Vegas there were arguments that he should never again be licensed to fight in Nevada, that even in a city for which turning a profit was as fundamental as breathing there was a limit to how far the civic conscience could be stretched.

He was back in the ring in 18 months, of course, and where else but Las Vegas? After some showy agonising, the commission handed back his licence after hearing Tyson's acts of contrition. The first one was expressed a week after the fight when, abandoning his argument that Holyfield had provoked the horror with his headbutting, he announced on television, 'I just snapped. I couldn't tell you why I acted exactly as I did.'

But if Tyson got back his right to fight, there was no doubt that he had lost something integral to his meaning in the ring. It was also true that a respected member of the Athletic Commission would soon receive a phone call from the governor of Nevada, Kenny Guinn, telling him that his services were no longer required. It was Jim Nave, a vet who had grown up in Missouri and ran an animal hospital out on Tropicana Avenue. He was the one commissioner to say no to Tyson. The governor thanked him for his services and told him that he would be replaced by Amy Ayoub, who had been occasionally seen at the fights but was better known for her political work, which included some on the governor's election campaign. She would be the new colleague of the chairman, Dr Elias Ghanem, a general practitioner, Luther Mack, the multi-millionaire owner of a hamburger franchise, and two big men in the casino industry, Glen Carano and Lorenzo Fertitta.

Nave's dismissal caused considerable shock in boxing circles in the city and the nation. He was widely seen as a stalwart fighter for decent values in sport, and John McCain, Republican Senator for Arizona and presidential candidate, said that Dr Nave had been a great force in legislation aimed at tightening controls in boxing.

After some initial reluctance Nave agreed to speak to me. He said that he made his decision after several days of 'rassling' with his conscience. He said he would make no judgement on his fellow commission members and suggested that the economic impact of one fight, even a Mike Tyson fight, tended to be overestimated. 'I wouldn't have spent ten years of my life working with people capable of making such a decision simply for money, one night's profits. People sneer at Las Vegas all the time. I'm used to it. The casinos are one thing and there is another side to this city. But the point is I had my own position on Tyson. I turned him down on three points which I thought were too important to ignore.

'The main reason I said no to Tyson was that I couldn't get one question out of my head. Why had all his counselling and psychiatric help come so late? What had been happening in the 15 months since the Holyfield incident? Of course, that cast doubts in my mind about Tyson's remorse. Did he not think he had a problem? There was also the question of premeditation in the act of biting Holyfield's ears. Was he truly sorry for what happened? Then there was the business in Maryland.' That was Tyson's road rage attack when he was alleged to have struck two men in the wake of a fender-bender on a day when he said he was preoccupied by a desire to buy a Harley-Davidson motorbike. He was sentenced to a year in jail, reduced to three months after the pleading of his lawyers that he was facing myriad financial disasters.

Despite the admirable Nave's defence of his former commission colleagues, it was still hard not to conclude that Vegas had considered the degree of notoriety Tyson had brought to the city with his cannibalistic antics and then measured it against the extraordinary columns of commercial profit the event had created. There was, however, one certainty. If the commodity was still financially viable, it had undoubtedly undergone a profound change.

Curiosity over his next performance, his next outrage, would be immense, and if it generated anything approaching the profits of Tyson–Holyfield II, well, that reality still carried more weight than a thousand platitudes. The bite fight had shattered all records. It produced the biggest gross in boxing history. More than 18,000 fans in the MGM Garden Arena paid $17,227,000. Household pay-per-view soared to 1.99 million and brought in $99,822,000. Six million dollars more came from 1,625 closed circuit locations in the United States. Foreign sales in 97 countries generated another $21,240,000. The gambling 'drop' in the casinos was huge.

Such was the underpinning of the final phase of Mike Tyson's career. It would stretch eight years beyond the moment he first bit into Holyfield's ear and cast himself forever in the role of the most ungovernable of all major fighters.

For those of us who would follow him to the end, who joined him in boxing outposts like Louisville, Kentucky, and Memphis, Tennessee, there would be the implicit understanding that we were no longer around to record his achievements but, rather, his ability to avoid one ultimate misadventure. We understood, deep down, that he would never again win another significant fight. He would never again be promoted by Don King; never again have the belief that he could break all the rules and still emerge with a triumph measured easily enough in material terms. It would take him six years to win his legal action against King, charging serial underpayment of ring earnings. He claimed $100 million, but when he was awarded $19 million it was immediately claimed by the US tax authorities.

And so it went down the years – a win here, an eruption there, and, in its last reaches, an unstoppable tide of defeat, a breaking of the fierce spell that, with each convulsion, you were a little more certain he would never be able to restore.

His first fight after the biting was against the workmanlike South African Frans Botha, who laboured diligently to forge a lead on all scorecards until he was devastated in the fifth round by a right-hand blow Tyson unearthed from somewhere in his past. Botha, advancing with a growing confidence, walked into the punch. He made two attempts to get back on his feet before subsiding. He had been undone by his premature belief that he was doing enough to take his share of the plunder from what was left of Mike Tyson.

Tyson, perhaps fretting that an obligation to produce another brutal sensation had not been met, shone a little light on an incident at the end of the first round that had cost him a deduction of two points. Tyson held Botha's arm in a grasp, which his opponent punched out of with his free hand. 'What I was trying to do,' Tyson deadpanned, 'was break his arm.'

Ten months later Tyson was paid $8 million for a few seconds more than three minutes' work against the short and cowed Orlin Norris. Again Tyson was deducted two points, this time for knocking his opponent down after the bell had sounded for the end of the first round. Norris didn't come out for the second, telling the fight doctor that he had injured his knee when going down. Tyson was outraged, saying that Norris had invented his injury to avoid certain defeat. Tyson had certainly dominated the first round. The ruling was no contest, and the commission threatened to withhold the purse of the erring Tyson. They relented after a week of deliberation but, still, it seemed like the end of something. And so it was. Tyson would never again fight in Las Vegas. Instead he was taking us on the road; a diminished circus but one that still carried a certain compulsion.

He fought the obscure Julius Francis in Manchester. Francis announced his serious intent by cutting a deal with the *Sun*, which paid him to advertise the newspaper on the soles of his boxing boots. Francis delivered satisfactorily enough, laying prone before the fight was ended by TKO in the second round.

The British promoter Frank Warren, for one, still believed there was some considerable cachet – and profit – in owning Tyson's rights. He entertained Tyson royally in London, buying him a watch said to be worth hundreds of thousands of pounds. Perhaps unsurprisingly, Tyson was back in Britain six months later, dismantling Lou Savarese in all of 32 seconds at Hampden Park, Glasgow.

It wasn't easy to believe Tyson was fighting with much serious intent any more. What, you had to ask, was any longer at stake beyond the last pickings, which were to be taken as comfortably as he could?

Andrew Golota, in his tumultuous way, might have threatened that ambition three months later in Auburn Hills, Michigan, but at the end of the second round he claimed to have suffered a broken bone in his head. This caused a degree of cynical speculation, but the fact was that until his withdrawal he clearly represented a threat with his wild but potentially destructive punching. Tyson was given the decision but that was wiped away when he was found to have tested positive for marijuana. So it was another no contest, a little more slippage in the meaning and the fading momentum of Tyson's career.

In another year he was in Copenhagen, partying more strenuously than he was required to perform in the ring, where the local hero, Brian Nielsen, quit on his stool before the start of the sixth round.

I found I couldn't abandon the Tyson watch. I couldn't spend so much time trying to absorb and tell a story that had been so compelling for so long, had carried me so far beyond the dramas of the boxing ring, and then just drift away. It had, after all, been a story that had filled me with both wonder and despair. Wonder at the furies and the resilience of one young man's life. Despair at the elusiveness of a sense that any of it – the brutal glory or the unshakeable pain – would find a moment of resolution, still less the likelihood of some softening of the light at the end of the road.

It was also true that not all the last miles – the sitting around in hotel rooms soiled, to his amusement, by his companion pigeons – were marked by an absence of some of the old force. Or the belief that around him there were still stories to be told that made him, right to the end, someone who could not be casually assigned to the past.

Chapter Twenty-two

New York, March 1999

Once, I walked down Seventh Avenue in the company of Muhammad Ali, and now as I did so with Lennox Lewis I couldn't but remember again the exhilaration of that time 22 years earlier. That had been one of the most uplifting days of my professional life. I was strolling with someone who could not only bring Manhattan to a halt but also make a passable claim to being the king of the world. However, who could deny that the big man now walking in his footsteps carried a certain lustre of his own?

No, it wasn't that of Ali. Lewis had neither conquered nor beguiled the world beyond the boxing ring and, indeed, he was yet to be crowned the undisputed heavyweight champion of the world. He couldn't reinvent himself as easily as he might pick out a new tie. He couldn't stare down the world and then make it laugh. What he had done, though – and it was an achievement that for me made him uniquely admirable at this late stage of the history of his sport – was to get where he wanted to be without compromise. He could say that in his moment of triumph he would have no backroom deals to honour, no favours to repay.

He would fight Evander Holyfield in Madison Square Garden to unify the three world titles for one simple reason. It was his absolute right, hard and honestly won. He had a mantra that was widely scorned both in the boxing trade and my own. He said he was on 'Mission Impossible', a quest to fight his way through all the politics and the duplicity, all the horse trading and the paybacks, and then to raise his arms to the sky.

Going to Madison Square Garden, an old memory flared. It was of being surprised by a pulverising bear hug from behind while standing in the lobby of the Mirage casino in Las Vegas. It was delivered by the big man, who the night before had beaten Levi Billups next door at Caesars on a unanimous decision. It wasn't a great fight against a great fighter but Lewis had shown again that he was a heavyweight of quality and much, if a little too often, latent power. He said he was on the trail of the new champion of the world, Evander Holyfield, and he would catch him soon enough. He said it with a boyish enthusiasm. But seven years had passed since then and the trail had gone cold with dismaying frequency. Now, though, Holyfield was in his sights and his intimidating range and it was easy to believe that his time had finally arrived.

That optimism on behalf of Lewis survived several visits to Holyfield workouts in a basement gym in the Bowery. Holyfield, as always, worked ferociously, but then it was also true that no 36-year-old on earth had made heavier demands on his own body. If someone as knowing as Teddy Atlas considered him a shell before his wars with Tyson, what could anyone make of him now? My belief was that he was a warrior who had come to the end of his time. However, he was emphatic that he would win, and he knew precisely when. It would be in the third round. He had been told this by an unimpeachable authority. His source was God.

'I'm anointed to win,' he said. 'I have confidence in the word of God. I'm not predicting, I'm telling you. I will knock him out in the third round.'

Unfortunately for Holyfield, God apparently had a prior engagement and was unable to enforce his fancy. Also missing was the justice of Solomon.

Holyfield didn't knock Lewis out in the third round, though he had one of his better rounds, and after 12 rounds he was awarded a draw. It was a decision that still has the power to sicken. Lewis won the fight so overwhelmingly that the only relief for my own share of rage came early the following morning when the New York newspapers were delivered to my hotel room, where I had spent the night attempting to define the scale of the injustice suffered by Lewis. The front page of the *Post* brought the reassurance that the world hadn't gone entirely mad. A huge banner headline proclaimed, 'It Stinks.' New York mayor Rudy Giuliani was among the outraged, saying, 'I am embarrassed as a New Yorker. I know boxing as well as I know being mayor. This is a travesty of what happened.'

In the first shock of the announcement I turned to my good friend Sri Sen, the boxing correspondent of *The Times* who won a Blue at Oxford, and said, 'Surely to God this is wrong.' He nodded solemnly and said, 'Lewis boxed his ears off.'

The South African judge, Stanley Christodoulou, scored it 116–113 for Lewis. Eugenia Williams of New Jersey gave it to Holyfield 115–113. Britain's Larry O'Connell made it a draw. Williams won 'substantial' damages after the London *Sunday Mirror* alleged her scoring was the result of bribes worth thousands of dollars. My allegation was fortunately not actionable. I merely said that she could not have had any serious knowledge of that which she had been asked to judge.

The case of O'Connell was more complicated. He was an experienced fight man, a referee, but he brought to New York considerable pressure. Just how much was underlined for me by Don Majeski, the ubiquitous matchmaker and fight man, who had helped O'Connell check into his hotel room and then taken him to a nearby coffee shop.

As they talked Majeski noticed tears forming in O'Connell's eyes. He believed they were the result of a combination of exhilaration and relief; exhilaration to be working one of the biggest fights in years and relief that he had survived what many believed to be a poor night's work at the Thomas & Mack Center in Las Vegas a month earlier, when he was the only judge to give the Ghanaian welterweight Ike Quartey the verdict over the coruscating world champion Oscar De La Hoya. 'I thought that might have been the end of my judging in America,' he told Majeski. 'Now I can hardly believe I'm doing the biggest fight of them all, Lewis versus Holyfield. It really is amazing.'

Majeski, who had close contact with the boxing authorities, had formed the view that O'Connell's reprieve was an example of WBC president José Sulaimán's belief that when a good judge had a bad night the best reaction was to send him straight back into the firing line. But if it was a good move for an embattled ringside official, it was a disaster for Lennox Lewis. Afterwards, O'Connell was almost as stunned as the victim. He said, 'I scored it as I saw it. I thought Lennox Lewis won the fight but I scored it round by round.'

There might have been considerably more heat on O'Connell but for the even more bizarre scoring of Eugenia Williams. She reacted defiantly to a huge tide of criticism, sued the English newspaper and defended herself vigorously when the FBI investigated her financial affairs. However, there was one charge she could not rebut. It was written down, in her own hand on her own scorecard. It said that she had given the fifth round to Holyfield. The fifth round was the one Lewis dominated most profoundly, the one that made it look like Holyfield was growing old before our eyes, the one that left Emanuel Steward in a fever of regret that his man had not applied a brutal coup de grâce.

Williams said she wasn't interested in what television said. She didn't have the benefit of television when she scored the fight. She scored the punches and she saw Holyfield land more of them through the fight and, yes, in the fifth round. In her defence it was claimed that her view was partly obscured by photographers. Unimpressed, Hugh McIlvanney suggested that a reasonably competent judge could have scored such a one-sided fight with the help of pictures from a space satellite.

The more the night wore on, the more the rage intensified. I was back in San Antonio, recoiling at the injustice heaped upon Pernell Whitaker as it now descended on Lennox Lewis. Wherever you turned there was an angry denunciation of the party line of promoter Don King, whose influence here at Madison Square Garden seemed to have been no less pervasive than it had on that night of ignominy in Texas.

When the fighters emerged from their dressing rooms there was a fresh surge of disbelief over the decision. Lewis looked as though he had taken a stroll in Central Park. Holyfield was battered and ready for hospital, where he would be taken almost immediately. He left praising the performance of Lewis before adding, 'I did all I could, the judges make the decision. I can still get him. I guess I did the best I could, this was not my best though.'

King said that of course there would be a rematch. The public would demand it. It would be a desire rising in the blood of the people. Lewis shook his head and his manager Frank Maloney shouted, 'Lennox Lewis, the people's champion, is now leaving the building.' King's response was sotto voce. 'Not a smart move,' he said. But we had had enough smart moves for one night. We had also seen a fight for the undisputed heavyweight championship of the world stolen so blatantly it might have been a mugging.

One of New York's finest offered an unequivocal view. He said he had been on anti-pickpocket duty but there had been nothing he could do to prevent the grand larceny. George Foreman sent his commiserations to Buckingham Palace, saying, 'The Queen and all her subjects can be proud. Lennox Lewis undoubtedly proved that he is the best heavyweight in the world today. He should forget about tonight, it's over, just get up, dust your pants off, fight him again and knock him out next time.'

The tide of criticism flowed ceaselessly. The gifted world light-heavyweight champion Roy Jones said, 'I just feel ashamed about what happened tonight. I love Evander Holyfield but Lennox Lewis did not lose it.' Richie Giachetti, who had trained Larry Holmes and for a little time had been asked to try to contain the furies of Mike Tyson, slammed his scribbled scorecard on my ringside desk. It made Lewis a huge winner.

Budd Schulberg, my ringside companion when Marvin Hagler and Tommy Hearns had so spectacularly relegated the scoring judges to the role of slacked-jawed spectators, was also among the bemused. 'What's happened to the British?' he asked me. 'Why aren't they rioting?'

Those normally reserved about the value of statistics could only read the figures and shake their heads once more. Lewis threw 364 jabs and landed 187. Holyfield responded with 171, 52 of which scored. Lewis connected with 161 of 249 power punches, Holyfield with 78 of 214 thrown.

Before he left the building, Lewis said it would be some time before he could properly absorb what had happened to him. 'Right now,' he told me, 'I just find it too hard to believe that they did that.'

If he had solace in the night it was maybe the view of the one judge, Christodoulou, to score in his favour. He spoke soberly but with a sharp tone in his voice. He said, 'I don't want to comment on the scoring of my fellow judges but I've been around boxing for a long time, 36 years, and I think I know how to score a fight. In my view Lewis won the fight.'

Going back to the hotel, my yellow cab driver was silent. But he had noted my accent and when I paid him he grimaced and said, 'I saw the fight in a bar. Boy, did they do a number on your guy.'

Then, as the sun rose over Manhattan, I took another look at the newspapers strewn across the desk. The veteran columnist, and dogged critic of Don King, Jack Newfield, wrote under the headline 'Robbery', 'It was the worst decision I have ever seen in any championship. I watched every punch and I had Lennox Lewis ahead by ten rounds to two. There is no shadow of doubt he should have won. I believed the world heavyweight crown was sacred but not any more. It was like the Vatican had been burgled. It was a disgusting decision. It was the crime of the century. Don King had everything to lose if Lewis won because he controls Evander Holyfield. Now he is looking for another pay day when the rematch is staged . . .'

I'd seen enough, read enough, felt angry enough, written enough, and so I went down to have a coffee and then walked to Fifth Avenue to attend Mass at St Patrick's Cathedral. When it was time to make the sign of peace with a handshake, the man in the next pew looked at me dubiously and declined. Maybe I was a little worn down by the New York night, perhaps he thought I was a panhandler who had wandered in from the street. However, I did muster the grace not to say that if I looked bad perhaps he should have seen Evander Holyfield.

Eight months later at the Thomas & Mack Center in Las Vegas, I couldn't speak for myself but Holyfield looked impressively healed. And Lewis? He carried the serenity of someone who believed it was within his power to put right a terrible wrong. I shared his faith, picking him to win in the sixth round. It was, looking back, something I wanted to believe with a fervency that had maybe never quite gripped me so strongly before. The rematch, I suppose, had become in my eyes rather more than a fight. I saw it – maybe eccentrically, given all the years I had been around this business – as a potential last, and particularly satisfying, chapter in a morality tale.

Perhaps it was partly to do with this that I sought out again the company of Jim Nave, the man who had stood so firmly against the relicensing of Mike Tyson and paid for it with his place on the Nevada Athletic Commission. We had breakfast at the Mirage, one that stretched out for some hours. It was not necessary to force him on the issue of boxing's latest crisis of ethics. First, though, he told me something of his life in Missouri as a farm boy whose love of animals – which would lead to his election as the president of the American association of veterinarians – was matched only by his passion for the sport he had come to defend so selflessly. 'I helped my mother bring up three other children after our father was murdered,' he said. 'He was shot, coldly, in the chest five times, and after that life was quite hard. I worked the farm, paid my way through college and then volunteered for Vietnam. Before leaving for that unpopular war – I thought my country needed me – I was stationed in New Jersey and spent all my leave walking around New York City. For a country boy, it was the most wonderful place to see. I barely had the funds to ride the subway but I didn't need money. I could walk and I could see and on one occasion I went into the restaurant of the great Jack Dempsey and shook hands with him.

'Boxing has always been my inspiration and I want the best for it now as ever. People ask me if I'm bitter but I ask them, "Why should I be?" I had 12 great years doing something I loved and my feeling for the sport was never conditioned by the privileges it gave me. Sometimes I think of boxing as an alcoholic. It has got to go right down before it can heal itself. It has got to kiss the concrete. There have been so many blows, so many scandals. I don't say, "I told you so," when I discuss the Tyson affair. I just did what I thought was right at the time. If it hadn't been proved that he assaulted those motorists in Washington, if he didn't go back to prison, if he didn't behave in the way he did in the Botha and Norris fights, I would still believe I made the right decision. When you are dealing with a situation like that you have just one option. You do the best you can with the facts you have.'

Talking with Nave was to have a decent perspective served with the black coffee. It was one of a man who had said that boxing meant more than the conveniences of Mike Tyson and Don King. This was a view he didn't offer as a passing soundbite but as a stand on which he knew one of the most rewarding aspects of his life might well founder. It did soon enough but, as Nave was quick to say, he would always have chosen that over a single betrayal of the sport that had become so entwined in his broader view of life.

This was Nave on his memory of the great Hagler–Hearns fight of 1985: 'As long as I live, I will remember the moment Hearns hit Hagler with a perfect shot. It was everything Hearns wanted it to be. It hit Hagler flush in the face as he was coming in. Hagler stopped, momentarily, and then he kept on coming. What a lesson in life, in determination, in taking a shot that went into your bones and questioned every ounce of your resolve. It was extraordinary. It was the greatest fighting I had ever seen and when it was over I just sat in my seat for so long thinking about all of it. They were cleaning up the arena when I walked out.'

Nave's point, again, was that when you see something like that you are obliged to make a covenant with that which produced it. The essential elements of the deal were surely self-evident. It had to be bound in honour and respect.

Nave was at Madison Square Garden for Lewis–Holyfield I. He took his daughter and they sat some way from ringside. At the end of the fight she turned to him and said, 'Well, Lewis won that easily.' But Nave wasn't so sure. He had his opera glasses trained on the ring and then he shook his head and said, 'I think there may be a problem.' He could see Sulaimán, the WBC president, holding his head in his hands. 'I think they may be calling it a draw.'

Now, he said, 'I can't remember a time when boxing was in bigger need of great fights and undisputed champions, men who are looked up to right across their sport and in the wider world. We really need those great fights. We need for people to be reminded how great boxing can be. We can't keep having one scandal after another. I read this morning that this fight might not make a million pay-per-view sales. If this is so, it is a most serious warning. We are in a crisis if the best fight out there cannot make a million sales. There is a hardcore of fight fans but they are no longer captive. Maybe a guy has three choices. He can buy the fight for $49, he can watch a nice movie, or he can really please his wife by taking her out for dinner. With the kind of fights we have been having recently, it is getting harder to convince the fight fan that he should make the first choice. I find this tragic.'

There was plenty to digest when I took some desert air, and still more when I collided with Mickey Duff, who for so many years had been the most influential and best connected British fight man at home and abroad. Duff had handled 20 world champions. Unlike the self-appointed protector and aficionado Nave, he had been involved in boxing at every level and in every aspect. A boy refugee from the pogroms of Poland, the grandson of a rabbi, he was a fighter in his youth, a manager, matchmaker, promoter and, when his instincts were strong enough, a prodigious gambler.

It was in that last capacity that he still so fiercely despised the scoring of a draw at Madison Square Garden. He had lost heavily but here he would confidently seek to both recoup and profit. He gave me a copy of his recently published autobiography before continuing his trawl of the fight fauna of the boxing capital, with whom no doubt he would spend much of the day trading old stories and theories on the coming fight. He insisted Lewis would win again but this time he would get the decision.

I riffled the pages of Duff's book and came to a passage that returned me to the breakfast table I'd shared with Jim Nave. It started with a question that could rarely have been more relevant to the future of boxing. 'How would I like to be remembered by boxing people?' Duff asked himself. 'I would like to be remembered as someone who knew his business as a tough but fair negotiator, who always acted in what he thought were the best interests of his boxers as a good manager and matchmaker. I don't expect to be remembered as a man who only made life-and-death matches. Hopefully, I will be remembered as someone who made fights in the best interests of the boxers I was representing but at all times with regard for the public who were paying money to watch.'

It didn't seem too much to ask of a sport that, after two decades of mouth-watering profit, was indeed passing through the crisis Jim Nave had feared. Lewis–Holyfield II would not make a million sales. It would fail by no less than 150,000. However, if the financial horizons had contracted, and Don King had been required to cover Holyfield's $15 million half-share of the fighters' purse, it had been at no cost to the fascination of those of us who had arrived in Las Vegas still deeply exercised by the sense of injustice that had filled Madison Square Garden.

Before Lewis broke training camp in the Poconos I had driven up from New York to see him run through the late-fall woods of russet and gold and work with impressive composure – and power – under the rapt attention of Emanuel Steward. It seemed to me there was one key question: how much more aggressive and commanding would he be in the rematch? There was a trace of irritation in the answer he gave while stretched out in his luxurious log cabin. Its source was the implication that his performance in New York, for all its technical mastery, had lacked a certain authority and, yes, maybe a little moral courage.

He was also irked by the weight of American opinion that Holyfield had suffered a bad night in the Garden and that he would be restored to full working order in Las Vegas. This viewpoint was led by the former editor of *The Ring* magazine, the loquacious but always quotable Bert Randolph Sugar, who had declared, 'Evander had a bad night in the

Garden but he doesn't ever have two in a row. Lennox has a lot of talent but Evander is just more of a fighter.'

Lewis said, 'For me, for most fighters, it is not a question of courage, that's just not part of it. You prove your courage every time you step into the ring. If you didn't have it, you wouldn't go in, full stop. Once you're in the ring you have decisions to make and the most important one, I'll always believe, is to do with how you're going to win the fight. Knockouts, how good you look, all that stuff, may be important for your profile with the public, it might affect your next paycheque, but first you win. So how do you do it? I was very sure about what was I going to do at the Garden. And I did it. I wasn't going to go inside, at least not in the early stages, because that was what Riddick Bowe did the one time he lost to Holyfield.

'Evander wants you to go inside, he wants you to come to him, that's his game – hey, against someone like me or Bowe, with our build and weapons, it's his only game. So there I was fighting for the undisputed heavyweight title of the world, the thing for which I'd gone through all those trials and tribulations, and was I going to give Holyfield any advantages, was I going to play his game? Why would I do that? My job wasn't to play hero, it was to win, just to win.

'People keep telling me I should have finished off Holyfield when I appeared to have him beaten in the fifth round. But they weren't in the ring. They didn't have all their life's hopes at stake, and they didn't know how completely in command I felt. Maybe in the second fight I will be less cautious, more assertive when I know I have hurt him, but basically I still believe I was right in the Garden.'

Lewis's logic, while plainly at odds with the instincts of his hugely experienced trainer, was sound as far as it went, but it didn't stop me feeling uneasy on the drive back to New York – and all the way to the moment I took my seat at ringside in Las Vegas with that sixth-round knockout prediction already in stone.

It didn't help that in some of his pre-fight interrogations Lewis had been less emphatic about the sweep of his strategy. In one of them he said, 'Maybe I was a bit cautious in the first fight – I will be less so this time.' That certainly was the urging of Emanuel Steward, who on the eve of the fight said, 'Usually I have a dream, a vision. I can see it very clearly, but not this time. I just have this feeling that there will be some kind of sensation, maybe something like Hagler and Hearns, something wild, off the graph.'

It almost was, at least the one I had charted in my mind ever since that shocking announcement in Madison Square Garden. Certainly, I would never be so drained, so enervated through the course of watching a single fight. You may say, probably correctly, that I was in the grip of a cardinal sin. I had come not to see a fight, in all its raw and sometimes mysterious originality, but the re-enactment of something of the past. I wanted the old story but with a new, more satisfactory ending, and somewhere between Madison Square Garden and the Thomas & Mack Center I had mislaid the old reality that fighting, like the life from which it springs so viscerally, rarely comes with such a guarantee.

The truth, whatever your feelings about the eccentric workings of natural justice, was simply not negotiable. It said that not only had Holyfield come to fight, he had also brought the serious intention, and maybe the means, of winning. That was his opening statement, and so I marked down the first round quite unequivocally. It was Holyfield's.

In the Garden Lewis had exerted immediate command, scoring freely with his jab and landing right hands with an apparently easy poise. Here, he stormed into the centre of the ring but without that kind of authority. It seemed, disturbingly, to be bluster, an impression strengthened when Holyfield moved inside and delivered a combination that sang with some of his old bite and conviction. Lewis connected with a right hand of some force to Holyfield's chin but it did not disturb the victim's momentum. This wasn't the Holyfield of New York; it might have been the one of the heavyweight ages.

The worry, so soon, was that maybe Lewis had drawn too much reassurance from the understanding that three experienced judges – Jerry Roth, Chuck Giampa and Bill Graham – had never been more obliged to record every significant nuance of the fight unfolding before them. And that, perhaps like some of those who supported him most keenly, he believed his task was to rearrange an old injustice rather than present a fresh and unanswerable assertion of his superiority.

In the second round, though, there were stirrings of a more dominant Lewis, but then it was also true that when he delivered a textbook uppercut it barely registered on Holyfield's intent expression. It was, however, undoubtedly Lewis's round. He was also edging ahead in the third, with solid jabs and another well thrown uppercut, until Holyfield scored with a heavy overhand right to Lewis's head and then drove him into the ropes as the bell sounded.

And so it went, shifting on a fine balance until the seventh round, the best of the fight. It saw Holyfield doing so much of what he had promised in the Bowery gym before the first fight, dancing and hitting in the face of the Lewis cannonades. They were heavy assaults by Lewis but Holyfield handled them so well that another round had to be placed in his column. The eighth was almost too close to call. It meant that going into the last four rounds it was entirely possible that Holyfield led by five rounds to three.

Lewis rallied well in the later rounds, however, and I gave him the ninth, tenth and 11th. He had only to win the last round to confirm his edge. But he didn't do that, not on my card, and when the last bell sounded my friend Tom Archdeacon from Ohio, a man whose judgement I respected deeply, tapped me on the shoulder, raised his arms in the air and said, 'I gave it to Holyfield.'

It was the trigger to anxiously review my notes – and confront maybe the greatest irony of my nights at ringside. I had scored it a draw. Six rounds to Holyfield, six to Lewis, and when the scorecards were read out there was a haunting question: do two wrongs ever make a right?

Some American writers claimed the scoring was as outrageous as it had been in New York, and it was hard to argue when you looked at the margins awarded Lewis in his victory by unanimous decision. Most astonishingly, the veteran Graham had given it to Lewis by six rounds, an atrocity to rival that of Eugenia Williams in the Garden. Giampa's margin was four rounds and Roth had it at two.

Well, did this latest batch of bizarre scorecards clear away a scandal or simply compound one? It was not the kind of post-fight discussion I had imagined when I called it for Lewis by a knockout and a thunderous confirmation of his right to be numbered among the great heavyweights.

Nor had Emanuel Steward, who was encountered later as he passed through the Mandalay Bay lobby on his way to a celebration party. I asked him how deeply he would celebrate. He gave a small grimace and said, 'Oh, deep enough. It wasn't the fight or the performance from Lennox I wanted but he won the fight all right and he deserves to be called the undisputed heavyweight champion of the world. He is a good man and an intelligent fighter and no one could have worked harder than he has over the last few years. He had a lot of work to do and he did it without complaint. I love him like a son and I think he loves me and we can go on from here and do more – a lot more.'

A week later, back home in Detroit and after some extended reflection, Steward was more precise. 'I think I can get 50 per cent more from Lennox,' he said.

Lewis was happy enough with his three belts, though he conceded the acquiring of them had been harder than he expected. Holyfield said he was pleased with his performance, and that was the important thing. How the judges scored was out of a fighter's control.

For me, there was a sense that the certainties of my ringside affair were beginning to dwindle. Of course, the old compulsions would never die, and least of all that surge of the blood and the knot in the pit of my stomach when the first bell sounded – and it was also true there were still many miles to cover. But then it had been a hard year and it brought an unwelcome conclusion in the debate over the meaning of the verdict at the Thomas & Mack Center.

In the end, I decided that rough justice had been served. No, two wrongs do not make a right, but in this case who could deny that an eminently decent man, and still potentially great champion, had not been delivered from a most outrageous fate? If they had scored a draw in Las Vegas, as well they might have done, Lennox Lewis would have been denied the prize that had been stolen from him in New York. In an imperfect world, Lennox Lewis had finally triumphed. It was something to lighten the baggage on the way to the airport and to ease, for a little while at least, the growing weight of accumulating regrets.

Chapter Twenty-three

Memphis, Tennessee, June 2002

Mike Tyson versus Lennox Lewis on a bank of the Mississippi at an arena known as the Pyramid may have been an afterthought of boxing history but then some fascination is proofed against the passage of the years. Here, much of it was no doubt attached morbidly to Tyson's continued capacity to outrage the sensitivities of polite society, a knack of his that he proved was still in full working order when the fight was announced in New York six months earlier.

First, he bit Lewis's leg. Then he drew a $56 million lawsuit from WBC president José Sulaimán, who hit his head on a table and was knocked unconscious in the subsequent mêlée. There were other inconveniences. The Nevada Athletic Commission, despite the departure of Jim Nave, voted 4–1 against licensing the fight in Las Vegas. California, New York and Texas also said they would draw a line at serial cannibalism.

The *Independent* newspaper was less squeamish. I was told to interrupt my work at the World Cup in Japan and South Korea and fly to Memphis. It was no great sacrifice. I returned in time to see David Beckham jump out of a tackle and cough up a ball that enabled a ten-man Brazil to end England's latest futile participation, this time in the

272

quarter-finals. Beside the Mississippi, at least you knew that whatever else you saw that turned the stomach it wouldn't be such milky surrender. You also knew that for Lewis fighting Tyson, and beating him in any ring at any time, was still integral to how he wanted to see himself at the end of a career that in so many other ways was now fulfilled.

There were also reasons to be in Memphis other than for the self-anointing of a fighter who had so often represented a breath of dignity in a business that had compromised itself to the brink of self-destruction. One was the need to be around for what might be the last of Mike Tyson the fighter, if not the freak show, to see what he had left at the core of his combative nature. The suspicion had to be that – however much it had been dissipated by the years of neglect and self-abuse – it might just flare again in a way to remind you, albeit briefly, that once this was a force of nature that had superior fighters beaten before their gloves were tied.

For Lewis, it would also be to re-engage a phenomenon that had threatened to break him when he was still a boy. His first boxing trainer, Arnie Boehm – who set him on the road to his Olympic gold when he arrived at the police gym in Kitchener, Ontario, as a gangling young immigrant from England – had taken him down to Catskill to spar with the teenaged Tyson. He remembered the occasion vividly as a statement of his protégé's extraordinary determination. Tyson, who was more physically mature, dominated and hurt Lewis in their first session, and Boehm's instinct was to immediately shepherd him safely back over the Canadian border. But Lewis was defiant, returned to the gym to face Tyson and gave a much better account of himself.

It meant that for Boehm, too, the late date in Memphis carried a powerful resonance. He recalled, 'Lennox was a young man of tremendous pride – and quite fearless. I remember when some kids came to the gym causing trouble and he knocked one of them down, just like that. I had to give him a good talking-to about the need for discipline, but you couldn't help being drawn to a boy who had such a strong idea of what was right and wrong and who was ready to work so hard for what he wanted. I remember his impatience to drive. He got in a car once and he didn't really know how to drive but he was so set on the idea. I looked at him with his hands clenched around the steering wheel so tightly and I could imagine him driving to the other end of Canada in one go.'

Over breakfast in Memphis one morning, Lewis looked out at the wide river glinting in the sunshine and said, yes, it was true that victory in this fight would probably mean more than any of the others. It would give a sense of his being close to the end of a journey that, for all its frustrations and cul-de-sacs and the two defeats he had been able to avenge, had finally given him all that he had sought. 'Since those few days in Catskill I've always had Tyson in my sights,' he said. 'He has always been on my mind. I have always wanted to say that I fought and beat everyone that mattered. It is late, now, the fight should have happened five, even ten years in the past, but it didn't, and all I've been able to say is, "Maybe one day it will be me and him in the ring again like when we were still kids, maybe it will happen." Now it is happening, and I've never been so ready.'

Readier, certainly, than on a South African dawn 14 months earlier when we saw his one betrayal of the meaning of the night in Las Vegas when he was declared the undisputed heavyweight champion of the world. It had been more than anything a triumphal parade until the moment in the fifth round when Hasim Rahman landed a stunning right hand to Lewis's jaw. Lewis, a 20-1 favourite, blustered afterwards that it was the kind of thing that can happen when two big men trade blows in a confined space. He was kidding only himself. The ill-considered man from Baltimore hadn't got lucky. He had done his work. Lewis hadn't.

Driving back to Johannesburg – the fight had been at a casino 5,000 feet above sea level on the Transvaal plateau – I carried the feelings of an exasperated father dismayed by the behaviour of an errant but much-loved son. If that sounds absurdly proprietorial, there is maybe something of the inevitable in at least a touch of such emotion. You travel from one scene of heightened action to another over many years and there are times when the line between detached observer and impassioned disciple can become somewhat blurred. If not, why would hardened old pros have had tears in their eyes at ringside when they came to realise they were seeing the last of the best of Muhammad Ali? No doubt there was a little of that on the dawn drive across the veld.

The terrible nag was that Lewis had conspired in his own downfall. Rahman had been adjusting to the altitude for the best part of a month. Lewis had come in barely two weeks before the fight. He did most of his training in Las Vegas, where one day I attended a press conference at which discussion of the threat posed by Rahman seemed less important than an account of the filming of his walk-on part in the big-budget remake of the old Rat Pack *Ocean's Eleven*, which featured such Hollywood luminaries as George Clooney, Brad Pitt and Matt Damon. Though Lewis brushed away my worries, it was disquieting. Heavyweight champions do not train on a movie set. When he weighed in he was 17 stones, his heaviest ever, and by the fifth round he was heaving in his breath.

What put an expression on my face as glum as those worn by the day workers riding in the back of the open-topped trucks to the factories and building sites of Johannesburg was the sense of waste. I couldn't shake the idea that the fighter I had admired for so long had carelessly thrown away the potential for a magnificent climax to his career.

Before the Rahman débâcle he had been faultless, imperious even, since the second Holyfield fight. Some fancied the chances of the young first challenger Michael Grant and when I went to his training camp in the woods of North Carolina it seemed that Lewis would have some serious work to do at Madison Square Garden. Grant was big and he punched hard but what he produced against some bedraggled sparring partners was utterly beyond him when he stepped in with Lewis. He was destroyed in the second round.

South Africa's Frans Botha met precisely the same fate when Lewis brought his title belts home to the London Arena.

Against the fierce Samoan David Tua, who many felt had the power to ambush Lewis, he made the Las Vegas crowd restive with the degree of his control, his masterful extinguishing of the threat. It was a performance that spoke of a majestic passage to the end of a career that had come to carry a mark of greatness. Then he reported for duty on the set of *Ocean's Eleven* and somehow mislaid the imperative of avoiding the best right hand ever thrown by Hasim Rahman.

He had to wait seven months, and go to court, before getting the chance to respond but, when he did so in Las Vegas, revenge had rarely come so thunderously. Again, it was a right hand that did the damage. Lewis threw it in the fourth round and the image of Rahman draped star-shaped on the canvas was not so much a symbol of defeat as obliteration. Lewis claimed this as vindication of his belief that he had been the victim of a lucky punch in South Africa, a reaction from him that was unusually graceless and had most to do, no doubt, with Rahman's attempts to dodge the rematch clause in their contract.

The reality was that Lewis had suffered not from ill fortune but a neglect of his own best values. That understanding, however reluctant he was to concede it publicly, suffused his performance in the rematch. It was the work of a restored champion of great boxing quality and inordinate strength and when he arrived in Memphis to face Tyson he carried the sheen of a man reacquainted with all of his powers.

Yet, so long after his venomous peak, there was still the mystique of Mike Tyson. Even Lewis's now-devoted trainer, Emanuel Steward, conceded that – while he believed Lennox Lewis had moved into a higher class, that he was demonstrably fitter and stronger than Tyson – there was something in this fight that, more than any other in his life, had been disturbing him in the night. He said, 'I haven't slept too good. I'm more nervous about this fight than any I've been involved with. Mike Tyson didn't get to where he is, being as small as he is, without being a very good fighter. And I think he will go to the top of his game and use whatever he has left in this fight. Either guy could land a big punch in the first ten or 20 seconds and the fight could be over. I do worry about Tyson cold-cocking Lennox. Anyone fighting Tyson who doesn't worry about this is crazy. So, yes, there is a possibility Lennox will get hurt, and we have discussed this. You don't beat Mike Tyson easy.'

Steward had his apprehensions, no doubt, and the odds-makers had Lewis a surprisingly narrow 2-1 favourite, but he also agreed that if Tyson had any serious chance it would have to come at some early flashpoint. Indeed, the sound of the bell for the end of the first round might well signal that his last chance had already come and gone.

'Everyone is holding onto an image of Mike Tyson from ten or fifteen years ago,' Steward added. 'But that Mike Tyson is gone. The natural, instinctive moves are gone. To be honest, I don't think he deserves to be fighting for the world title now. There is only one thing he can do, based on his skills and his physical structure. It is to just come out and attack. And when a fighter rushes you from the opening bell, you have got to fight with him. But then if you look at the record – big fights, tough fights, dangerous fights – that's when Lennox is at his best. Plus, you must challenge Tyson, not give him time to set his traps and make him fight when he doesn't want to fight.'

Before the fight, Tyson did not disturb the warm summer nights beside the Mississippi. There was none of the rampage that he had produced so vigorously in New York. He was clipped, surly in response to routine pre-fight questions. He looked like a man brooding over these moments, which would do so much to shape the rest of a progressively chaotic life. He said, 'I know what is at stake here. I know what

I have got to do. Lennox Lewis is a good champion but he has never faced anyone like me before. He is stepping into the unknown.'

No one could deny that Tyson had explored uncharted territory more thoroughly than any contemporary rival, but it was the certainties that had to be worrying him most, the certainties of power and reach and confidence that had been restored so impressively by Lewis the last time he had stepped into the ring.

Plainly, Lewis had brought all of it to Memphis. When he came into the ring, one split by a screen of security guards assigned to keep the fighters separated before the sound of the first bell, he had the demeanour of a champion of the world. Tyson no longer prowled with a look of venomous intent, the kind that so long ago froze the blood of a fine champion like Michael Spinks. He stood blinking under the television lights like a man considering his fate as his past raced before his eyes.

As Steward predicted, Tyson came rushing across the ring, throwing hooks and clearly hoping to conjure some of the old terror. He threw hard from his familiar, crouching position and he did enough to take the first round. But he had wanted so much more. He had needed to invade both the body and the psyche of Lewis in the way he had 20 years earlier in the gym in Catskill where it all began. All he had done, though, was state his presence, and when Lewis returned to his corner he showed no trace of intimidation. Indeed, his body language framed the question: Mike, is this the best you can do?

It was. He maintained a show of business in the second and third, but his speed of foot and hand was winding down at dismaying rate. And as Tyson ebbed, and threw his last significant punch in the second round – an arching hook that Lewis absorbed comfortably – you had to begin to wonder if this was indeed the last time you would see in the ring the man who, for 15 years, had been the dark but most magnetic force in his sport.

In the third round Lewis's control was nearing the absolute. He set the first blood flowing on Tyson's face with a jab and a right hand that brought a cut over his right eye.

The final question was formed the moment the fight was made, and now, in the fourth round, when Tyson struggled to muster the last of his power and his breath, when he had to will his every straining fibre into the effort of throwing a punch, we were about to get the answer. How would Mike Tyson take his beating? Would he unfurl a white flag like so many of his beaten, overwhelmed opponents? Would he go quietly, resignedly into his dark night? No, he would take whatever had been stored up for him, as he always said he would when he looked to the future and anticipated some of its worst possibilities.

Lewis delivered it without mercy. If he had been criticised for being too passive when Oliver McCall fell apart in the ring they shared, there could be no such charge now. By the sixth round Tyson was bleeding copiously from cuts over his eye, on his face and in his mouth. In the eighth he was defenceless. Lewis hit Tyson with a cluster of uppercuts and then a crashing right to the chin that sent him down. There were 35 seconds left in the round but as referee Eddie Cotton, who it had been feared by the Lewis camp would do all he could to protect Tyson's cause, started the count, nobody needed telling, and least of all the man on the canvas, that it was the end.

In what might have been a forlorn desire for some fleeting privacy, Tyson had his right hand over his face throughout the count to ten and then he slowly moved it to his side. Revealed was the beaten, blood-smeared face of the fighter who had, in another life, provoked a thousand fears with one sidelong glance.

Now, maybe for the last time, he had some post-fight rituals to perform, which he did, given all his circumstances, with remarkable amiability. He embraced his conqueror and kissed Lewis's mother, Violet. 'I am happy for him and I'm thankful of the chance he gave me,' he said. 'He knows I love him and I hope he gives me the opportunity to fight him one more time.' Lewis did not rule out the possibility of a rematch but, as it would be for the rest of the world, it seemed to be low on his priorities. He was more concerned with the significance of this victory in the long sweep of his career.

'This guy bit me,' he said, 'and he was going to get some discipline. After the fight, he apologised to me and said I was a masterful boxer and that he admired and respected me. Mike at 19 ruled the world but, like a fine wine, I came along later and I'm the ruling man.'

The rhetoric, as it so often did in boxing, paled in the wake of the brutally explicit action. Tyson's interest in a rematch was poignant in its defiance of the realities that Lewis had imposed so emphatically. There was nothing left for Tyson in the ring beyond pain and humiliation, anybody could tell you that. Lewis's hyperbole was at least founded in a certain historic truth, but here too was a case of a fighter whose continued presence in the ring would surely be subject to the law of diminishing returns, certainly in terms of his historic reputation. And for a man whose financial affairs had been secured as carefully as Tyson's had been devastated by 15 years of unbridled excess and plundering, this was surely the last vital consideration.

As I flew back to Japan for the conclusion of the World Cup, it certainly felt like the end of something. No doubt there would be other fights to cover, other stories to tell, but with the same intensity, the same sense of being bound to unending drama that simply could not be ignored? It didn't seem so likely on the descent path to Osaka airport.

Yet some of my assumptions were premature. I hadn't seen the last of Lewis or Tyson – and nor, more surprisingly, of Memphis and its great, leisurely river, its haunting Blues and twice-daily parade of mallard ducks through the lobby of the Peabody Hotel. I was back there eight months later to see Tyson fight again, although this was perhaps to pay excessive tribute to the resistance provided by his opponent, Clifford

Etienne. It was over in just 49 seconds of the first round, and it seemed to mean as little to Tyson as to anyone who saw it.

Freddie Roach, Tyson's latest trainer, had advised a postponement of the fight. He said that his man's condition was poor and that defeat against such an ordinary opponent would surely bring down the last curtain. Several members of Etienne's camp had left town by the time Tyson arrived late but apparently prepared to go into the ring. Etienne took his turn to waver, agonising over whether he should fight. When he did, it was a travesty, a desperate jumble of eroded skills, and when Tyson finally landed a punch – a right hand of some force after a flurry of wildly inaccurate hooks – Etienne went down with the finality of a discarded sack.

What did it mean? Not triumph for Tyson. He was asked about the possibility of a Lewis rematch and he was evasive. He was in the first stages of his $100 million lawsuit against Don King, his marriage to Dr Monica Turner was dissolving at potentially huge cost, his creditors had become an army, and his own trainer, the respected Roach, had questioned his fight-worthiness against an opponent as slight as Etienne. Where was there to go? Only to the end of the road that was now crumbling beneath his feet. Remarkably, it would take him two more fights, and more than two more years, to know finally, beyond all doubt or manufactured hope, that the ground had given way beneath him.

Lewis, as anticipated, left the ring in rather better order but not, it had to be reported from Los Angeles a year after his victory over Tyson, quite as majestically as he would have liked. He was trailing on all three cards when the ringside doctor ordered the referee to stop the fight at the end of the sixth after inspecting a cut over the left eye of Vitali Klitschko.

The number-one contender from Ukraine had fought with courage and power and in the second round he threatened a sensation with some stunning right hands to Lewis's head. The champion had come in at his heaviest, at 18 stone 4 pounds, provoking questions over his condition and his commitment, but there was no doubt that he had retained his ability to cause hurt. After the fight, Klitschko needed 60 stitches on cuts on his face and in his mouth. He had, though, launched himself on a long and honourable career as Lewis went away to think about what he would do with the rest of his life.

Lewis lingered over his decision for nine months but each new day of ease made the case for retirement more attractive. When he announced that he had fought for the last time, he did it as a man who could say that everything he had wanted had come to pass. He had done his work and now he could enjoy the results. He had made himself one of the great heavyweight champions. He shared with Gene Tunney the distinction of having a record free from a single unavenged defeat.

It was terrain that, I could not help thinking, might have belonged in another universe when I packed my bags and went on the road again for the last desperate fighting days of Mike Tyson.

Lewis had survived the worst of his days and triumphed. Tyson had still to find the depths of his failure. He would discover them first in Louisville, the birthplace of Muhammad Ali, and then Washington DC. In both places there seemed to be no limit to reasons for the most profound regret.

Tyson did, however, make a fair show of philosophical equilibrium in his hotel suite in Louisville a few days before he fought Britain's obscure Danny Williams. From time to time he fondled his pet pigeons, which flew unfettered from room to room.

Tyson's financial affairs, it was true, had never been in such a dire state, but if a bankruptcy arrangement now before a court was approved he would keep $2 million of his $8 million purse. Seventeen months had passed since the crudities of his victory over Etienne but, who knew, a lively showing here might set up a late surge of major income. Promoter Bob Arum, for one, had been talking up a big deal – which might rise to $80 million, more than double his estimated debts – to cover his last fighting days. He was 38, everyone said he was washed up, but we should remember that life was strange. 'Sometimes funny things happen,' Tyson said, with a slight trace of mirth.

But not at the Freedom Hall State fairground. There, we had an image that seemed to push beyond all doubt the certainty that this was the last we would see of Mike Tyson as an active fighter. With nine seconds of the fourth round left, he sat on the canvas with his back to the ropes, his right arm resting on the lower strand and his right leg stretched out before him. It was not so much an attitude of defeat as abandonment. He looked out into the middle distance, ignoring completely the mechanical count of the referee. It was as if it was all happening to someone else, someone beyond rousing, beyond help.

Williams, who before the fight admitted that he sometimes wept under the pressure of having to go into the ring, had delivered a stream of unanswered punches to send Tyson down. 'People forgot this wasn't a peak Mike Tyson,' Williams said later. 'I always gave myself a chance.' Tyson's trainer, Freddie Roach, said Williams had taken the opportunity of a lifetime. That was one way of putting it. Another, at that moment, would have been to say he happened to be around when Mike Tyson reached down and found that nothing, absolutely nothing, was left. But then, 11 months later in Washington DC, so too was a big raw Irishman named Kevin McBride.

Muhammad Ali was in attendance, pushed in a wheelchair, and what Tyson did in his desperate extremes seemed nothing so much as a prolonged act of sacrilege before a man whose very presence was enough to reconjure so much that was best and most thrilling in heavy-weight boxing.

At various times Tyson attempted to break McBride's arm, succeeded in a head butt that cost him, academically, two points and then, somewhat half-heartedly, bit one of his opponent's nipples. He had one last resort, which he took at the end of the sixth round, by which time he appeared to have reached a state of unutterable weariness. He quit on his stool.

It was 18 years since I had ridden with Tyson to the New York high school and heard him tell of the desolation of the streets of his native Brownsville and how so many of those he had grown up with were dead or in prison or ravaged by drugs. The memory of that brought only an old dimension of sadness to any consideration of his current plight, one illustration of which was that of his $5.5 million purse the most he could expect to receive, in his sea of debt and disappearing horizons, was $250,000. The rest, after tax, would go to his ex-wife Dr Monica Turner and some lucky creditors.

No, he was not a suitable case for sympathy. The possibilities of redemption had stalked him as relentlessly as the temptations that had kept bringing him down. He had been given the world and he had thrown it away. But then wouldn't it be comfortable if every life, every fight, could be so easily assigned to the columns of win and loss, glory and shame?

It was something to think about as Mike Tyson retreated from the capital of the nation founded on hope. And as, maybe inevitably, I began to wonder how much was left to make my affair with boxing linger on.

Epilogue

Who can say when a great affair is truly over? When it no longer has the power to stir some of the strongest emotions you have ever felt? When it cannot again summon in you the uncomplicated wonder of an expectant schoolboy?

Still now, more than 40 years since I first went to Madison Square Garden to see Muhammad Ali fight, I cannot say it.

Sometimes I feel badly about this. I wonder if somewhere along the road I became desensitised to some of boxing's worst affects. If I mourned the death of Ali and, like so many of his admirers, was saddened by all the years of his physical decline, did I pay sufficient attention to the mounting medical evidence that insisted he fought on too long, too damagingly? Did I celebrate too easily, too blindly, the courage that condemned him to a twilit world?

It is not so comfortable asking such questions, and this is especially so when you suspect – no, let us be honest, when you *know* – the answer is yes.

There were, after all, so many times when boxing cried out for more than passing rebuke. Times when Mike Tyson seemed intent on dragging the sport into the very entrails of the worst of life, and where was his discouragement when each new outrage was used as a bargaining tool by his promoter Don King? When it was said by a rival promoter, 'Boxing is squeezing the cantaloupe so hard now you can hear the pips squeak.'

Yes, there were plenty of questions to ask, and some of them were indeed posed in the heat of controversy or disaster, but too often the answers went unpursued or simply blew in the wind.

That was the fate of one I raised from ringside at the London Arena in 1995, when the American Gerald McClellan, arguably the best pound-for-pound fighter of the day, collapsed under the weight of Nigel Benn's punching.

The onslaught condemned McClellan to a wheelchair and near-total blindness and I sat a few feet away as the paramedics did what they could. That night I wrote, 'When they gave Gerald McClellan his fourth injection in the corner of that zoo of a ring, when they put the brace on his neck and the oxygen mask over his face and all the demons of a brutal business came crowding in, you were left with the question that will never go away. How long can the old game go on?'

More than 20 years later, the answer is as self-evident as it was then. It will go on so long as enough people buy the tickets and the pay-per-view slots. And while others skirt, or disregard, a reality that is as old as boxing. It is the one that says there will never be sufficient medical safeguards to remove the certainty that men will continue to pay for the excitements of the ring with their ruined health and, too often, their lives.

I wish I could say that such ambivalence weighed on me more heavily in the last years of my odyssey through boxing. But I cannot say that, not in all conscience. It would be to forget, for one thing, that travelling back from the London Arena through the early-morning streets I wondered if anything in the name of sport could ever justify such devastation of a man's life. And wondered, indeed, if it were time to say I had covered my last fight.

But then a year or so after the darkness closed in on Gerald McClellan I was riding a camel beside the pyramids in Cairo the morning before Chris Eubank knocked out an overmatched Argentinian, Luis Barrera, in a vast marble hall to which thousands of Egyptian army cadets had been marched to fill in some of the empty spaces. Boxing rolled along, making its profits where it might, and I was willing enough to follow in its wake.

In 2008 I twice followed Joe Calzaghe to America, first to Las Vegas, then New York, to see him fight the great but aged performers Bernard Hopkins and Roy Jones Junior. Seven years earlier, in Copenhagen, I had asked him why, at the prime of his career and impressive talent, he was not fighting men of the quality of Hopkins and Jones but defending his world super-middleweight title against the obscure American Will McIntyre on a Mike Tyson undercard. I asked him if he did not understand that an admiring public wanted to see him fight real fights against real opponents. And he asked me, 'Don't you understand that boxing is a business?'

He outpointed both Hopkins and Jones all those years later. Both fights are faint in the memory, which is not so surprising when you note that Hopkins was 43 and Jones 39. Calzaghe came to them so late that the meaning of their scalps was inevitably reduced.

Indeed, I remember that time in New York not for Calzaghe's victory, and the preservation of his unbeaten record, but for the taxi ride to Harlem I took when it became clear that Barack Obama had been elected as America's first black president. They were popping champagne corks and, very briefly, I danced with a man in the street. For a little while you had the feeling that you were at the centre of a suddenly more hopeful world.

I stopped at the old terrace house of Sugar Ray Robinson, a place of homage from where the great middleweight champion – for some old men still the most dazzling fighter they ever saw – would ride out as an emperor in a pink Cadillac.

Robinson may have been a glory of another America, one in which no one on these Harlem streets could have imagined there would come the day of a black president, or that a world champion would say that what happened in the ring was a business and not a recurring glory of the blood. And still less, maybe, that anyone standing on the steps of the house of Sugar Ray Robinson, with a passport in his pocket that had carried him through maybe the last great age of boxing, should feel the merest twinge of regret.

Who ever said, after all, that even the most unforgettable affair would be free from at least a trace or two of guilt.

James Lawton,
Padua, Italy, June 2017

Acknowledgements

My first thanks must go to the sports editors of the *Daily Express*, the *Vancouver Sun* and *The Independent* who for more than 30 years made attendance at the big-fight ringsides across the world an integral part of my routine working life. They bestowed an astonishing privilege which, I hope, was never taken too much for granted.

The companionship and help of my British and American colleagues was another huge gift.

They were a warm and talented, if sometimes raucous, brotherhood and they will always inhabit vividly my memories of the unforgettable occasions we shared in the shadow of so many great fighters.

Roy Collins and Jeff Powell were especially close companions and my debt to the help and the authority of such as Hugh McIlvanney, Colin Hart and Ken Jones will never be exhausted. Of the Americans, Ed Schuyler Jr, Pat Putnam, William Nack, George Kimball, Tom Archdeacon, Royce Feour and Michael Katz never stinted in their welcome or their generosity or their humour.

Beyond the press room, such knowledgeable denizens of the fight crowd as Don Majeski, Gene Kilroy and Tony Dowling were always happy to give their help and their insights.

Hopefully, my appreciation of the access granted – and my admiration for some of the greatest fighters and trainers boxing has ever known – has already been adequately expressed on these pages.

In the writing of this book I was most grateful for the wise counsel of Charlotte Atyeo at Bloomsbury, the skill of copy-editor Ian Preece and the unfailing support of my agent David Luxton. My wife Linda, as always, was both kind and patient.

Index